Learning with INTERACTIVE MULTIMEDIA

*Developing and Using
Multimedia Tools in Education*

Edited by
Sueann Ambron and Kristina Hooper
Apple Computer, Inc.

PUBLISHED BY
Microsoft Press
A Division of Microsoft Corporation
One Microsoft Way
Redmond, Washington 98052-6399

Library of Congress Cataloging-in-Publication Data
Learning with interactive multimedia : developing and using multimedia
  tools in education / Sueann Ambron and Kristina Hooper, eds.
     p.   cm.
   ISBN 1-55615-282-5
   1. Computer-assisted instruction.   2. HyperCard (Computer program)
 I. Ambron, Sueann Robinson.   II. Hooper, Kristina.
 LB1028.5.L389   1990
 371.3'34--dc20   89-77543
                                        CIP

Printed and bound in the United States of America.

1 2 3 4 5 6 7 8 9 RARA 4 3 2 1 0

Distributed to the book trade in Canada by General Publishing Company, Ltd.

Distributed to the book trade outside the United States and Canada by Penguin Books Ltd.

Penguin Books Ltd., Harmondsworth, Middlesex, England
Penguin Books Australia Ltd., Ringwood, Victoria, Australia
Penguin Books N.Z. Ltd., 182–190 Wairau Road, Auckland 10, New Zealand

British Cataloging-in-Publication Data available

Acquisitions Editor: Dean Holmes   **Project Editor:** Jack Litewka

Thank you, Bill Atkinson,
for creating HyperCard,
a tool for sharing within a community of explorers,
and for making a difference in education.

Contents

Preface

Our first book, *Interactive Multimedia,* provides an overview of the field; this second book, *Learning with Interactive Multimedia,* looks at the impact of multimedia tools, especially HyperCard, on the development of educational materials.

This book was compiled after an invitational conference on HyperCard and Education held in Cupertino, California, in October, 1988. Participants had the opportunity to reflect on their presentations and conversations with colleagues and then write their essay. Participants at the conference are users of HyperCard and other multimedia tools. They work in educational research labs, elementary schools, high schools, universities, and publishing companies. Many of them had experience building multimedia educational applications with HyperCard.

We thank our authors for the insights and thoughtfulness that they have put into their chapters and for their patience in working with us through several deadlines. We also thank Rachel Cohen—for this book would not have materialized without her support, useful suggestions, and perseverance.

While we are excited about the results of the conference, the opinions expressed by the participants do not necessarily represent Apple Computer, Inc.'s point of view. As with any joint effort, the thoughts expressed are the diverse views of some of the best people in the field of interactive multimedia. The ideas are presented to give readers a sampling of current issues from labs, schools, and publishers.

Our hope is that this book will be of interest and value to researchers, teachers, students, software developers, filmmakers, television broadcasters, book publishers, and others interested in interactive multimedia and learning. We believe that interactive multimedia gives us an opportunity to learn in new, more dynamic, and more exciting ways.

We hope this book contributes to making that happen.

> *Sueann Ambron, Ed.D.*
> *Manager, New Technology in Education*
> *Apple Computer, Inc.*
>
> *Kristina Hooper, Ph.D.*
> *Director, Multimedia Lab*
> *Apple Computer, Inc.*

Introduction

"Multimedia: What the Excitement is All About"
(Electronic Learning, June, 1989)

"It's a PC, It's a TV, It's Multimedia"
(Business Week, October 9, 1989)

"Interactive Multimedia: The Next Wave"
(Classroom Computer Learning, September 9, 1989)

"Multimedia Doubters Taught a Thing or Two"
(Wall Street Journal, November 15, 1989)

"Couch Potatoes! Now It's Smart TV"
(Fortune, November 20, 1989)

In the last few months, a lot of space in both business and educational publications has been devoted to "interactive multimedia." The attention stems from the technological capabilities of computers and televisions, which are being enhanced and "fused" into hybrids such as video computers and interactive televisions. These powerful new advancements are fostering changes that, in turn, present exciting and profound business and education opportunities.

It is still not clear whether the most successful hardware platforms for multimedia in the 1990s will come from the computer, television, or telephone industries. Perhaps, initially, multimedia platforms will be produced by a combination of talents. We think the computer industry has an edge because of its focus on ease of use of the human-machine interface. Nevertheless, *what is clear is that learning in schools, businesses, and homes will take on a new dimension when integrated hardware is less expensive and when easy-to-use and "capable" multimedia software is readily available.* Imagine what the future of this technology can do to release human potential!

But what is "interactive multimedia"? It is a collection of computer-centered technologies that give a user the capability to access and manipulate text, sounds, and images. Just as word-processing programs today enable users to integrate text and graphics, multimedia programs in the near future will enable users to access not only libraries of text documents but also storehouses of music, sound effects, speech, still images, animations, and movies. In addition, multimedia users will be able to manipulate this lexicon of material and add their own material. Initially, we will see extensions of existing conventions such as interactive fiction, video notebooks, surrogate travel, and browsable movies. Gradually, producers and users will discover new ways to use multimedia.

This book focuses on multimedia tools, especially HyperCard, as used in labs and schools and by publishers. HyperCard is an extremely popular end-user programming language. Since its release into the market in August 1987, HyperCard has opened the door to a new class of capabilities. From the viewpoint of the current multimedia environment, it is ideal software for controlling external multimedia devices such as videodisc and CD-ROM players. You will see examples of multimedia applications written with HyperCard.

The book is organized into three sections: "Applications Researchers," "Teachers and Students," and "Publishers and Producers." The book provides a sampling of work from labs, schools, and publishers, giving a glimpse of the thinking of the pioneer developers of HyperCard for educational multimedia applications. The essays describe what has worked and what has not worked as well as what is generalizable to other multimedia tools and what is not.

Keep two questions in mind as you read the chapters: What is learning with interactive multimedia? What is required to realize the possibilities? We hope you go on to answer the questions on your own after you put the book down because the answers we come up with together will shape how learning occurs in the future.

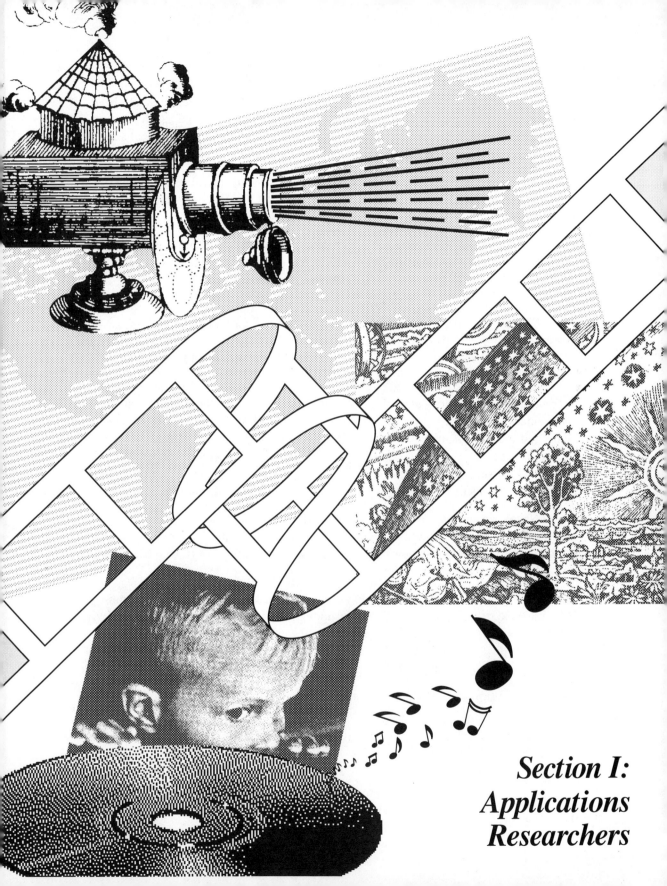

Section I:
Applications
Researchers

Over the last few years, several individuals at Apple Computer, Inc., research labs have used HyperCard as a multimedia tool to create interactive multimedia educational applications. The papers in this section reflect their observations of the philosophical and design issues in developing applications with multimedia tools, especially HyperCard.

Kristina Hooper, director of the Multimedia Lab, traces the historical roots of HyperCard and uses applications developed at the lab to illustrate her messages about HyperCard as an educational tool.

Fabrice Florin brings his expertise as a television producer to developing new interactive information landscapes using computers. His article describes five frameworks for information landscapes. Each framework is illustrated by applications.

Rob Semper, director of the collaboration between Apple and Lucasfilm, Ltd., writes about three characteristics of HyperCard as an educational tool. First, HyperCard provides the possibility of truly multimodal presentation. Second, HyperCard functions as a do-it-yourself medium. And third, HyperCard is useful as a tool for thinking and learning.

In the near future, people who work in education and business will use multimedia for communicating. In her chapter, Sueann Ambron, cofounder of the Multimedia Lab, explores multimedia composition. What will school and the workplace be like when technology gives people easy-to-use tools for manipulating images, sounds, and text? How do people feel when they are confronted with these opportunities now? What do people compose in multimedia? What are some principles of multimedia composition?

Margo Nanny, an educator and designer, has worked extensively with visual images. She uses interactive images to manipulate space and time, thereby altering the point of view and allowing people to make new connections. She illustrates her work with examples from The Visual Almanac™.

At a time when schools across the country are cutting back on art and music programs, Mike Liebhold, from Apple's Advanced Technology Group, offers comments on why visual arts should be a continuing, integral part of the curriculum in the 1990s. He argues that hypermedia requires media technology and interactive-media-literate teachers, students, domain experts, and producers.

Yolanda Jenkins, experienced in technology and educational research, proposes a role for technology in the education of young children. In this chapter she briefly discusses research and theories that relate to the use of computers with young children. Then she describes The Magic Classroom, an example of how multimedia could be used effectively in preschools.

Tim Oren is at the forefront of issues regarding information retrieval and hypertext architecture. In this paper he discusses his concern about cognitive load in hypermedia: What happens when we give users exploratory freedom in hypermedia? They can be overwhelmed by the task of digesting and organizing vast amounts of information. This paper discusses several techniques for reducing cognitive load.

HyperCard:
A Key to
Educational Computing

Kristina Hooper

KRISTINA HOOPER

Kristina Hooper, director of Apple Computer, Inc.'s Multimedia Lab, was trained as a cognitive scientist. In her work during the past 20 years, she has extended this perspective into the areas of picture recognition, imagery, and visual technology.

She earned an A.B. in cognitive psychology from Stanford University and a Ph.D. in cognitive science from the University of California at San Diego. She also was the recipient of a post-doctoral fellowship in architecture from the University of California at Berkeley.

Prior to joining Apple Computer, she was on the faculty of the University of California at Santa Cruz and was a visiting professor at Massachusetts Institute of Technology. She was also the director of research at the Atari Sunnyvale Research Lab in California.

In 1985, she joined Apple Computer, where she initially was principal engineer for the Advanced Technology Group and later was principal engineer for the Human Interface Group and also a senior researcher. As director of the Multimedia Lab, she is in charge of projects that explore the development and application of interactive multimedia systems as tools for thinking, learning, and communication. She is co-editor with Sueann Ambron of Interactive Multimedia *(Microsoft Press, 1988), a book that addresses multimedia from the perspectives of computer science, education, publishing, and television production.*

It is an exciting time for educational computing. We have behind us now more than 10 years of experience with this medium. We have accomplished some great successes and accumulated a number of failures. We are no longer as naive as we once were, and yet we are still idealistic enough to keep trying out some wildly new things.

Whether or not actual historic precedents for this stage of development exist in other endeavors, it's clear to me that we are finally at a launching pad from which we can "enhance educational opportunities for all."

HyperCard, and tools similar to it, are key to our current opportunities. For HyperCard is fundamentally designed to address how people think rather than how processors might work effectively. We can now design pedagogical surrounds with tools designed to be compatible with mental activities.

In this paper I will discuss some personal views of the use of HyperCard, formed over the last few years while working on the development of this product as well as uses for it. My goal is to provide the reader with a number of specific examples that illustrate exactly how HyperCard and related tools might greatly enhance educational computing at a very basic level.

Early Developments

It was interesting to be an insider at Apple Computer, Inc., as HyperCard (initially titled WildCard) was being developed. When one discussed this new tool that Bill Atkinson was developing, one was faced with a range of very interesting questions:

- Who, exactly, is the market for this product?
- Be clear: Is it or is it not a database?
- Why are you considering both users and authors? Can't you simply focus on one or the other?
- What is the purpose of linking things together? Why can't you have some discipline and specify the kinds of parameters that will be used?
- Which other applications will HyperCard compete with? Is it or is it not an application? What do you mean when you say that HyperCard is similar to system software?
- Why have you developed external command structures? Are we hiding some weakness within HyperCard?

- The use of so many graphics give HyperCard a toylike character. How can you expect it to be taken seriously, particularly in the business market?
- Why are you working with videodiscs? This is such an old, failed technology. What use is this? HyperCard surely isn't powerful enough to work with our new CD-ROM players, is it?
- Why should we include HyperCard with all machines? Isn't it worth anything on its own?
- Why doesn't the desktop interface appear in this product? HyperCard seems completely inconsistent with the Macintosh interface.

And so on, and so on, and so on. Each of these questions triggered an animated conversation, if not an argument. For the most part it was fun to discuss these issues before the release of HyperCard. We began to develop the new kinds of reasoning that would be required to transform this innovative product into a commercial success.

To my mind the core argument was that HyperCard is a tool that is absolutely fantastic for education, be it the education of small children or adults, including adults who work in corporations. HyperCard did not fit neatly into the prevalent application categories: Strictly speaking, it wasn't a database or a spreadsheet or a word processor or a graphics program or a desktop-publishing application—yet it didn't seem all that strange to me.

At about this point in my arguments with people, I realized that even though HyperCard wasn't strange to me—recall, I am trained as a cognitive psychologist and not as an engineer or a software marketer—it was indeed totally new to many within Apple Computer. The mainstream personal computing revolution, within which many Apple people were trained, had not yet approached such a mentalistic product. During 1986–87, most educational computing was not done on the Macintosh, and most of what was successful on the Macintosh were databases, spreadsheets, word-processing and graphics programs, and desktop-publishing applications.

One Explanatory Approach: Historical

Early on I found that I could use two basic approaches to describe HyperCard: The first was historical and the second was pedagogical. (See Figure 1.)

The historical issues are intriguing, because HyperCard can be thought of as the convergence of a number of exciting traditions.

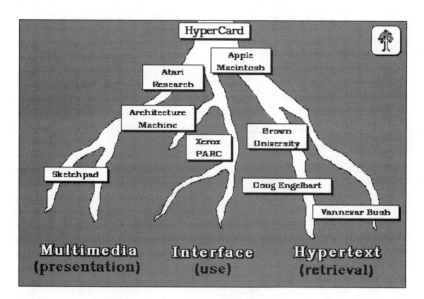

FIGURE 1. This diagram is a HyperCard card that was used in a live presentation to a large audience at MacWorld in 1987, on the occasion of the introduction of HyperCard. Each of the labels on the diagram acts as a button: When the user clicks on a button, a short video clip shows related historical materials. This constitutes the "roots" part of this presentation. A "fruits" section, showing the top of this "tree," illustrates a range of HyperCard presentations that demonstrate the possibilities of HyperCard-based applications.

Hypertext Traditions

At HyperCard's basis is the hypertext tradition. Briefly described, this tradition asserts that information, linked and cross-referenced in many different ways, will be widely available to end users. Vannevar Bush elegantly described the basic ideas for this formulation in 1945 in a classic article in *The Atlantic Monthly* titled "As We May Think" (reprinted in *CD-ROM: The New Papyrus,* Microsoft Press, 1986). He suggested that there would be a tool that would enhance human memory and thinking and that would allow people to retrieve information from a computer in many of the same ways in which retrieval is accomplished within human memory. One could, for example, find associations to ideas quite easily and browse related materials.

Ted Nelson and Doug Engelbart extended these basic ideas in the 1960s. Ted coined the term "hypertext" to suggest that, in the future, literatures will not be constrained to linear-document form, that instead they will allow the conscious flights of fancy that are possible within people's mind. Doug extended these notions, developing working models of quite extensive hypertext systems on large-scale computing systems. Contextualizing these models within his own concept of the computer as a tool for "augmenting the human intellect," he provided a range of examples in which hypertext systems were used to enhance the thinking of individuals involved in collaborative work.

Human Interface Traditions

HyperCard also included a basic focus on the design of a human interface that would encourage the use of computers by a very wide range of individuals (rather than only by highly trained people). This tradition, at its most obvious in some of the early systems designed at Xerox PARC and in the design of the Apple Macintosh computer, is key to the design of HyperCard. It reflects a basic belief that anyone can be a programmer. And although the debate still rages as to just how "English-like" HyperTalk (the HyperCard programming language) is, it is certainly far more approachable than many programming languages. In addition, the highly graphical nature of HyperCard means that a sensitive designer is likely to produce an understandable interface for an end user.

Multimedia Traditions

A multimedia presentation tradition is also available in HyperCard. Its external command structure allows easy access to highly visual and acoustic presentations—using videodisc drivers and CD-ROM drivers, for example. This allows HyperCard to be central in easily producing multimedia presentations, including presentations like those created more than 10 years ago in research labs such as Nicholas Negroponte's Architecture Machine Group (which is now a part of the MIT Media Lab). The incorporation of movies, still images, and sounds in the computing environment makes available a new general medium for expression and, as Negroponte argues often, the convergence of the television, computer, and publishing industries.

HyperCard brought together the traditions of hypertext, interface developments, and multimedia opportunities. Each of these traditions was well developed by 1986, allowing this new tool to build on what was learned in the related activities and to make the traditions available to the mainstream user of the Apple Macintosh computer. The availability was new, although the concepts were well worn and well known to researchers in the general field of "human-enhanced computing."

Another Approach: Pedagogical

The historical frameworks proved quite useful in explaining HyperCard to people who found it alarmingly strange. The idea that elements of HyperCard had been experimented with earlier and that it was a new element that fell within a range of established traditions made people feel comfortable.

It was, however, the pedagogical arguments that I found, and still find, the most exciting to convey. With the capabilities of HyperCard, some significant pedagogical ideas are finally "given a voice" in quite simple contexts.

Maps and Territories

My favorite of these ideas is the general idea of "maps and territories." The sense of this distinction, and complementarity, is that a range of ideas can be well expressed in terms of an abstract concept (a map) and a specific exemplar (the territory). Obviously, these are not the same (as many a philosopher has pointed out); yet the ability to manipulate the relationship between them seems to be integral to what we typically mean when we say that someone is "well educated."

The most obvious example of a map-and-territory pairing in a HyperCard application can be found in the literal sense of these terms, as a simple click on a geographic map can bring forth a picture of a landscape. (See Figure 2 on the following page.) Both Mike Liebhold and Fabrice Florin (each of whom has an essay in this section) pursued this use of HyperCard, which is clearly the archetypal (and profound) use of this tool, very early on in its development.

However, the map-and-territory theme is not limited to such a literal translation. The graphical nature of HyperCard, plus its linkage metaphor, coupled with interactions with optical media, allow the user to produce a range of such effects quite easily. For example, the user can click on a diagram of a cellular structure and see microscopic images of the biological elements included in the cell; the user can click on a timeline and see a short movie clip of an event that occurred in the selected year; or the user can click on a musical score and hear specific notes.

One can extend this map-and-territory theme from content-specific examples to general media tools. A prime example of this is the "movie map" example that Margo Nanny (whose essay appears in this section) developed as part of her master's thesis. (See Figure 3 on page 13.) This movie map lets a viewer access any part of a 20-minute movie at any time. This allows a teacher, for example, to show brief segments on a particular topic of interest to a class, oftentimes in a context unrelated to that of the entire narrative

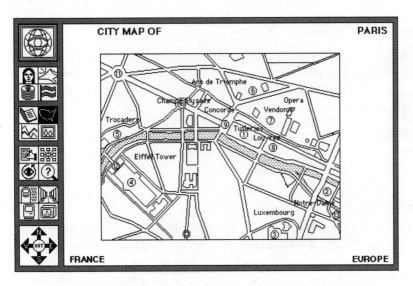

FIGURE 2. This screen is from Worldview, an application prepared by Fabrice Florin alongside HyperCard. This application helped to formulate and test the ways in which HyperCard could be used. Clicking on a numbered section in the map brings up a picture of a related scene. The interface elements on the left of the screen bring up other "territories," including economic data, information about the population, and other similar atlaslike elements.

of the movie. The movie map also will allow a student to independently review the entire movie or only sections of it.

A Linkage Medium

Another aspect of HyperCard well suited for the educational environment is its content focus and its inherent linkage metaphor. Most computer applications have been tool oriented. Clearly, this is important for learning, as students have used easy-to-learn word processors to extend their communications and thinking abilities, as students have used graphics packages to extend their expressions beyond text, and as students of all ages have used spreadsheets to play "what if" games that allow them to explore the consequences of different classes of actions.

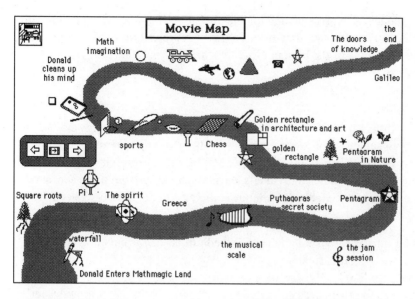

FIGURE 3. This "movie map" is a card in a HyperCard-based demonstration prototype developed by Margo Nanny and Apple Computer, Inc., in conjunction with The Walt Disney Computer Software Company. It makes a movie (in this case Disney's Donald in Mathmagic Land) *available for browsing, presentation, and analysis. The long, shaded, curving line represents the entire movie, from the beginning to the end. Clicking on any location along this line, labeled with key scenes, accesses the corresponding section of this movie for the viewer. [*Donald in Mathmagic Land: *Copyright © 1959 by The Walt Disney Company.]*

HyperCard can be used as a tool by HyperCard authors, but it can also be the basis for content presentations prepared by these authors and then explored by end users. These end users need not have any familiarity with HyperCard as a tool; they explore topics that have been linked together for their browsing. In this sense a prepared HyperCard stack can be like the paper that someone outputs from a word processor; however, it is different in that nonlinear, linked messages can be presented by the author and then can be viewed by the end user in a variety of ways.

This nonlinear exploratory presentation style can, if used in a disciplined fashion, be extremely useful in education. An author can acknowledge the grouping of messages and the interlinkages of ideas explicitly in a prepared document. Similarly, contexts of presentations can be explicitly noted. "Readers" can examine ideas in manners that are suited to their own abilities and knowledgebases, even as they take hints from the authors as to preferred modes of exploration.

Clearly, these new modes of expression and understanding will not be absorbed immediately into conventional use, although they offer modes of representation that are possibly more similar to the workings of the human mind than are the spatial arrays afforded by pages and pages of paper.

Images and Sounds

One can learn many things from texts and from blackboards, yet other things are better learned in dynamic visual and acoustic media, especially media that are user controlled. Similarly, some individuals learn well using paper and pencil or from viewing linear movies or other narratives, yet other individuals learn much better from more sensory media—media that incorporate sights and sounds at their core, not simply as decorative facades.

HyperCard offers an inherently visual and spatial medium, as one is encouraged to render an idea graphically that is linked to others and to lay out a set of ideas systematically on a card. Similarly, HyperCard's ease in linking to images and sounds on optical media as well as to other cards enhances this sensory capability. It provides an entry vehicle for many in education who have not yet dealt directly with sensory presentations as well as a vehicle for effective communications by those who are comfortable with sensory media. In any case, recent research suggests that the multiplicity of sensory media available can be used significantly for critical educational effect.

Learning by Making

A critical prescription for learning—more often stated than followed—is that of *active learning*. The basic proposition is that "to do" is to understand, that active involvement by students in manipulating information is key to their success in learning.

Papert and others have argued strongly for active learning in the educational-technology domain. Before the arrival of HyperCard, the Macintosh computer offered students little opportunity to program the machine directly. Partly because of the huge demands of the Macintosh desktop interface, the Macintosh is a difficult machine to program. With HyperCard, this is no longer the case. As you will note in chapters throughout this book, a wide range of nonprogrammers are now actively pursuing the creation of HyperCard stacks. Many designers who previously were computer adverse have found HyperCard to be an accessible and useful tool in developing creative presentations. Students and teachers are also finding it to be useful in representing their educational ideas, at both simple and complex levels.

This active participation in creating presentations of ideas is good news for education. When a person dwells on a concept and considers how to present it well, the concept will probably be understood when it is presented. The capability of HyperCard to assist people in creating casual custom presentations quickly is very compelling.

Performance/Presentation

Computers have typically been used in individual or small group settings. With Hyper-Card we have witnessed the use of computers in many large-group presentations. In some cases computers are used simply to display a set of bullet points that a speaker wants to emphasize, and in others they are used simply to display a set of video clips amidst a talk. Yet computers can also be used in quite complex ways; audiences can be encouraged to participate in one or another form of interaction, be it in the selection of one of many options or in the calculation of a range of possible responses to a dilemma.

However, even simple interactions can be very exciting. If the content is profound and the delivery engaging, even the simplest HyperCard structure can enhance a presentation. Ever since I made my first large-audience HyperCard and videodisc presentation at MacWorld in 1987, I have felt completely inadequate if I do not use these media in large group presentations. Although speaking from notes or overheads or slides can be compelling, these media fall short of the dramatic impact that is possible when the presenter uses HyperCard stacks.

Teachers can design HyperCard stacks that allow direct access to a wide range of materials. As follow-up to certain questions, materials can be traversed quickly (when one is lucky) to uncover the materials relevant to a particular point that has been raised. Hyper-Card can then provide a fluid medium that is a resource to the teachers in a large-group presentation, as preparation or follow-up to smaller-group interactions.

Multimedia Design with HyperCard (1988–89)

The above-mentioned and other equally compelling pedagogical properties of HyperCard made it, from its inception, an exciting tool to use in creating learning presentations and in creating tools that could be used for learning. Given the potential of this tool, we explored its use in multimedia contexts extensively on its release. Specifically, Sueann Ambron and I set up the Multimedia Lab in San Francisco in late 1987 to explore the use of HyperCard, videodiscs, and CD-ROM in designing compelling educational experiences. HyperCard allowed us to articulate many of the properties of computer-centered environments that we considered important to future developments at Apple Computer.

(Note: Although a wide range of HyperCard designs are not multimedia in character, our awareness of HyperCard's power and flexibility as a multimedia tool drove our work in this area.)

Our intents were three-fold. First, we wanted to understand the design opportunities offered by this tool so that we could show potential developers what they could produce. Second, we wanted to show end users in education and in business the opportunities available with this off-the-shelf tool. Third, we wanted to gain enough experience with this tool so that we could suggest to the engineering staff at Apple the hardware, soft-ware, and interface elements to elaborate in future systems.

The Multimedia Lab focused on creating a set of *design examples*. Each design example allowed us to explore some particular idea, typically in collaboration with a group or groups whose talents complemented ours. Initially, each example was also designed to be a brief sketch of a set of central ideas. Our sense was that products could be con-sidered only after we had experienced what these projects would "feel like" and that to get this sense we would need to build some working systems. Not uncoincidentally, HyperCard provides a superb prototyping tool for the creation of design examples defined in this way.

We have learned a number of lessons from producing these design examples and from the feedback we received after showing them to others. I will describe a few of these lessons, including:

- HyperCard as an accessible tool
- The use of drama in a HyperCard project
- The incorporation of images in educational discourse
- The use of multiple representations in displays
- The usefulness of HyperCard in acessing time-based phenomena
- The interface and navigational opportunities available with HyperCard

An Accessible Tool

I have become convinced that HyperCard is indeed accessible to professionals in a variety of areas. Video producers, graphics designers, and teachers take readily to this tool, producing some amazing projects. And students, in their typically casual fashion, learn the intricacies of this tool quite naturally and seem to enjoy being end users of HyperCard presentations that have been prepared for them.

Pat Hanlon and Bob Campbell, a high-school English teacher and retired librarian respectively, have linked a set of materials—named Grapevine—related to John Steinbeck's *The Grapes of Wrath* that has been invaluable to me (as one very specific audience) in learning about the 1930s in America. (See "HyperCard: A New Deal in the Classroom" in Section II.) Their materials have also provided a framework for those students who want to learn more about this author.

The most important aspect of their work is that the Grapevine materials that they gathered do not seem like computer materials. Instead, they seem to be engaging materials that just happen to be gathered together on a computer. The content is in the foreground; the tool and the machine drift into the background inconspicuously. Equally impressive to me is that these individuals have put this project together for their own use, to extend their own interests and those around them. I hope we will find a way to make this project more widely available, because it is a remarkable piece of work, providing a wonderful inspiration for other people "to make their own materials."

Drama and Character Development

Producers of educational materials can all too easily become very serious and unimaginative in creating such materials. This is understandable because education *is* a serious endeavor. Viewed from a traditional perspective, students must learn so many things that it is proper to deal with these directly, especially in the fields of science and mathematics.

We decided to try a few other tacks in a number of projects, to see if we could make the materials "lighter" and more enjoyable to use while at the same time maintaining high standards for the educational integrity of presentation. We chose the techniques of dramatic depiction typical of television, movies, and cartoons rather than the techniques related to the computer screen.

In a collaboration with the Smithsonian Institution and Lucasfilm, Ltd., we examined how an extremely well-done dramatic episode—in our case, Life Story, a depiction of the discovery of DNA—could be structured and elaborated to encourage scientific understanding and to provide dramatic enjoyment. We combined elements of the movie with additional elements—including interviews with the scientists, simulations of simple equipment, questions and answers about important ideas, and concept maps of scientific inquiry—to give a sense of the depth of this scientific enterprise.

These additional elements are ideas that people have been talking about for years. Yet these ideas have typically not been demonstrated, usually because of the perceived expense involved. In those cases in which the ideas were demonstrated, the demonstrations usually have been ineffective, apparently because of inadequate tools or the unavailability of a team that could adequately address computer programming, design, scientific inquiry, and dramatic presentation.

With HyperCard we produced the Life Story demonstration with great effect. (Fabrice Florin, one of the lead designers on the project, summarizes this project in the next essay in this book.) HyperCard provides a new electronic form of a blank piece of paper. One is challenged to represent ideas simply and directly and to develop structures that are appropriate for a particular use. One is encouraged to put together diverse teams and to quickly sketch the main aspects of some very complex ideas.

Our collaboration with Lucasfilm and the Audubon Society produced another successful demonstration of the use of character development in the presentation of scientific material. In this instance, the topic was ecology, and the character was not an actor but rather a custom-designed cartoon presence named Paul Parkranger. Paul's existence added excitement to the problems associated with vanishing natural habitats, drawing students into careful examinations of scientific principles and making this biological topic "come alive." The graphics and, particularly, the sounds in this example caused otherwise mundane notions to become controversial and engaging. They also transformed obtuse, experimental work into topics that were understandable and even fun!

Images, Images, and More Images

In most endeavors we are consumers of images—visual and acoustic—rather than producers of them. For example, we view movies and cartoons, we stroll through art galleries, and we listen to great symphonies on the radio and in our concert halls. Although few of us are trained to produce images, most of us are visually and acoustically sophisticated. This duality is a cultural phenomenon, but it is also a technological and economic phenomenon: The technologies for image manipulation are usually difficult to use, quite expensive, and unavailable to most of us.

HyperCard, when considered along with videodiscs and CD-audio discs, eliminates this duality: This combination of media gives all of us access to a wide range of still and moving images as well as sounds.

We initiated a project we titled The Visual Almanac™ to examine what people might be able to do if they were provided with a large number of visual and sound images as well as some tools built with HyperCard that let them combine these according to their own interests and intents. As described in much more detail in other chapters in this book (including chapters by Margo Nanny and Sueann Ambron), people have found these materials extremely engaging. Teachers and students are drawn strongly to this image resource and quickly master the required methodology to become expressive multimedia composers.

The Visual Almanac contains a range of activities and sample compositions, included as initial explorations of how this particular image resource might be used in many topic areas to explain ideas. I look forward to viewing the ways in which people use these resources, especially those ways which are quite different from any we have anticipated!

Interestingly, we have already learned that all the people we have worked with seem to have both the talent and inclination needed to put together their own materials. I suggest this concurrence is partly due to the simplicity of the tools that we have built using HyperCard and partly due to the straightforwardness of the methodology we have employed in the creation of a composition and the use of an activity. I would guess that the concurrence is also a function of the readiness in our culture to work directly with images. If this guess is correct, we will surely see some very new classes of communication that enter the mainstream of education.

Multiple Representations

Many cognitive psychologists are now arguing for the importance of multiple representations in the understanding of a concept. Although there is little controversy about the correctness of this argument, the examples typically used in experimentation are limited. HyperCard, coupled with optical media, places multiple representations within the reach of the practitioner. It also provides the cognitive researcher in this area with a wide range of opportunities to examine how people do work with a broad set of examples.

We demonstrated the use of multiple representations in many of our design examples. It was most straightforwardly illustrated in The Visual Almanac, as shown in Figure 4 on the following page. In this example we found (in casual observation) that people were enchanted with these different representations. Some seemed to learn something about physics by playing with this demonstration. Others seemed to understand quite a bit more about graphs, or at least they began to feel that they might someday be able to understand these strange representations. Still others imagined a range of pedagogical instances in which a similar technique might be used to advantage.

We don't have systematic evidence from any of the examples we built that multiple representations are critical for thinking or understanding. We know that people like them, and these people tell us that they learn from them. With examples such as these, which are now possible with HyperCard, a set of instances appears that researchers can investigate to determine the usefulness of these displays.

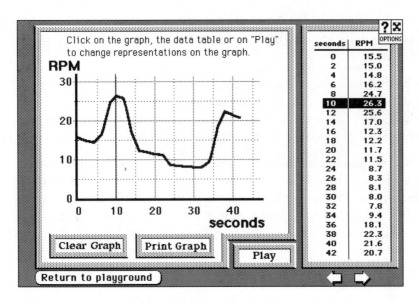

Click on the graph, the data table or on "Play" to change representations on the graph.

seconds	RPM
0	15.5
2	15.0
4	14.8
6	16.2
8	24.7
10	26.3
12	25.6
14	17.0
16	12.3
18	12.2
20	11.7
22	11.5
24	8.7
26	8.3
28	8.1
30	8.0
32	7.8
34	9.4
36	18.1
38	22.3
40	21.6
42	20.7

FIGURE 4. This HyperCard card accompanies an activity called Playground Physics in The Visual Almanac. The card demonstrates how multiple representations of a single event might encourage understanding both of the event and of the representations of the event. This card accompanies a short movie of a merry-go-round spinning around, which is displayed by a videodisc. As those of you with highly developed graph-reading skills will imagine, the people on the playground merry-go-round are moving in and out, causing the merry-go-round to go faster (did they move in or out?), then slower, and then faster again. The graph develops as the movie plays. After the graph is drawn, any point on the graph or in the table can be accessed; each selection shows the corresponding element in the other representation, including the appropriate still frame from the movie.

Time-Based Phenomena

The example described in Figure 4 seems to be particularly useful because it directly addresses a time-based phenomenon, which many people have difficulty in understanding.

A critical aspect of understanding time-based phenomena, which encompass most of one's everyday experience, is the ability to control these phenomena directly. Yet such control is usually unavailable in normal (everyday) experience. However, we have found that a combination of HyperCard and optical media allows us to provide viewers with direct manipulation of complex events. People report that they gain, readily and directly, an understanding of the events that they examine in this context, although they are often unable to articulate exactly what they mean by "understanding."

A number of possible events can be examined in a HyperCard context. These include such events as meetings, psychotherapy sessions, dance choreography, and sports activities. Each event is fundamentally a visual–kinesthetic experience that is typically

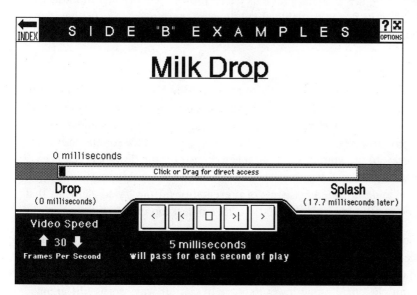

FIGURE 5. This screen is one of many from the Durations activity in The Visual Almanac. It shows a controller, which lets the user examine an event—in this case, a milk drop. This event, which lasts 17.7 milliseconds (note the end of the timeline), can be viewed at a number of speeds by changing the Video Speed indicator; each choice of speed will result in a certain playback rate, which is shown beneath the videocontroller. (For example, 5 milliseconds will pass for each second of play at a playback rate of 30 frames per second on the videodisc player.) An opportunity for some enjoyable arithmetic presents itself here, as well as an opportunity to directly deal with (and hopefully understand) the differences between initial sampling rates of a camera and final playback rates of a playback device such as a videodisc. In observing a number of users, the profound "understandings" are reported as the viewer directly manipulates the event by moving the indicator on the timeline (hence, accessing a different stage of the event). Note the ?-X-Options "superbutton" in the upper right corner of the screen; this superbutton is referred to in Figure 6.

unavailable for analysis in normal experience. However, the simple combination of a HyperCard controller and a videodisc or CD-audio disc makes it very possible to systematically analyze these events and others. In The Visual Almanac, for example, we included a large number of time-based movie clips—time-lapse photographs of sunsets, slow-motion records of action sequences such as cars crashing, high-speed photography of quickly occurring events such as a bullet going through an egg. A single HyperCard controller, as shown in Figure 5 on the previous page, allows access to any of these events. Simple modifications would enable annotations of these events for further discussion and analysis.

Interface Opportunities

One great curse and great opportunity we discovered in using HyperCard is that we can invent an interface to accomplish whatever task we have in mind. The curse is that one spends much too much time considering, again and again, exactly how a subject might be presented most effectively; the advantages of a consistent interface for end users (such as the Macintosh desktop) are simply not available to constrain the designers' choices. The opportunity is that invention is encouraged in the interface domain, particularly in regards to navigation and multimedia aspects of presentations, time-based elements that are hardly addressed at all in the more spatially oriented desktop interface.

The interface elements of HyperCard stacks are beginning to be standardized, through use and through the encouragement of documents such as the *HyperCard Style Guidelines* provided by Apple Computer, Inc. Arrows are being used in standard manners for navigation—for example, enabling a viewer to move in similar ways across different stacks. Overview navigational maps, such as the one shown in Figure 6, are also becoming widely available for user movement through a system. Help systems are being provided in many HyperCard systems, to provide the least-experienced users with some guidelines about what elements in a system are "clickable."

Multimedia presentations are beginning to include a range of very similar video controllers and video editors, as well as note takers, annotation indicators, and "book-markers." This range of tools is being used differently by each multimedia producer, but great similarities in the paradigms that are available are becoming evident. In our own work in the Multimedia Lab, we are finding that the tools we developed for The Visual Almanac are migrating across many of our projects, as are the interfaces we invented for this project. It will be interesting to note whether a new set of interface conventions and standardized tools, available to all multimedia users, emerges in the near future.

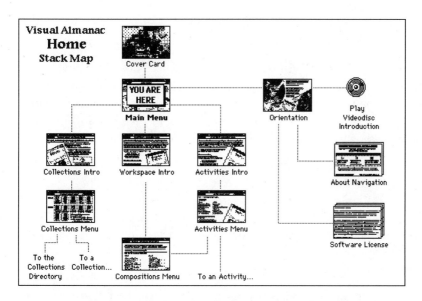

FIGURE 6. A map of The Visual Almanac is available at all times in this product via a "superbutton" (see Figure 5) that appears on all cards. This particular map is available from the Main Menu. This map is active; clicking on a location brings the viewer to that location.

Off to School (1989–90)

Even as we learned the lessons involved in HyperCard design very well, we found the issues involved in HyperCard multimedia product design to be substantial (although highly engaging). We found HyperCard to be remarkably scalable to large amounts of materials. We also were surprised to learn that, in producing multimedia products, we had to face both the perils of software production and those of television production, rather than some interaction of the two that was simpler than either.

With most uses of HyperCard—within a single classroom or school, by a few people, as examples—these production issues are irrelevant. HyperCard provides a "fluid medium" for representing one's casual thoughts and for communication among students and teachers. As projects and expectations expand, we will have to address serious production issues.

As with most media, HyperCard does give rise to a number of professional products and personal tools. The good news about HyperCard products, particularly the multimedia products, is that they are reconstitutable—that is, they can be examined, then disassembled, and then reassembled in a variety of ways.

It is this flexibility of HyperCard that will make new multimedia "titles" (a convenient name for professionally prepared HyperCard and multimedia presentations, which typically contain their own tools) very engaging in the school environment. Multimedia titles will provide a particular point of view on a topic as well as the raw materials to examine these points of view and to constitute an individual point of view.

A number of multimedia titles on the Macintosh platform will be announced in 1990, including three in which the Multimedia Lab has been centrally involved. The Visual Almanac will be made available by Apple Computer, Inc., for experimental use in the schools. WGBH-NOVA will introduce the first Interactive NOVA in collaboration with the Multimedia Lab. The National Geographic Society and Lucasfilm will be introducing a Macintosh geography-television product (GTV™), based on one of the early design examples of the Multimedia Lab.

Each of these products will offer great opportunities to explore the use of multimedia in human thinking. Each will introduce its own experiment. As people view these and other products, their experience with this new HyperCard medium will expand, and their own experimentations with this medium will change. Even as you read this book about ongoing work with HyperCard, you will imagine new opportunities that are now available to you—and hopefully soon seek them out.

In Closing

The excitement now is in watching people use the new technologies and tools and learning from these observations to create even better technologies and tools—to take one more step away from being "flatlanders," for most of us are truly limited in this area by our imaginations.

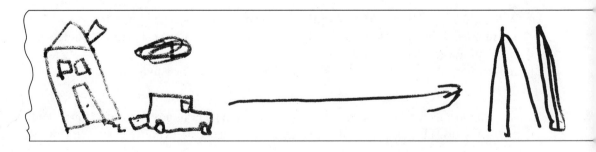

The timeline drawing, below, was done by my son when he was five years old. The linear format of this "cash register receipt" encouraged him to put together a pictorial narrative (about our trip to the mountains to go swimming, and then our return), something that is not present in most of his drawings. One must acknowledge how the form of a medium affects that which is communicated. Even with this acknowledgment, it is difficult to imagine exactly what kinds of communication will be afforded by presentation formats such as those merely hinted at by HyperCard.

Those of us born before, say, 1960 have been raised and educated without computers. Even if we have used computers, we have not had much experience with the highly sensory, nonlinear formats that are available today with HyperCard and other tools similar to it (for example, Silicon Beach's Supercard, Macromind's Director, and Authorware's Course of Action).

Our children will be the first real users of the systems we provide, and they will be the ones who can keep all our intuitions in line as well as keep each of us honest. We must laugh at ourselves as they take for granted those things that we consider amazing.

In my closing remarks in *Interactive Multimedia* (Microsoft Press, 1988), I wrote that it was bound to be an exciting era in the multimedia business. Little did I realize that within the 2 years following the writing of that book, I would see multimedia rise from obscurity to the limelight as a marketplace hit. I had thought that this ascent would take another 10 years or so. HyperCard has converted many fanciful dreams to concrete, accessible, and demonstrable realities. I can barely imagine what the coming years will bring!

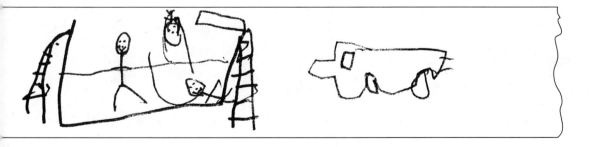

Information Landscapes

Fabrice Florin

FABRICE FLORIN

Fabrice Florin is a producer–designer at Apple Computer, Inc.'s Multimedia Lab, where he designs information environments. He began working with Apple in 1986 while producing an electronic atlas prototype called Worldview, developed with Apple fellow Bill Atkinson, to test interactive video applications of HyperCard.

Prior to joining Apple Computer, he was an independent television producer for 10 years. From 1978 to 1984, he headed Videowest Productions, Inc., a production company specializing in magazine-style TV programming for young adults. As executive producer, he supervised the development, production, and distribution of several television series for ABC stations, MTV, ON-TV, public television, and the USA Cable Network. He also oversaw the production of various specials shown on the Arts & Entertainment Network, the BBC, and Showtime, as well as a number of music videos. He personally produced, wrote, and directed many of the above programs and also worked as free-lance producer on television specials for the ABC Television Network, the Disney Channel, HBO, and Twentieth Century Fox Television.

He fell in love with interactive media in 1985, while producing "Hackers—Wizards of the Electronic Age," a public-television documentary about computer programmers.

In 1985, I had the unique opportunity to develop one of the first videodisc applications of HyperCard, in collaboration with HyperCard's developer, Bill Atkinson. A television producer by trade, I knew little then about computers. Bill's revolutionary authoring tool opened up a new form of expression as well as a different way of thinking. It also led to an unexpected turn in my career: I have been working ever since at Apple Computer, Inc.'s Multimedia Lab as a designer of HyperCard information environments. In this article I would like to share what we have learned about creating these new interactive structures.*

The charter of our research group is to try out new ideas by creating *design examples.* Typically, design examples are prototypes of educational multimedia systems using HyperCard and custom-made videodiscs; we build them to simulate interactive applications of the future and to address key design issues in the process. This article refers to three specific projects for which I was lead designer: Worldview, an electronic atlas developed with the help of Bill Atkinson and Kristina Hooper; The Living Constitution, an electronic museum developed in collaboration with Optical Data Corp. and Scholastic Inc. Software; and Life Story, an annotated movie developed in collaboration with Adrian Malone, the Smithsonian Institution, and Lucasfilm, Ltd. I also refer to The Visual Almanac™, a demonstration kit produced by the Multimedia Lab under Kristina Hooper's direction.

As a designer, what attracts me to HyperCard is that it makes possible a whole new class of information environments, which can be created and delivered with relative ease through interactive presentations of images, sounds, and words. As a user, I am fascinated by the prospect of exploring these environments, which respond to me and help me understand things more intuitively. HyperCard provides a rare opportunity to both present and discover knowledge in ways that turn the learning process into an adventure.

Information Landscapes

How do people present knowledge so that others can understand it? The traditional method is a linear, narrative unfolding of sequential information—for example, lectures and textbooks. Other methods rely on a nonlinear, spatial layout of information—for

* Some of the concepts presented here were discussed at length during the past few years with Sueann Ambron, Steve Gano, Nancy Hechinger, Kristina Hooper, Kristee Kreitman, Bob Mohl, Mike Naimark, Margo Nanny, Rob Semper, and other designers at the Apple Multimedia Lab. I would like to thank them for many open-minded and stimulating conversations. I particularly wish to thank Kristina, for fostering a forum in which such ideas could be discussed and experimented with so freely, and Bill Atkinson, for giving us HyperCard and a new design medium.

example, diagrams and maps. We are still discovering more sophisticated approaches: for example, conversational methods, in which one person queries another in no particular order and in which the other responds with specific answers; and hands-on activities and simulations that let people learn by trying things out or by building interactive models of the world. Although HyperCard tends to work better with some presentation modes than others, the projects I have worked on to date have used at least one of those methods.

In trying to grasp those different modes of presentation, I have begun to think of our HyperCard environments as *information landscapes,* which can be thought of as virtual towns or intellectual amusement parks. (See Figure 1.) The analogy is quite intriguing and helps us to visualize many abstract concepts within a single metaphor.

As you visit an information landscape, you can merely walk along pathways and look at roadside attractions, or you can choose from many different options. Some of the options take you on linear trails, which you experience passively from start to finish, as you would a ride in a bus. Other activities give you local control—similar to driving a car. Maps can show you a bird's-eye view of the territory, and guides can take you on tours or give you more conversational assistance.

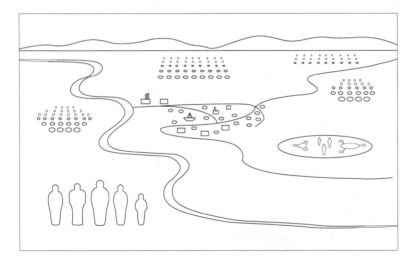

FIGURE 1. This is one way to represent an information landscape. Fields of raw data alternate with more structured information clusters. Various paths and trails traverse the environment and connect nodes. Guides and activities are also on hand.

The terrain on which the information landscape is built is the raw database, rich with various materials, from which the "visitor" can create new documents or exhibits. However, the information structure is what gives the landscape its distinctive features.

Searching for Structures

In designing these new environments, we have been searching for structures that work well and can be expressed in a few basic templates or recipes. During the past few years, I have encountered five types of structures, which I call:

1. Collections of data
2. Interactive documentaries
3. Annotated movies
4. Networks of guides
5. Hands-on activities

Each structure corresponds to a slightly different information framework and lends itself to different modes of exploration by the user. Information landscapes often combine several of these structures at once, as interconnected but separate tiers in a multilayered environment. Therefore, I have superimposed them one after the other in the rough diagrams that follow. In the comments below, I have referred to raw images, sounds, text, and film clips as *data,* regardless of media type. Meaningful arrangements of such data into thoughtful presentations are referred to as *information.*

Collections of Data

The simplest way to present knowledge is to break it down into collections of similar data or materials. Each collection has one or more main axes along which the data can be arranged. (See Figure 2 on the following page.) The axes let you measure common denominators shared by all the data, which can then be lined up against generic yardsticks. You can thus list items from A through Z, by size, place, time, theme, or in some other order of your choice. For instance, a timeline can represent materials in a database by showing data points arranged chronologically along its axis.

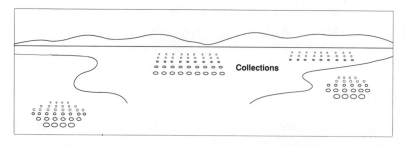

FIGURE 2. In an information landscape, collections can be viewed as fields of raw data, which can be arranged in different ways. In this illustration, one axis might be time, *with recent data shown in the foreground and older data shown in the background.*

In the Worldview electronic atlas prototype, I combined several axes to form a multi-dimensional grid. In this map browser, users can fly around the globe, zoom down to the region of their choice, and view materials in that particular place. (See Figure 3.) The materials are represented by thematic icons on a "touch and see" map, which you can click on with a mouse to display the appropriate pictures. I first used two spatial axes (*longitude* and *latitude*) and a *size* axis (zoom from big to small) to represent the data.

I later added another axis to define a spectrum of data *types* (maps, pictures, facts, and graphs) available for a particular place; I also put in a *theme* axis to break up materials related to people, land, economy, and history for that place. It is interesting to note that the *size* axis could be used in combination with either spatial or thematic axes. With spatial axes, you would zoom in and out from whole continents to single cities and back again. Along the *theme* axis, the scope of display would expand or narrow—from broad themes, such as *economy,* to subsidiary topics, such as *trade* and other subtopics nested deeper in this hierarchical tree structure.

By combining two axes, you define a two-dimensional grid, against which data can be laid out like pieces on a chessboard: This allows you to intersect, as above, *size* and *theme* or *theme* and *time,* by simply assigning different criteria to the *x* and *y* axes. Add a third axis, and you have a three-dimensional "data cube" in which you can map, say, *themes* over *time,* alphabetically. This is exactly what Steve Gano did in one section of our Living Constitution prototype called the Time Gallery. In his *data cube,* he presented

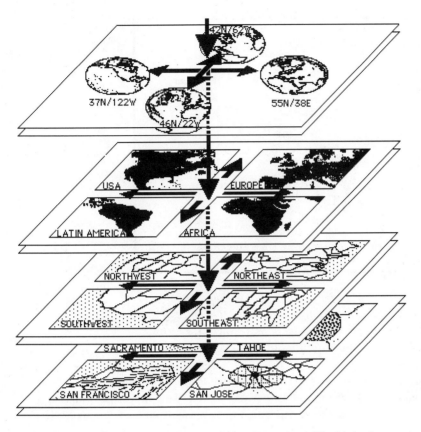

*FIGURE 3. As shown in this descent to San Francisco, Worldview's
prototype lets you discover the world at different scale levels: planet,
continents, countries, cities, and so on. By clicking with a mouse on
"hot" areas of the computer screen, you can zoom in and out to the
location of your choice.*

data chronologically along its length, thematically along its width, and alphabetically
along its height. (See Figure 4 on the following page.) Users could choose between a top,
side, or front view of the cube and then pick a slice of their choice, dive into it, and slide
back and forth along either axis to change their view.

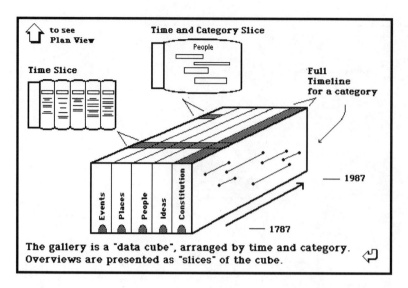

FIGURE 4. This data cube *provides the user with various methods to access materials about the United States Constitution. One face of the cube is a timeline, while the other has a set of predefined categories: Events, Places, People, Ideas, and Constitution.*

The beauty of such multidimensional structures is that they can organize vast amounts of disconnected data along fairly simple lines, without requiring much editorial work. (See Figure 5.) Users should be able to navigate easily through such a framework: For

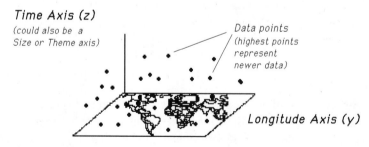

FIGURE 5. This crude space–time framework represents the contents of its database as data points in a three-dimensional model; each item is shown above its place on the world map, at a height corresponding to its time period.

instance, they could zip through images of world history with a simple time-machine control, sliding up and down the z axis, or they could compare two regions at the same point in time. You could also replace the vertical *time* axis with a *size* axis for spatial navigation or with a *theme* axis for thematic browsing.

However, this kind of representation has obvious limitations. Most databases require more than three axes, which is difficult to represent graphically on a two-dimensional screen; and although this framework makes your database appear more orderly, it does not necessarily make it more interesting. The initial exhilaration of flying through vast territories of data soon gives way to a feeling of frustration, due to the lack of depth and meaningful connections once you stop somewhere. As you look at an isolated picture or data set, you want to find out more about the people or ideas related to it, yet often you get only a terse caption with subject, place, time, and other keywords, with little substantive commentary and no meaningful linkages to other data points.

Space, time, and size measurements are too generic to be very useful when studying complex systems. The arbitrary breakdown of knowledge into themes or categories familiar to the designers might not match the users' own mental constructs, no matter how good the editors are. Therefore, the teacher and the student must create meaningful connections between data with special annotation and composition tools. Such connections are often difficult to establish because either the data do not exist to make a case or no point can be made with the available data. In my view, this framework is most useful in the first stages of building an information landscape, as a way to stockpile materials for further refinement.

By trial and error, we have discovered some general rules of thumb about this kind of structure:

- Clusters of tightly interconnected materials focused on specific topics are more satisfying than thin layers of data covering broad subjects. For example, isolated pictures are not as interesting as sets of five or more, where each picture in the set adds meaning to the others, exposing relations hidden in the single shot.
- In most cases, pictures with no good captions or data are not very useful.
- Still pictures and text can often be perceived as lifeless unless they are combined with sound or motion footage. I highly recommend that great care be given to the selection of a rich audio track and, if possible, film or video clips that bring a subject to life.

Interactive Documentaries

A more elaborate structure for an information landscape is the *interactive documentary,* which centers all data around modular presentations. These presentations can be short stories or interactive diagrams linked to related materials. By focusing on such presentations as building blocks of an information landscape, more meaning is given to the materials, connecting data points to each other along specific lines of thought (See Figure 6.) These nodes of information can now be browsed as integrated documents, rather than as disconnected data. Moreover, users can choose the order in which these presentations appear and interrupt them at will.

In the Living Constitution prototype, for example, I created an environment containing gripping news footage of James Meredith, a black man who was originally denied admission to the University of Mississippi in 1961 due to his race. We edited a two-minute excerpt from the PBS series "Eyes on the Prize" to show dramatic confrontations between James Meredith, segregationist governor John Barnett, and President John F. Kennedy, fighting over radically different interpretations of the U.S. Constitution. (See Figure 7.) This film clip is very moving, and it succeeds where traditional textbooks and other

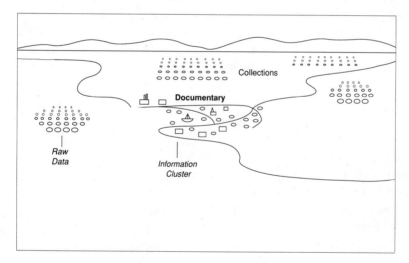

FIGURE 6. In an information landscape, a documentary could be represented as a small town or settlement. This structure lets designers integrate raw data *from adjoining collections into modular* information clusters. *Various paths through this virtual town relate materials to each other and define subject areas.*

1962

Video Clip - James Meredith

| James Meredith files for admission | Governor Ross Barnett stops him | Meredith tries again, Barnett interposes | President Kennedy intervenes |

| Old Miss turns into a battlefield | Kennedy & Barnett argue. | The army restores order | Meredith admitted to Old Miss Univ. Moral of the story |

FIGURE 7. This interactive storyboard represents a two-minute mini-documentary about James Meredith, which tells the true story of a human being caught up in an emotionally charged situation. Each miniature picture in this time-based presentation gives access to a different scene, such as the one shown in Figure 8.

educational materials often fail. The issues of federalism and civil rights become relevant to the user. Because the footage is emotionally compelling, you want to learn more on the subject; and because it lets you experience historical moments as if you were a witness to them, it opens the door to deeper levels of understanding. But what is most significant here is that the story gives you a *reason* to study the materials.

The important issues underlying this event can also be viewed in ways other than traditional linear storytelling. For example, interactive diagrams and concept maps can add new meanings to the same materials. We supplemented the Meredith story with conceptual diagrams illustrating the opposing interpretations of the Constitution put forth by Kennedy and Barnett. (See Figure 8 on the following page.) Set against a map of the United States, the diagrams show the importance each assigned to federal government and to state government under constitutional law. The diagrams could also play back on-camera statements presenting their opposing points of view, which could be viewed in any order. After comparing them, you could easily dive into the main database and slide along the *time* axis to discover other events related to civil rights in American history or to consult related documents, such as the full text of the Constitution.

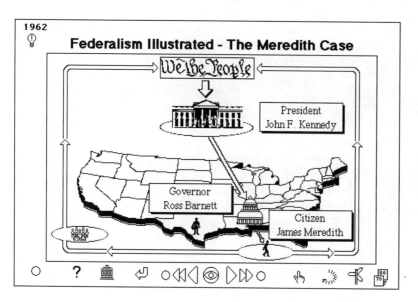

FIGURE 8. *This diagram demonstrates the concept of federalism by showing the relationships between the state, the citizen, and the federal government. Clicking on the Citizen plays a brief video clip of James Meredith explaining his position; clicking on the President plays an excerpt from John F. Kennedy's televised address.*

An information landscape based on this modular structure might feature up to a dozen related short presentations, meant to introduce key concepts and act as entryways into the underlying database. The presentations do not necessarily have to be film clips or linear stories; they could also be nonlinear exhibits or virtual places. What matters is that they be organized arrangements of ideas connecting a set of multimedia materials. For instance, the Living Constitution prototype uses the spatial metaphor of a museum, in which Exhibit Rooms are modular containers for documents related to different eras. (See Figure 9.) Scholastic's designers gave each Exhibit Room a blackboard for lesson plans, historical guides for narrated tours, pictures on the walls for short sequences of images, and so on. As does the Meredith film clip described above, the Exhibit Room provides an intriguing front-end to the data that it connects.

An interactive documentary is not an interruptible television program. It is a collection of experiences and ideas about a given subject, available to users in either linear or nonlinear modules: *story* modules organize materials against a temporal axis, whereas *place* modules arrange them in a spatial layout. Each module is self-contained, takes at most a couple of minutes to introduce, and therefore lends itself quite nicely to classroom

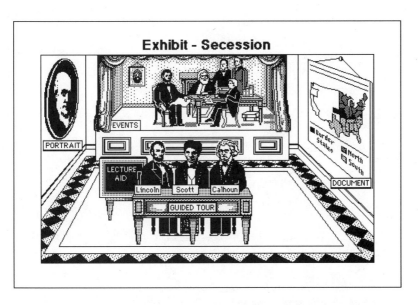

FIGURE 9. This Exhibit Room is a spatial representation of a multi-media database about the Secession Era. The walls, the people, and the plaques in the Exhibit Room are active buttons; clicking on any of these objects takes you into an exhibit trail—a sequence of multi-media HyperCard exhibit cards that contain text, picture, sound, and video segments. In this case, a "place" module acts as a front-end to various "story" modules.

applications. Teachers could present a different module (or unit) every week, extending the useful life of the information environment through the entire school year. Modules can be an extremely powerful resource for group discussions; teachers can decide the order in which they will present the materials as the discussion evolves. A clear draw-back, however, is that often no easy way exists for first-time users to know which mod-ules to try first, and some time needs to be spent poking around and playing clips at random before discovering what is available.

Annotated Movies

Another structure for an information landscape is the *annotated movie*. In this structure, a feature-length movie is the main backbone of the landscape. Unlike the free-form browsing approach of the interactive documentary, the annotated movie has a strong linear structure. (See Figure 10 on the following page.) Viewers are encouraged to view

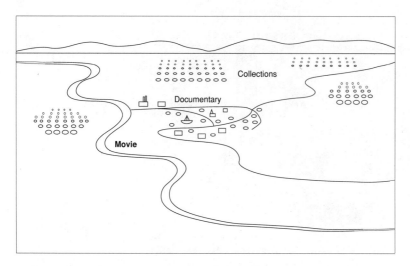

FIGURE 10. As its story unfolds, the movie flows like a stream through the information landscape and redefines it in the process. This simple linear structure is a good starting point for creating a new environment. The storyline provides a common thread to which all materials in the landscape can be connected.

the entire movie and then to use the interactive information environment surrounding the movie to revisit it and explore the issues that it raises. The idea here is that the excitement of a good motion picture can engage people to learn more about its subject matter.

The germ of this idea was presented to us by Adrian Malone and Ed Bastian of the Smithsonian Institution and, together with Rob Semper, director of an Apple–Lucasfilm research project, we developed it one step further in the Life Story prototype. *Life Story* is a BBC television drama about the discovery of DNA by Jim Watson and Francis Crick, presented in the United States on the Arts & Entertainment Cable Network. Producer–director Mick Jackson and the rest of the cast and crew did such a wonderful job that this movie can be viewed a number of times and still retain its freshness.

An annotated movie's storyline is the major feature of the information landscape, through which it flows like a stream. In this example, we chose to represent it with a plot map shaped like a double helix. (See Figure 11.) One strand retraces the story of Jim Watson and Francis Crick at Cambridge's Cavendish Lab in England. The other strand follows the parallel storyline of another team of researchers, Rosalind Franklin and Maurice Wilkins, at King's College in London. Both stories intertwine throughout the drama, as the two teams puzzle over this seemingly unsolvable mystery. The round

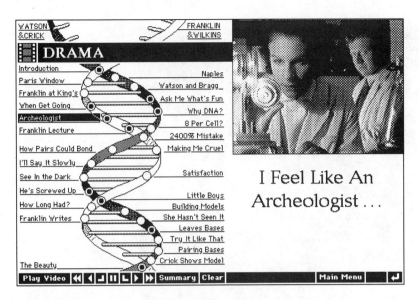

FIGURE 11. This plot map shows the entire Life Story drama at a glance. Each strand of the double helix represents a different story. Key scenes are represented by round buttons. This scene shows Rosalind Franklin preparing DNA fibers for X-ray diffraction.

buttons along each strand represent key scenes in the drama; you can click on any of them to jump directly to that scene, which can then be played back at the touch of a button. It occurred to us later that the double-helix shape of our plot map could also be used to represent other stories, as classic dramatic structures confront protagonists with antagonists in much the same pattern.

After users locate a scene of interest from the plot map, they can inquire about that scene in a number of ways. One of the most compelling approaches in this example lets users query the video frame directly through a video digitizer or graphic overlay card, which can bring the video image onto the Macintosh screen. This allows designers to define hot spots, which users can click on to find out more about the people or objects in a given picture. (See Figure 12 on the following page.) For example, when you click on one of the characters in the drama, a narrator whispers a few words of information about that person and an identifying label is superimposed on the video picture. The narrator then suggests you click again to see an interview with Raymond Gosling, a real-life scientist portrayed in the drama; this calls up a BBC interview with Gosling, describing 20 years later what he was doing in that scene. Similarly, double-clicking on the object that Rosalind Franklin is holding in her hand calls up a HyperCard animation illustrating

FIGURE 12. In the one-screen version of Life Story, users can click on hot spots to find out more about this scene. For instance, clicking on the man in the background calls up a voice-over and overlays a label identifying him as Raymond Gosling. Clicking on him again brings an interview with the real-life scientist portrayed here.

how X-ray diffraction cameras work. This very intuitive method of browsing through audio-visual materials shows a lot of promise for future multimedia applications.

Each key scene and related subject in the movie is documented in our HyperCard information landscape through what we call a *pamphlet*. All pamphlets in the system have the same structure, which includes Summary, Questions, Links, See Also, and Exhibits. The Summary screen tells you what the pamphlet is about and lists its contents, called Exhibits, which you can access by clicking on their name. The Questions screen offers a choice of frequently asked questions about that scene or subject, along with Hints that give you clues about where to look for answers. The Links screen highlights related pamphlets and lets you jump to the most important ones by simply clicking on their name or the picture that illustrates them. See Also gives you even more options, listing other interesting pamphlets, as well as external resources such as articles, books, films, and other useful publications.

One of the main advantages of the annotated movie structure is that the narrative provides a common thread that ties together all subjects in the information landscape. Having to build around a specific storyline encourages the interactive designers to go for depth rather than breadth, which makes for a richer environment. The opportunity to find out more about a movie you like is a thrill in itself. One can foresee a time when filmmakers will take such interactive applications as seriously as, say, merchandising. If you consider the phenomenal amount of research that goes into a film script or set design, you can't help but wish there were a way for people to access that information. The annotated movie structure lets you do that.

Of course, there are many outstanding questions about this structure. How many great movies can be repurposed for interactive applications? Will audiences want to revisit a movie to learn about its related subjects? Will filmmakers want the public to know the real facts behind a movie? Will teachers mind that most movies only cover a limited knowledge domain, with few ties to the curriculum? Will we have an affordable technology that gives access to a feature-length movie plus documentary footage in a simple format for a wide range of users?

I think these questions will be resolved in time, due to the incredible power of this structure. Because they engage users emotionally as well as intellectually, annotated movies can empower people to investigate subjects they would never have cared to explore otherwise. This structure also brings together the worlds of entertainment and education to deliver a whole new type of experience, one that could be the basis of a "crossover" market for movie studios and book publishers.

Networks of Guides

Looming on the horizon is a fascinating challenge, that of building information landscapes containing individual *guides* who provide users with personalized assistance. Although much talked about in research circles for several decades, the concept of guides or agents has yet to become a practical reality. The mere notion of an anthropomorphic guide can raise users' expectations beyond what today's computers can deliver. Nonetheless, this remains a very compelling goal—one that I think can be achieved incrementally if we begin with human, rather than artificial, intelligence.

In the Life Story example, we explored the notion of guides with an existing on-camera commentary by Jacob Bronowski, host of the BBC science series "The Ascent of Man," in which he tells his own account of the discovery of DNA. Rob Semper and I drew a rough concept map of his lecture, which weaves yet another strand through the Life

Story drama and its surrounding materials. However, the filmed lecture did not lend itself as well as the drama to repurposing as an interactive presentation. I think of a guide as more than a narrative train of thoughts broken down into small chunks. I want my guide to be more responsive to my individual needs than a scripted, one-way lecture can be, no matter how good the lecturer is.

This presents a very difficult challenge: How does one convey the knowledge of a good thinker so that it can be explored interactively through our information landscapes? One approach is to have the guide "anticipate" the users' questions—by prerecording a large number of voice or text annotations for playback in the environment. These notes can then be linked to each other and to related materials as part of a "guided tour." Another approach is to extend the environment with communication channels to the real world, allowing users to consult the actual guide (or its assistants and interpreters) in person or via mail, phone, and telecommunication networks. This gives many users an interactive introduction to a great thinker's ideas, without replacing subsequent person-to-person communication between student and teacher; it enhances the educational system instead of competing with it.

One of the biggest limitations to date with any publication (be it in print, on tape, on videodisc, or on CD-ROM) is that the information it contains is frozen long before it is sent to press. The best way for an information landscape to grow is through live channels of communication to and from the outside world, allowing for feedback, editing, updates, and so on. In such a scenario, the process becomes more important than the actual product. The system becomes a focal point for the development of a community of interested users and authors who collectively extend the shared knowledgebase. This requires a simple but powerful set of composition tools that allow content experts and novice users to mark, annotate, link, and otherwise interconnect various parts of the information landscape. Such tools would let users compare different points of view and develop their own through essays, diagrams, tours, and other custom presentations. Ultimately, any user could become a guide to the environment.

To illustrate this concept, I have added guides to the landscape in my diagram. (See Figure 13.) These guides add their knowledge to the environment by connecting various information nodes and data points; the webs they weave reach deep within the shared landscape, but they also extend out into the real world.

Much like a small town, an information landscape cannot come to life until it becomes populated with users who feel at home in it; as the community settles and grows in that environment, more users become guides and blaze new trails that add meaning to the landscape, which makes the landscape more attractive to newcomers. The human factor is what makes the difference here, because we tend to trust people more than machines.

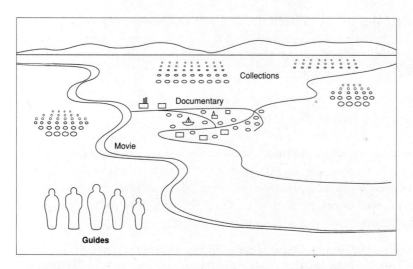

Collections

Documentary

Movie

Guides

FIGURE 13. Overlooking the entire information landscape, guides offer their viewpoints to integrate the various materials in the environment. They can blaze new trails to connect related collections, movies, or documentaries.

For the same reason that I would rather use a product that was recommended by a friend or trusted columnist, I would prefer to follow a local guide's recommendation of items to see in the system, instead of searching for arbitrary keywords in a database or browsing aimlessly in the information landscape. The guide's personality, viewpoints, and values are easier for me to relate to in my quest for knowledge than a set of abstract search criteria.

As larger user communities gather around our information landscapes, different classes of guides are likely to emerge, including:

- *System operators, information brokers,* and *editors*—who provide general services to help connect users with what they are looking for
- *Specialists and content experts*—who concentrate on specific subjects and report on their particular knowledge domain
- *Interdisciplinary authors*—who provide editorial commentaries and personal insights across a wide range of subjects
- *Other users*—who share tips with each other about interesting information they have found or added to the system

We are only now beginning to learn what is possible when a community grows up around a shared information landscape. I can't wait to see what happens when people start interconnecting movies, images, and sounds for public discourse, much as they do with text in today's computer networks.

Hands-On Activities

This brings us to our final structure, an information landscape centered around hands-on activities. (See Figure 14.) These activities let users learn by trying things out themselves and drawing their own conclusions. This structure seems like a great opportunity for interactive information landscapes, because it has the potential to turn passive consumers of audio-visual experiences into active seekers of knowledge.

As defined here, activities are enjoyable exercises with an educational outcome, max-imized for what the computer does best—supporting interactive experiences. Activities can range from simple games to complex simulations. The guiding principle is that they be fun and that they help users gain new insights. The Multimedia Lab's Visual Almanac offers several good examples. For instance, in the Planetary Highway activity, you learn

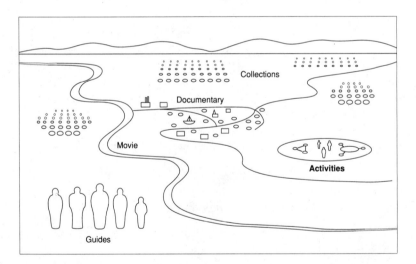

FIGURE 14. In an information landscape, activities are like play-grounds that allow guides and users to learn by playing with each other and the surrounding materials. Designing environments to support such human interactions directly addresses the important psychological and social issues of how people use information landscapes.

about the conservation of angular momentum by riding a merry-go-round; in the Playground Physics activity, you experience the size of the solar system by driving through a six-mile stretch of desert highway, along which planetary signposts are drawn to scale.

These activities are very compelling because they let users participate as players in the environment, not merely as spectators. The locus of control is shifted from the designers back to the users. Rather than absorb someone else's ideas, users now determine the outcome of their individual experiences: They make choices and reach their own conclusions. This deepens their understanding of the subject, because that knowledge was discovered "hands-on" and is now *theirs*.

Gaming is an important element of this activity framework. Turning serious assignments into playful exercises seems to relax the users and take some of the drudgery out of learning. This lighter approach also cuts through preconceived notions and invites users to re-examine the world from different perspectives.

Although they can become pretty complex, simulations and dynamic models of the world show a lot of promise as well. Even if they are not very accurate, these models can reveal interesting patterns by letting users experiment with different assumptions for a particular scenario. This helps them discover important processes and relationships within a system. Building an information landscape around such a simulation would give users the best of two worlds—a "what if" forecasting tool and a multimedia learning environment to explain the results.

The richest activities, to my mind, are the ones that also take place in the real world, not only on the computer screen. The Life Story project features one such activity, which lets students build their own DNA model with paper cut outs. The students first watch a scene from the *Life Story* movie, where Jim Watson uses the same paper cut outs to solve the structure of DNA. They can then browse through a HyperCard stack to learn about the atomic structure of the parts that they are holding. Finally the students are asked to piece the parts together to build a DNA molecule—*with their own hands*. The result is very encouraging: A freshman biology class in our first test site earned higher test scores than ever before after using this activity for merely a few days. As one student said, "You feel like *you actually discovered DNA*."

The reason such activities seem so important is that they suggest different modes of interaction between users and their information environment. An activity provides an arena for people to play in and materials to play with; most importantly, however, it gives people ideas of *what to do* in that context. Activities set the stage for experiences that involve people and computers in meaningful ways. Defining these human interactions is perhaps the ultimate challenge for this new medium.

Design Tips

As novice architects in a foreign territory, we are still struggling to understand what constitutes a good design for these new landscapes. I don't know if any of the ideas expressed here will stand the test of time, but I hope they will assist other designers in this emerging field.

The first step in designing an information landscape is to define its primary purpose: Is it meant as a generic resource or to teach a specific topic? How broad does it have to be? Who is the intended user group? How will users interact with it? Where do they need the most help? The next step is to identify the materials available for that project: How much data is provided for each item? Are the items cataloged? Are they cross-indexed? Have they been annotated or edited together with a single commentary? Are they disparate documents, or have they been carefully researched and sorted?

You now have to select a particular structure as the main framework of the landscape. The purpose of the project and the nature of the materials may suggest one, but more often it is a creative call. This process feels somewhat like landscaping or urban design: Which primary features do you want to build around? Which secondary features do you want to emphasize? How do you balance these different elements? How do people move from one to another?

I like to think of the different structures presented above as different types of space in a rural landscape. (See Figure 15.) For example, *collections* could be fields of raw

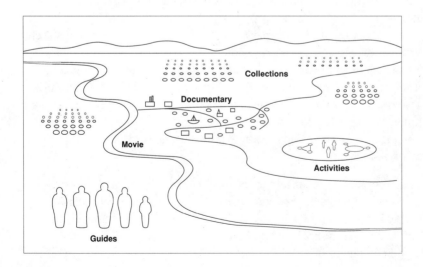

FIGURE 15.

materials, a *documentary* could be seen as a small town, a *movie* might flow like a stream through the landscape, *guides* might be shown as figures on a hilltop, and *activities* might be represented by a playground.

It doesn't really matter that the analogies be exact; what is more important is that as a designer you start getting a good feel for those structures as distinct classes of environments that people tend to use in different ways. After you have developed that intuitive understanding of what each structure does best, you can start mixing them together to produce a richer landscape. For instance, you might want to spread fields around the town or combine a playground with a stream.

Like a city planner, you are designing not only the structure of the information landscape, but also the flows and processes that take place in and around that environment. In the end, you really are shaping the culture of a user group, not just its database.

HyperCard and Education: Reflections on the HyperBoom

Rob Semper

ROB SEMPER

Rob Semper earned a Ph.D. in physics from Johns Hopkins University in 1973. After a number of years of college and university teaching and research in solid-state and nuclear physics at Johns Hopkins, St. Olaf College in Northfield, Minnesota, Lawrence Berkeley Laboratory in California, and the University of California at San Francisco, he joined the Exploratorium (San Francisco) in 1977 to help train college teachers in interactive exhibit development. He became deputy director of the museum in 1985. In 1988, during a leave of absence, he was director of a creative collaboration between Apple Computer, Inc., and Lucasfilm, Ltd., concerning the development of interactive-multimedia education projects combining computer graphics with film and video technology.

The HyperBoom is all around us. The number of products with "Hyper" in their title is fast approaching the number which have "Mac" in a similar position. Hypermedia is taking over as the buzzword of computing. *Newsweek* magazine calls Hypermedia "computer heaven"! Everyone seems to be producing HyperCard-based programs.

When something catches on this quickly and with this much gusto, it is instructive to examine what exactly is causing such high interest. And thinking about the nature of HyperCard itself might help us figure out what its utility in education might be.

So why is everyone so excited about HyperCard? I thought of a number of possibilities. Maybe this fuss is all the result of mass hypnosis. You know, Bill Atkinson might be going around to people's houses and places of work and hypnotizing them. Everyone wakes up the next day and begins to program applications in HyperCard. Or Apple is doing this with magical electrical fields (emanating from the Macintosh computer) that interact with our nerve cells. But on further reflection, that is probably not it. I've met Bill. He seems like a likable guy, and I don't think he hypnotized me. And I know enough physics to be suspicious of the electrical-field theory. So I don't think that's it.

Perhaps it's mass Hyperhype, and the emperor has no clothing. That might appear to be closer to the truth, because there has been an awful lot of hype about HyperCard over the last year. But I don't really think that's the case either.

Of course, any program of this power, which is distributed free with each computer, is going to be popular—if for no other reason than because of its large installed base. But I think there is much more to it. I believe that HyperCard is as popular as it is because it is indeed a unique and innovative program, and people intuitively sense that. And I believe that HyperCard has a significant role to play in education.

The Characteristics of HyperCard

When I began to examine what makes HyperCard intriguing as an educational tool, three characteristics stood out for me. (There are actually a lot of key features to choose from, but I picked the three that seemed most important to me.) First, HyperCard provides the possibility of truly multimodal presentation. It can control and present sounds, images, text, and graphics in a dynamic or static manner under user control. This means that it can be a full-fledged partner in learning, where learning abilities and styles are clearly multimodal in nature.

Second, HyperCard is the ultimate do-it-yourself medium. It allows you to design screens, deal with text and images, and create your own links—all with tools built into the program. The things you can do, even if you are a fairly naive user, are very powerful. In effect, HyperCard provides novice programmers access to much of the full power of the Macintosh interface. The quickness with which you can create a meaningful program and user interface means that it is ideal for prototyping. Much of the interest in HyperCard has come from developers because it is a tool that finally lets them demonstrate what they had in mind to do all along—without incredible programming hassle.

Third, the structure of HyperCard mirrors some of the successful strategies for learning, and it therefore becomes a useful tool for thinking and developing reasoning. Toward the end of this paper I will describe how we have carried HyperCard structure explicitly into an interactive multimedia project.

Multimodal Interactions

One of the powerful features of HyperCard is that it allows the integrated access and control of material in multiple modes. These include graphics, text, sound, control of videodiscs, CD-Audio, and computer and film animation. There is something for everybody. This multiple-modality capability is very important for education. Harvard cognitive psychologist Howard Gardner makes this point exceedingly well in his book *Frames of Mind*.[1] Gardner points out that there are lots of ways that people learn or areas within which they might be considered intelligent. People can be very good in some of these areas—and not very good in others. The seven areas that he discusses, although not necessarily an exhaustive list, are: linguistic, musical, logical–mathematical, spatial, bodily–kinetic, intrapersonal (knowing your inner self, knowing your emotions), and interpersonal (knowing the inner self of others, knowing how other people are reacting to you). A rich educational environment should involve experiences with all of these modalities.

HyperCard allows us to use the computer to support many of these modes of learning and various sensory inputs. It can provide material in many formats. There are easy ways to present text and text-manipulation opportunities. Margo Nanny presents ways of using HyperCard to develop logical–mathematical reasoning. (See "Interactive Images for Education" in Section I.) HyperCard can support sound and music manipulations. The preschool example that is described by Yolanda Jenkins shows how a HyperCard-based program can stimulate preschool dance activity. (See "Multimedia Technology: Tools for Early Learning" in Section I.)

---

[1] Gardner, Howard. *Frames of Mind: The Theory of Multiple Intelligences.* New York: Basic Books, Inc., 1983.

It seems to me that many HyperCard projects can be made more effective by explicitly incorporating more of these modalities. We should be able to manipulate images a lot better than we do already. Easy merging of video images with computer images would be useful. Tools that allow image transformations of regions of the screen with mathematical functions would allow image-analysis possibilities and true visual thinking. We should also try to incorporate richer and more exciting sounds in our projects. The recently completed design example by Apple's Multimedia Lab, Lucasfilm, and the National Audubon Society—"Paul Parkranger and the Case of the Disappearing Ducks" (discussed later in this essay)—is an example in which sound and image as well as computer graphics and video have been integrated to a high degree.

As human beings, we naturally prefer an environment that is aesthetic. This is as true in education as it is in other areas. Therefore, we need to create high-quality images, sounds, and text materials for our educational projects, and we need to use nice photographs, a nicely crafted piece of film, and a high-quality image and/or sound rich in possibilities. Manipulating low-quality digitization of either images or sounds is simply not as enjoyable. The poor quality of film-projection systems in the schools is inexcusable. We need to pay attention to the quality of what we present as well as the content.

However, it is also true—as Kristina Hooper is fond of saying—that resolution is in the eye of the beholder. The right piece of an image at the right time can have a profound impact. And we don't want to send a message to users that if they cannot create high-quality "products," then they should not try to create products at all. People should be encouraged to create their own material—as crude as it might be—any way they want to. In such a case, much of the educational potential and aesthetic quality would be found in the *freedom* of the actual creation process.

This new medium should aim to support both professional-quality and do-it-yourself endeavors. These are much the same issues that arise when you realize that photography can be art or snapshots and films can be cinema or home movies. I believe that using high-quality material will encourage greater manipulation and learning and that using highly manipulable material will encourage the development of an aesthetic appreciation.

Learning By Doing-It-Yourself

The second significant educational feature of HyperCard is the fact that almost anyone can begin to make programs, or at least add to existing work. One of the nicest things about HyperCard when you are beginning to develop something is the blank card—the one that appears when you call up New Card. The paint tools, the field and button tools, and the XCMDs (special language subroutines you can access using HyperTalk) all provide a very rich palette. You can create a complex weave of images, sounds, and interconnections. HyperCard is one of the ultimate do-it-yourself mediums for the computer.

The possibility to create your own stories, your own links and connections, and your own applications is a very powerful educational experience. Significant learning happens in an environment where you have the opportunity to make meaningful choices. For people to figure out what the right path is, they must have opportunities to go off the path, to make their own mistakes, and to make their own connections. Using HyperCard, students from third grade through high school have been able to create mixed-media presentations using their own drawings and sounds mixed with those available on a videodisc or in memory.

HyperCard allows many more people access to the powerful features of the Macintosh interface. While novice programmers may have difficulty programming full-featured HyperCard stacks, it is possible for them to use the paint tools and the button makers to create their own maps and trails through material. And as more tools for searching and creating presentations are developed, quite sophisticated learner-created programs will be possible.

HyperCard is clearly very popular and successful with developers of educational applications. It lets educators and developers produce operating prototypes of many programs that they have always wanted to create but previously found very difficult to do. The energy in the HyperBoom is still strongest among the developers. One of HyperCard's great secrets, however, is that it can make a developer out of almost anybody. It is clearly fun to create this stuff. I notice that I enjoy making and demonstrating stacks that I am using even more than I enjoy using already developed stacks. Having a useful developing tool is incredibly important because it lets us show what our visions can be. And often the prototype is good enough to be the end result.

HyperCard Structure as a Framework for Learning

Finally, HyperCard serves as a framework for learning. The HyperCard structure actually mimics some of our thinking processes. For one thing, it tends to involve manipulating bite-sized pieces of information—a graphic, a sound, an image. There is something quite natural about using nuggets of information here and there rather than accessing page after page of information.

HyperCard is clearly a tool of associative thinking. Vannevar Bush describes associative thinking in his oft-quoted *Atlantic Monthly* article[2]: "The human mind... operates by association. With one item in its grasp it snaps instantly to the next that is suggested by the association of thoughts in accordance with some intricate web of trails carried by the cells of the brain." HyperCard, if nothing else, is about association. It is easy to link card to card by descriptive buttons, and this button linking structure can be quite complex.

We talk a lot about browsing through interactive programs. However, genuine browsing is difficult to do in computer programs because browsing requires the ability to see the overall extent of the territory from which to make a choice. When you look through a book, or visit a bookstore, library, or museum, or take a walk through the woods or a department store, there is a spatial distribution of objects, ideas, or paths from which you can choose. (See Figure 1.) You usually can get a sense of the boundaries, of the high

FIGURE 1. In the physical world, we navigate through space by making choices based on seeing the territory.

---

[2] Bush, Vannevar. "As We May Think." *Atlantic Monthly* 176, 1 (July 1945): 101–108.

points, and of the possible traversals, so that you can intelligently decide where you want to go. This spatial characteristic also helps you know where you have been and where you are in the midst of the whole thing—important features for learning and navigation.

In many computer-learning systems, however, it is very difficult to know what the boundaries are, where you have been, and where you want to go. Much of what passes for interactivity or browsing is nothing more than choosing from a predetermined (limited) selection menu or following a highly directed path.

HyperCard seems to me to offer support for some genuine browsing in a computer system. You can do some browsing by running through the cards by themselves. No matter what links are available, you can still do only a next card or a previous card. Interestingly, in this case, it is the uniformity of the basic HyperCard interface that allows more freedom to the user.

At a higher level, it is possible to introduce graphical elements in HyperCard that can give a sense of an overview. In the recent design example by Apple's Multimedia Lab, Lucasfilm Ltd., and the National Audubon Society, which combined HyperCard graphics and text with video material taken from a PBS program on the endangered wetlands, an interactive "room" in the cabin of a naturalist detective character, Paul Parkranger, is used to create a two-dimensional browsing space. (See Figure 2.) By accessing files in a file cabinet or items on Paul's desk, the user can locate different pieces and types of

FIGURE 2. *This interactive room from the "Paul Parkranger" design example serves as a two-dimensional map to the information in the database.*

information. The room helps to frame the overall program, an overview which in this case relates to a story line.

This is a two-dimensional spatial system. But in HyperCard, we can go one step further and create three-dimensional and even four-dimensional frameworks (if you count time as a dimension) that can greatly enhance the freedom of interaction for the user. The dynamic graphic capability of HyperCard allows for the easy development of active conceptual and story maps (that is, installed links to other parts of the program), which means that we can add a rich set of browsing features to the programs we create. It is possible to use the metaphor of HyperCard itself to help provide a three-dimensional matrix for information. This matrix can serve as a fixed structure or jungle gym that users can navigate through on their own. Paradoxically, this explicit structure can provide users with great freedom to follow their own ideas.

The "Life Story" Design Example

To show more explicitly how HyperCard can serve as a tool for intellectual development, I want to discuss the "Life Story" design example and the structure that we're trying to develop for it. The "Life Story" design example is a collaboration between the Smithsonian Institution, Adrian Malone Productions, Apple Computer, Inc. (through Apple's Multimedia Lab), and Lucasfilm Ltd. The idea is to design an interactive learning environment based on an existing television drama[3] about the discovery of the structure of DNA. We use scenes from this drama—in conjunction with filmed interviews with the scientists involved, stills, animations, text, and graphics—to create a tool for learning about DNA for high-school and college-level students. The drama serves as a motivator and stimulus for students to learn more about the discovery of DNA as well as to present the social and human side of scientific discovery.

This project contains a great number of individual elements such as scenes from the drama, film interviews, audio interviews, computer and film animation, texts, activities, bibliography, and a glossary. Many of these elements can be linked to other items, so much so that the whole thing was becoming a tangled web of ideas and links. The first structural element we developed was a set of maps, such as the plot map and the concept map. (See the discussion of "Life Story" in Fabrice Florin's essay in Section I.) These maps provide a method to access the material—such as by a scene-by-scene account of the story or by the general direction of scientific discovery—but they do not by themselves easily provide natural access to the wide variety of material available, nor do they let you browse easily through the elements on your own.

---

[3] "Life Story" is a 1987 B.B.C. Television production.

To create an internal structure, we used the HyperCard metaphor directly. Every item in the database—be it a scene from the drama, an interview, an animation, a piece of text, a scientific idea, an activity—becomes a stack. These stacks have explicitly similar structure so that you are pretty sure what to expect from each card in the stack. In addition, we developed navigation paths through the stack and between stacks at the same card level. In effect, we established a fixed matrix for all of the material in the system, with graphic indicators telling you where you are and how to get to where you want to go. (See Figure 3a.) Paradoxically, this rigid framework actually allows much more freedom for users to navigate wherever they want.

Each object in the system has a stack attached to it that is made up of at least eight cards. (See Figure 3b on the opposite page.) These cards include the Summary card, which gives a capsule summary of the scene, interview, or idea; the Highlights card, which tells you about four interesting things relating to this stack that you can investigate; the Questions card, which includes a number of questions and hints about this element; the Concept card, which presents the major scientific or social concepts being discussed; the Exhibit card, which is an index to the material which is specific to this scene, interview, or idea; the Index card, which presents an index of this stack; the See Also card, which lets you know what else in the database is related to the theme of this stack; and the Resource card, which points to resources outside the system such as books, films, and so on.

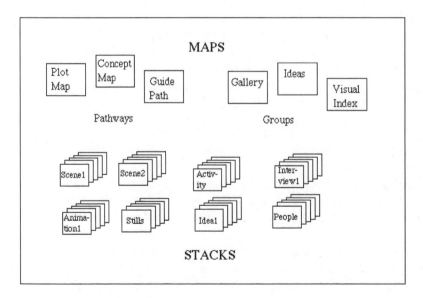

FIGURE 3. (a) Maps serve as pathway guides to a collection of stacks. Groups serve as collections of stacks.

FIGURE 3. *continued*

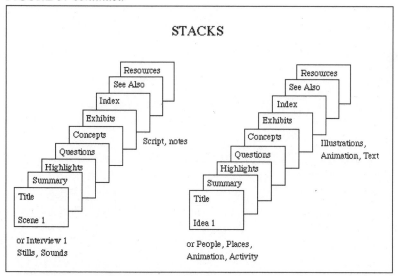

(b) Each multimedia element has its own stack, and the stacks are identical in structure.

This structure allows you to access the information by various routes. You might start at the Concept map level, for example. From the Concept map you might go to a Summary card of a particular idea—and perhaps get more information there or go to the Highlights card to see what we've got in here. (See Figures 4a–4d on the following pages.) You could also enter the Concept map and go into a Summary card for a specific idea, and then start moving from idea to idea—in other words, moving from stack to stack. You could come into a Summary card for an idea from the Concept map, but you might then go to a Highlights card, a summary card of a scene, and wind up out at the Plot map. With this structure, you can flow through a great cross-reference pathway, the kind that everyone talks about in Hypermedia but that is very difficult to program in advance.

This structure can be illustrated through this series of cards from the Franklin Lecture stack. (See Figures 5a–5d on pages 64–65.) This scene depicts Rosalind Franklin giving a lecture, in which she discussed her results in measuring the X-ray diffraction pattern of DNA. The Summary card provides the summary of the scene. The Highlights card tells you about other interesting things you can do. You can ask questions about what Franklin is doing in this particular scene; or you can go to the Exhibit card for this scene and, for example, discover a comparison between the lectures as presented in the drama and the actual text Rosalind Franklin used for her talk; or you can access another Exhibit card, which shows the structure of DNA.

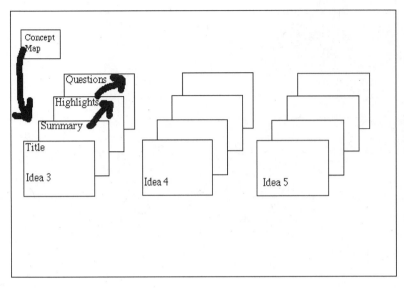

(a)

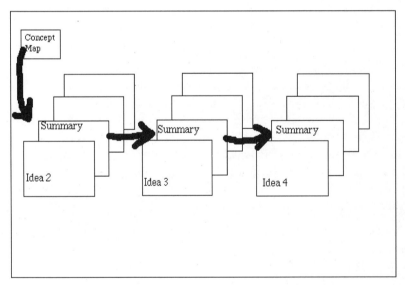

(b)

FIGURE 4. *(a)–(d) show various possible pathways through the stacks.*

FIGURE 4. (continued)

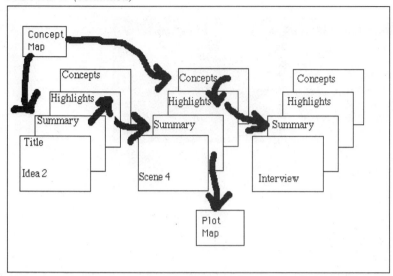

(c)

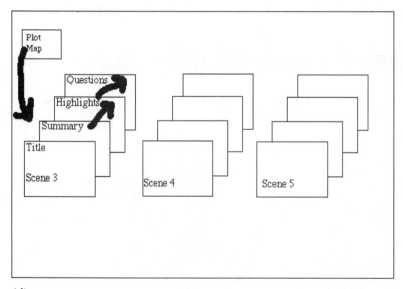

(d)

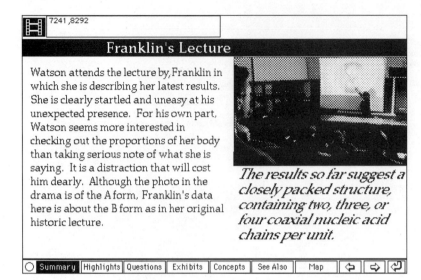

FIGURE 5. *(a) This Summary card for the Franklin Lecture scene summarizes this scene. It also provides controls to view the scene as well as direct access to other cards relevant to this scene.*

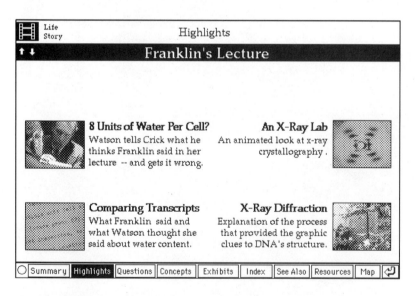

(b) This Highlights card for the Franklin Lecture scene provides viewers with direct access to four other views on the topics portrayed in this dramatic scene.

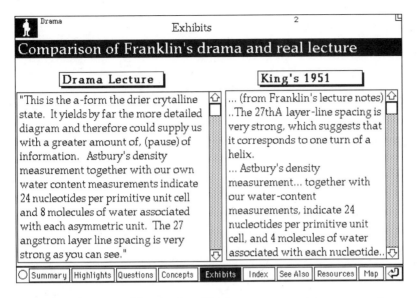

(c) This Exhibits card for the Franklin Lecture scene shows a textual comparison of the speech actually delivered by Rosalind Franklin in 1951 and the one presented in the drama.

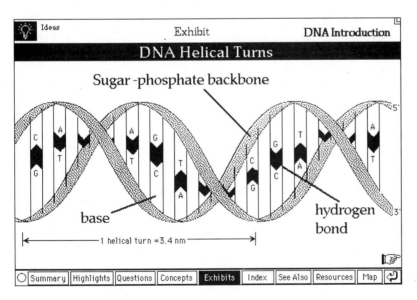

(d) This Exhibits card—very different from the Exhibits card in Figure 5c—provides viewers with a diagram of the DNA structure, designed to assist in the understanding of the scientific content of Franklin's lecture.

We are still developing this design example and investigating how best to structure the data. In particular, we want to develop the idea of the visual index as a three-dimensional index that allows users to get anywhere they want quickly and, just as importantly, provides users with a sense of the project's scope. Further work on these mapping structures is needed to develop the educational potential of these systems.

Thoughts for the Future

For HyperCard to continue to develop into a significant foundation for educational projects, a number of features and tools need to be pursued. First, we need to develop maps that let you know where you are, where you've been, and where you're going in a stack and between stacks. When browsing in real space, or reading a book, you always know generally what the boundaries of the information set is that you are using. However, with computer-based environments, it is very difficult to know the scope of the program. Each interaction replaces the one before it on the screen. Few clues exist that differentiate the experience. We need to develop a set of tools and spatial metaphors for our systems that help us see the boundaries and objectify our trails.

Secondly, we need to develop tools that help people create more of their own programs, particularly using sounds and images. In some ways, videodiscs are the worst media for interactive multimedia because they are a read-only medium. Controllable videotape players and video cameras along with simple visual digitizers are needed to complement the flatbed scanners and audio digitizers already available. We also need to develop HyperCard-based image and sound manipulation and analysis tools to help us think with sound and pictures. It would be wonderful to have hooks available into sophisticated image-transform programs to allow one to manipulate and merge parts of video images (such as high-frequency Fourier transforms) or to measure movement and scale in films.

Thirdly, we need to incorporate more of the thinking of filmmakers and graphic artists in our projects and impart those skills to the people who are going to create programs in the future. The creation of multimedia requires skills from many different disciplines and many of the design and presentation rules have already been worked out in other media. We also need to learn a lot more about how to use sound more effectively in our projects.

Finally, we need to develop the appropriate working ideas and metaphors for interactive Hypermedia. The rules for creating and viewing cinema turned out not to be the same as the rules for books. Films started out with chapters. They don't use chapters in films anymore; cinema has a whole new set of rules, which grew out of using the new media.

Hypermedia must develop its own set of rules if we are to be able to determine where it fits into the educational picture. The good news is that HyperCard is leading the way in these efforts.

Multimedia Composition: Is It Similar to Writing, Painting, and Composing Music? Or Is It Something Else Altogether?

Sueann Ambron

SUEANN AMBRON

Sueann Ambron is manager of New Technology in Education and co-founder of Apple Computer, Inc.'s Multimedia Lab. The lab has built prototype multimedia products that have influenced hardware and software design. The prototype development includes collaborations with organizations such as Lucasfilm, Ltd., National Geographic Society, WGBH, The Walt Disney Company, and others.

Previous to starting the lab, she managed software product development at Apple, new education product development at Atari, and computer products for industrial training.

She taught for 10 years at Stanford University. She earned an Ed.D. from Columbia University in education psychology, with emphasis on cognition. At Stanford she worked with colleagues at Xerox PARC on interface design for word processors.

She has authored several books and articles, including a best-selling college textbook on human development. She co-edited with Kristina Hooper Interactive Multimedia *(Microsoft Press, 1988).*

Computers are not just for computing! We are beginning to use computers, videodiscs, and CD-ROMs to communicate in new ways. Computers are not merely for manipulating numbers in a spreadsheet or words in a word processor; they can be used to access, manipulate, and display information in many forms (including motion pictures, animations, music, and sound effects). It is the combination of these forms that will evolve into a new medium of expression—the multimedia composition. The computer is the central controlling device for multimedia composition and can be the delivery platform for real-time interactions. The ability to communicate with multimedia will give a new dimension to information and will change how we think about problems.

This paper describes what it is like to compose with multimedia. While it is not like writing a book, it uses text; it is not like filming a movie, but it uses moving images; and it is not like making a recording, but it can have music and narration. It is like adding degrees of freedom to a painter's palette because it allows the use of movie clips, still pictures, text, music, narration, and animation. The purpose of a multimedia composition is the same as that of any form of communication—to tell a story, render an experience, play a game, or highlight information.

During the last year I have worked with adults and children to create multimedia compositions using the material from an experimental product, The Visual Almanac™, developed by the Multimedia Lab at Apple Computer, Inc. In that capacity, I was virtually a multimedia director. I believe a quick look at what people created by using the multimedia composition tools in The Visual Almanac can give us an indication of significant genres for multimedia compositions. Furthermore, the principles of design for multimedia composition with The Visual Almanac can be applied to other multimedia environments.

First, I will describe The Visual Almanac, so you will understand the context of the compositions. Next, I will illustrate the major categories of what people actually made. Finally, I will outline six principles of designing multimedia compositions that evolved from the experience of working on these compositions.

Source of Multimedia Material

The Visual Almanac was the source of the multimedia material and tools used for the multimedia compositions that are described in the paper. The Visual Almanac is an interactive multimedia product created at Apple's Multimedia Lab. (See Figure 1 on the following page.) It consists of a videodisc of 7000 still images and moving images, software for the Apple Macintosh computer based on HyperCard, and a companion book.

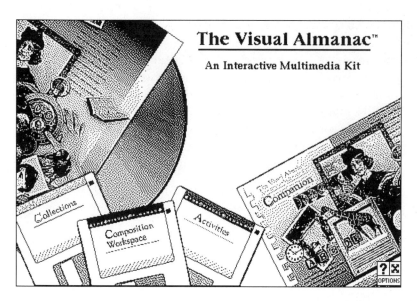

FIGURE 1. *The Visual Almanac includes a videodisc, software, and a book.*

The Visual Almanac software is divided into three parts: Collections, Composition Workspace, and Activities. (See Figure 2.) The images and sounds on the videodisc are organized into 12 collections that include a variety of science and social-science topics such as The Solar System, People Around the World, and Everyday Objects. In the Composition Workspace, users create their own compositions. The Activities include sample activities and compositions. As much as 40 percent of the material on the videodisc was original film footage shot by the Lab for interactive use with a computer. The other 60 percent was acquired from 35 other sources.

The Composition Workspace is the set of tools that allows you to create your own multimedia compositions. You browse the Collections for interesting images and sounds, save the images and sounds to a select sheet, and use the material in your select sheets for your composition. The Composition Workspace includes templates that you can choose for different types of compositions. The templates include several backgrounds and text possibilities. You can create your own multimedia composition with drawings, text, animations, music, sound effects, and images on one of the templates. In addition, you can edit the video and sound material from The Visual Almanac disc or add your own material. When you are done, you can walk away with a disk of your own multimedia composition.

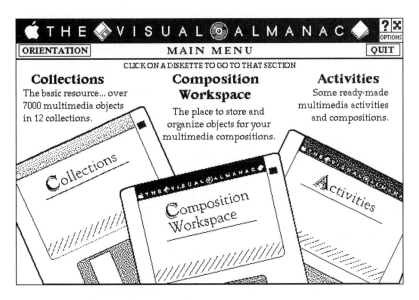

FIGURE 2. The Visual Almanac software is divided into three parts: Collections, Composition Workspace, and Activities.

The Visual Almanac is designed to give children, teachers, and developers the tools to use images and sounds to create reports, lessons, essays, poems, experiences, and new compositions. It is designed to be suggestive of the image- and sound-rich products that can be created for today's computers, videodiscs, and CD-ROMs. It is also indicative of what people are going to want to do with integrated multimedia technologies in the near future.

Categories of Multimedia Compositions

The following is a selection of multimedia compositions created by adults and children using tools from The Visual Almanac. The selection is presented in rough chronological order and is designed to be illustrative of particular categories. As the composition tools in the Composition Workspace became more robust, the compositions became more varied from a simple linear book presentation. The categories that are illustrated here include: Oral Report, Visual Poem, Visual Crossword Puzzle, Interactive Story, and Interactive Menu.

Oral Report

"Neal's Animal Book" was created when The Visual Almanac tools were nearing completion. Neal, age eight, was impressed with the Animal and Plant Collection images and wanted to make something with his favorite pictures. At first he was not sure what it was going to be. He went through the animal collection, saving his favorite images. Next, he went to the Composition Workspace and began grouping images of the same animal on a single card. He had cards for several animals. The final composition has four cards: frogs, toads, turtles, and whales. This selection of animals resulted from several iterations back and forth between the animal collection and the composition cards. Each card has a banner title, such as "Frogs," and a digitized image of a representative animal. (See Figure 3a.) The card also contains text statements about the frogs. An image can be accessed by clicking on the buttons in the text. (See Figure 3b.) Most of the animals in Neal's book are stills. A few dramatic motion clips are used. Neal was able, with the tools provided in The Visual Almanac, to slow down a motion clip of the Malaysian flying frog, so his friends could see how it flies. Neal also added sound narration to a motion clip about the hazards facing baby sea turtles, and he added the singing sound to the motion clip about the baby whale and his mother.

I have twice seen Neal give this oral report for an audience. The first time, the audience was his family. The second time, it was his class. Each time the report was quite different. What Neal said the first time was stimulated by the images: His attention was focused on the images that appeared on the video monitor—not on the text on the computer screen. His observations were rich and loaded with personal comments, and he elaborated on the details of the animals' appearance and behavior. While he began by discussing the images, his explanations went far beyond the image and information in The Visual Almanac: He was telling what he knew about his favorite animals.

In the oral report to the class, Neal changed his delivery style and just read the one line of text that appeared on the computer screen. While it was exciting for the class to see moving images accessible with a mouse click, the information had been much richer when Neal talked about his selected images, as he had done in the presentation to his family. He knew much more than one line of text about each animal, and his personal comments added much to the quality of the presentation.

The opportunity to put quick access to images, sounds, and text in the hands of a second-grader made an exciting oral report. Neal, however, thought it was more fun composing the report than delivering the report to the class.

FIGURE 3. (a) A Frogs card, containing a video image of a frog. When
you push the Leopard frog button, you see the leopard frog, shown
in (b), below.

(b) The leopard frog.

Visual Poem

Three people came to the Multimedia Lab to learn how to use The Visual Almanac. As we watched the time-lapse motion clip of a bowl of fruit rotting, the fruit appeared to breathe or pulsate as it was rotting. We decided to see if we could splice several clips together at the end of the rotting-fruit sequence and set it to music using The Visual Almanac composition tools. (See Figure 4.)

"Pulsating Fruit" was the result of this collaboration. It is a visual poem that consists of a spliced button in a field of words about the experience. A spliced button is made up of several image or sound clips played in sequence. Clicking on the button begins a time-lapse sequence of images of fruit rotting in a bowl, with musical accompaniment, followed by a woman's voice saying "Great" and a short rock-music clip.

Users may not know how to respond to "Pulsating Fruit." It feels like a new art form. It reminded me of something like a vignette from an old Monte Python sequence. You know, that same style of zany and outrageous humor. Some people are going to be very uncomfortable with this new form of expression; others will simply relax and have a good laugh. We should continue to experiment with new forms of multimedia expression.

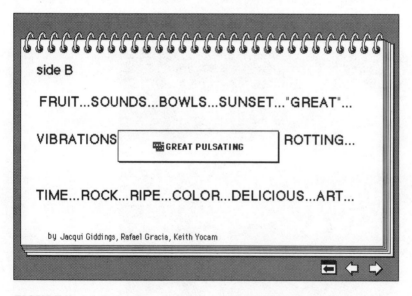

FIGURE 4. (a) A visual poem, activated by clicking on the button, that shows the "pulsing" of fruit as it rots and that contains voice and music.

(b) A videodisc image, taken from near the end of the sequence, showing rotting fruit.

Visual Crossword Puzzle

Bob Bayless, a local college teacher, likes to play games. He developed a crossword puzzle based on *images* of United States presidents since Lincoln. (See Figure 5 on the following page.) This crossword puzzle has clues that are still images; it includes the capability to generate your own crossword puzzle.

This is a great group or class activity. You'll be surprised by how many of the presidents go unrecognized. It is at least as much fun as Trivial Pursuit and Pictionary. The capability to generate your own crossword puzzles give this composition real extendability.

FIGURE 5. A multimedia crossword puzzle, with still images used as clues and with a capability to generate additional crossword puzzles.

Interactive Story

"Harry T. Spider's Party" is an interactive fable about a sowbug and a trapdoor spider. It was created by Maura, age 12, who likes to write stories and draw. She started with the elements of a cut-and-paste story called "The Sowbug and the Spider," which I coauthored with my husband, Brian Ambron. (See Figure 6.) She made new drawings, added new music, and changed the story.

Maura's new interactive story provides a completely different experience from the original story for the audience—even though it uses many of the same video clips. Clicking on a music button begins the story of a sowbug's quest for acceptance among her insect peers. (See Figure 7 on page 80.) The story is told in a series of cards integrated with text, music, sound effects, still images, video clips, and animations. Having two different stories use the same characters is somewhat like having two different painters paint the same scene.

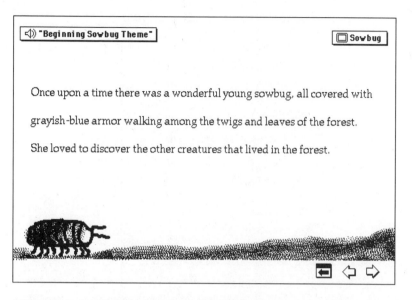

FIGURE 6. (a) The second card from "The Sowbug and the Spider."

(b) The video image of the sowbug.

FIGURE 7. The second card from "Harry T. Spider's Party," with a computer-digitized (rather than video) image.

Interactive Menu

"Chez Michelle" is an experience in virtual dining. (See Figure 8.) It was inspired by a demonstration called "EAT," created by Mike Naimark and his students at the San Francisco Art Institute. The dinner menu for Chez Michelle's was designed by Meghan, age 15. The dinner guest can choose items from among several categories of food: appetizers, entrees, vegetables, and desserts. Each selection is "offered" as a video image. After the meal, a bill is presented along with a comment from the waiter.

Virtual dinning at Chez Michelle's is ideal if you are trying to lose weight. You never eat the food; it only appears in video. Meghan had fun putting a little humor in the menu. She was interested in the replay value of the random buttons. You can see the celebrities that dine at Chez Michelle's, receive a bill, and have a fortune all come up randomly.

FIGURE 8. (a) The first card of "Chez Michelle," showing the face of the menu.

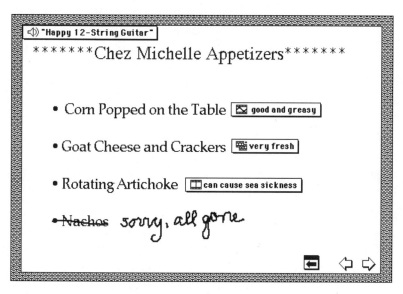

(b) The Appetizers card of "Chez Michelle."

Principles of Designing Multimedia Compositions

There are six principles of designing multimedia compositions that were evident in working in the Composition Workspace of The Visual Almanac. Although I have not applied them to other multimedia composition environments, I believe that they would be equally applicable in a variety of modes.

Composition Is Iterative

The most successful multimedia compositions were iterative in two ways. First, when people had an idea for the composition, they would explore the Collections. This was a back-and-forth process between their idea and the visual and sound resources in the Collections that would support or expand their idea. Sometimes they dropped the original idea because the visual material suggested another approach. Next, after selecting a template, they went through several iterations of images, sound, and text combinations before they were satisfied with the results.

Start with Images or Sounds and Then Add Text

The most successful compositions began with images and sounds rather than text. In a second-grade class, the children decided that they wanted to write a composition. They started by dictating a story about space and the environment on a hypothetical planet. They filled three cards with text before they realized that they were not using any images or sounds. They were used to a text composition world and were not quite sure what to do with the images and sounds available on the disc. On the other hand, when they started again and browsed through the Solar System Collection, they selected very rich images around which they composed an exciting story.

Sound Is More Intrusive Than Images or Text

If you do not like the image, you can ignore it. If you do not like the sound, it will drive you to turn off your computer. Music and sound effects in multimedia composition are little understood. They can add a great deal to the mood of a multimedia composition and give the feeling that the material is alive.

We found that users wanted the capability of turning sound on or off. This was especially true if users were going to replay a multimedia composition. In "Chez Michelle," we had ambient dinner music coming on as the user moved from course to course. The first time through, it was tolerated. After that, the users wanted to choose their music.

Images Have More Fluid Meanings Than Text

People in the film world already know that images can be used to mean very different things. This principle was very clear in the multimedia compositions. Text is fairly explicit—it means what it says. The same video clips and still images can be used to say several different things. This will be more evident as images become digital, allowing us to manipulate them easily with a computer.

For example, the video clip of the sunset can be played backwards to give you a sunrise. The still picture of a farm scene in Bolivia can be used to illustrate agriculture, mountains, sheep, and grass; and, if the multimedia composer takes license with the images, it could represent agriculture in any place that has snowcapped mountains.

We found it was important to ensure that images in The Visual Almanac carried data that identified the source and nature of the image.

Dynamic Elements Are Attention Getting

Dynamic elements attract more attention than text and still images. People creating multimedia compositions wanted more dynamic elements—that is, moving images, music, and sound effects. We have been conditioned by television to expect dynamic elements on a screen.

Additionally, some dynamic elements carry more information than others. The chameleon catching a fly with its tongue is a very short clip, but it was more interesting than long clips of horses walking.

Not all dynamic elements are equal. Just the right piece of compelling video, music, or sound effect for a particular composition is noticed by composer and user.

Artifacts of Multimedia Composition Are Primitive

We have not yet established multimedia artifacts equivalent to great books, movies, and symphonies. Multimedia composition is similar to playing chess, in that the process of creation is very involving, but the finished product simply "sits there." The product comes to life only when it interacts with a user. The fun, the challenge, and the learning is in playing the game—that is, in creating the multimedia composition. What is left behind is the weak artifact of someone else's chessboard.

I suspect this may change as we develop multimedia-composition ideas, better tools, and richer databases of information to explore.

Evolving a New Medium of Expression

Multimedia composition requires skills similar to those used in writing, painting, and composing music, but it also has additional elements that seem similar to filmmaking and choreography. At present, it is so new that we do not have the vocabulary to describe it. Perhaps it will be called media making or mediagraphy.

Technologies give us the opportunity to communicate in new ways. Multimedia composition with The Visual Almanac suggests a few things people will compose in multimedia when they have easy access to and the capability of manipulating images and sounds. We must continue to explore and to experiment with these new opportunities. We are at the beginning of an innovation in human communication as profound as the text page and the moving picture. We are evolving a new medium of expression.

Interactive Images
for Education

Margo Nanny

MARGO NANNY

Margo Nanny has a background in education. For 15 years she taught mathematics to a wide range of unique learners, from elementary-school through junior-college levels. Her classes included "Math Without Fear," math for blind students, and math for women reentering the job market. For several years she taught math in the bilingual program in Berkeley (California) schools. She has always focused on helping people use hands-on materials to visualize mathematics. As part of this effort, she also taught carpentry for girls and woodworking for teachers, and through a special grant helped schools in northern California set up carpentry programs for children.

In 1982 she became involved with computers and taught Logo to junior high school students, trained student teachers to set up computer programs in Oakland (California) schools, and worked as an associate to the Equals in the Computer Technology program at Lawrence Hall of Science in Berkeley. In 1985 she entered the Interdisciplinary Computer Science graduate program at Mills College in Oakland, California. There she became involved with multimedia and built one of the first HyperCard-based multimedia environments, using the repurposed Disney film Donald in Mathmagic Land. *Since that time she has worked on multimedia at Apple Computer, Inc., and is currently a designer at the Apple Multimedia Lab.*

The ideas in this chapter arose from my work at the Apple Multimedia Lab in San Francisco. For the last two years a team of us at the Lab, guided by Kristina Hooper, has been working on a project called The Visual Almanac: An Interactive Multimedia Kit. The Visual Almanac™ is one of the first large multimedia environments of its kind. It consists of a videodisc with a total of 7000 image and sound objects, HyperCard stacks including databases, on-line activities, and a "build your own" composition workspace. *The Visual Almanac Companion* is a book about multimedia and the use of this specific multimedia system.

Working on The Visual Almanac gave me a concrete opportunity to choose and design video images as well as to use these images in activities. One of the lessons I quickly learned was: Not all images are created equal. Some were naturally more compelling. They tickled my brain and begged to be watched over and over again. The more that I watched them, the more interesting they became. Finally, I noticed that certain types of images grabbed me. As I sorted and categorized them, I discovered that most of my categories could fit under the single broad heading: "Images that expand the viewer's point of view." But there was much more to it than that. Images became fascinating to think about. As a result, I feel compelled to offer my point of view on interactive images for education. The examples I use in this chapter are almost entirely from The Visual Almanac.

Interactive Images for Education

At the heart of multimedia systems are interactive images—particularly, video images that bring real-world visuals into the computer domain. They are full color, many have motion, and they can be played in any order, at any speed, and in any direction. Recently, such images have become more accessible through the use of HyperCard, videodiscs, and the Apple Macintosh computer. Soon such an abundance of these visuals will exist that we would be wise to keep a critical eye toward what kind of images we want to use and how we want to use them. One class of images that I've found valuable for use in multimedia systems are those that allow users to control some aspect of space or time in order to quickly change their point of view and see things in a new way. These are the images I wish to discuss in this chapter. However, let's first take a look at the context for using images in education.

Preparing for the Information Age

The information age brings with it the challenge of preparing learners for the vast amounts of information they will face in the coming years. A large portion of problem solving will involve sifting through information, seeking out relevant relationships, and finding coherent ways to represent the conclusions.

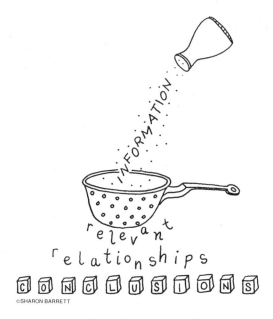

©SHARON BARRETT

Those who are able to express their ideas clearly and efficiently in a visual manner will be most successful at gaining an audience for their ideas.

Information users will scan for visuals that communicate ideas with a minimum of time invested. Teachers will seek more powerful visuals to help explain difficult concepts in an efficient manner. Students will learn to create and manipulate visual images to express relationships and connections between the information and the ideas that grow out of their research.

As this future becomes a reality, humans will invent ever more powerful tools to create a fluid environment in which images, text, graphics, data, sounds, and the connections between them can be easily accessed and manipulated. As these environments are created, images will become tools for the mind to bring clarity to ideas. The images will be like the head of the hammer, which drives the point home.

©SHARON BARRETT

Within multimedia environments, choosing and manipulating interactive images to express ideas will become akin to choosing words for a piece of writing. To paraphrase Sueann Ambron (of the Apple Multimedia Lab), just as the use of a dictionary of words doesn't guarantee a clear piece of writing, so the use of a multitude of images doesn't guarantee the coherent communication of an idea. As we begin to work with images, we must come to know how to choose the most valuable images to express an idea. And we must learn to create powerful interactions so that users can manipulate the images to explore the idea. In many cases, one successful criterion for selecting images is to choose those images that can expand a viewer's point of view by increasing her or his control over space and time.

The Human Point of View: Stuck in Space and Time

As humans we are limited by our necessarily human point of view. We are stuck with a few givens, with respect to space and time, that we cannot control—for instance, our location, our size, our moment in time, and the rate at which time passes. At any given point we are stuck in one location and cannot instantly see things in faraway places. We are stuck with our human size and cannot shrink ourselves to see microorganisms, nor can we become giants and stretch into space for a more global point of view. We are stuck at our given moment in time and cannot jump back through the years to reexperience historical events. And finally, we are stuck with the rate at which time passes; we cannot speed up a sunset, nor can we slow down a flash of lightning for better viewing. We are stuck with these limitations, and yet we have created a myriad of tools to help us overcome them. We have electron microscopes, space shuttles, high-speed photography, time-lapse photography, books, films, airplanes, and other devices that help us see things in different places, at different times, from different points of view. And now, with interactive images, we can bring some of the benefits of all these tools into one multimedia learning environment—an environment that enables us to change perspectives quickly and to discover new patterns, relationships, and connections between things. By manipulating images with respect to space and time, we can maintain a flexibility in our point of view and see things in ways that we've never seen them before.

For teachers and students, multimedia systems that provide this kind of interaction will become an important tool. Such systems will help students to get to the heart of information, ideas, and concepts more quickly. The visual images will provide the concrete examples that lead to greater understanding. They will enable teachers and students to show their ideas more clearly. Thus, less time will be spent merely trying to understand the meaning of an idea or concept, and more time will be spent exploring the many situations in which it manifests itself. As teachers and students become accustomed to manipulating images in this fashion, their thinking will be influenced. They will routinely use different points of view in presenting their explanations. It will occur to them more often to alter these points of view over space and time in order to get a wide range of interesting examples. They will become attuned to visuals to such a degree that multimedia will become a more efficient chalkboard for the explanation of concepts and ideas.

Controlling Space and Time

To discuss the interactive control of space and time, I have separated space into two controllable elements, location and size, and I have separated time into two other controllable elements, moment in time and the rate at which time passes. This certainly is not the only way to divide these two large concepts, but it's a way that works for the purpose of this discussion. The remainder of this chapter will illustrate how the manipulation of these elements with interactive images can alter our point of view and help us see things in unique ways.

Controlling Space

Location
Controlling location with interactive images simply means changing your position in space. The images could place you instantly in various parts of the world, from a mountain top to the ocean floor. They could give you a view of one place and let you move

around in it, visually walking or riding through the space or simply changing your perspective. By controlling your location you can control where you are, what you see, and what angle you see it from. Multimedia systems using HyperCard and videodiscs cannot give you complete control over your location. An infinite number of video images would be required to move in any direction at any time; however, that much power is seldom necessary. With careful thought about images, it is possible to create very interesting experiences with only a few perspectives on a given place.

Here's an example in which a viewer can manipulate location in order to understand the complexities involved in the concept of "frames of reference." Imagine trying to understand the path of a ball rolling across a rotating merry-go-round. (See Figure 1.) An image shows the point of view of being on the merry-go-round. The person on the left attempts to roll the ball to the person on the right while the merry-go-round is rotating clockwise.

FIGURE 1. A digitized image of three people on a merry-go-round. The person on the left tries to roll the ball to the person on the right. [Apple Multimedia Lab]

The ball ends up going to the person in the middle. From the viewpoint of sitting on the merry-go-round, we see the ball moving in a quarter-circle arc. (See Figure 2 on the following page.)

FIGURE 2. The path of the ball, as viewed from a sitting position on the merry-go-round. [Apple Multimedia Lab]

Now imagine the same scene being viewed from directly above the center of the merry-go-round. (See Figure 3.) Here, we see the same roll of the ball, yet this time the ball seems to move in a straight line. (Actually, due to friction the ball curves slightly in the direction that the merry-go-round is moving.)

It turns out that both views are actually occurring. The ball moves through space in a straight line, but its path on the moving merry-go-round is an arc. This is an example of a situation where the user, by manipulating images and changing points of view from a spatial perspective, can grasp a "frame of reference" problem that would be very difficult to understand otherwise. In fact, it is hardly possible to see that the path of the ball is a straight line if your point of view is that of a person riding on the merry-go-round. To perceive the straight-line path requires that viewers detach themselves from the rotating system and watch the ball from a point in space. This is not easy to do in the real world. Even if we happened to be sitting in a tree directly over the merry-go-round, our mind would still focus on the curved path. We would see the straight-line path only if we were able to ignore the rotation of the merry-go-round altogether and watch only the ball.

Controlling our location in this fashion is a powerful use of interactive images. The difficult concept behind "frames of reference" problems can be quickly displayed.

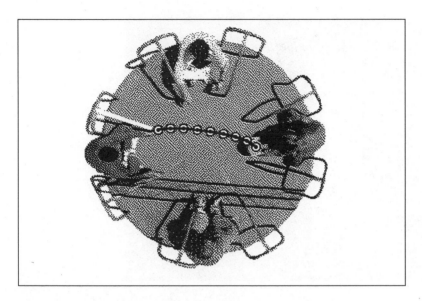

FIGURE 3. *The path of the ball, as viewed from directly above the center of the merry-go-round. [Apple Multimedia Lab]*

Although it's not easy to completely understand such a "frame of reference" problem, the manipulation of images enables us to view problems repeatedly in order to let the idea sink in. By manipulating space through the choice of our location, we change our point of view to see an event in an unusual way.

Size

The other aspect of space that is controllable is size. (More formally, it would be called *scale*.) Given that you can control your location and can observe the object you want to see, you might then want to size yourself up or down to get the proper view. For instance, if you want to see the earth, you could imagine stretching yourself way out into space and looking back.

If you want to see a microorganism, you could imagine shrinking yourself way down to get the proper view. Whether you want to imagine changing the size of yourself or the size of the object makes little difference. I choose to imagine changing my own size, because it has always been easier to suggest to children that they imagine becoming teeny weeny little people so that they can see blood cells or walk inside a seashell than it has been to ask them to scale the object up to the desired size.

Controlling size with interactive images allows us to see things that are too big or too small to view from our normal perspective. Size control offers the opportunity to observe visual patterns and relationships that are otherwise difficult to notice (such as the similarities between a city's freeway system and the circuits on a microchip). It gives us a point of view that can lead to creative solutions to problems that might not otherwise be solved.

Controlling Time

Moment in Time

The idea of time travel has long been imagined, and perhaps controlling interactive images is the closest we'll ever get to it. By choosing a moment in time, we can revisit historical events through images that were recorded on the scene. After we've chosen a moment to review, we can repeat it for close analysis. The famous "instant replay" has become a common example of taking an audience back to relive a moment. By using interactive images to reexperience the past, we can broaden our point of view and compare the past with the present to understand our future. We can also view events that occur rarely and that we might never see in our lifetime without the use of images—events such as the hatching of a bird's egg (see Figure 4) or the motion of a dramatic tornado.

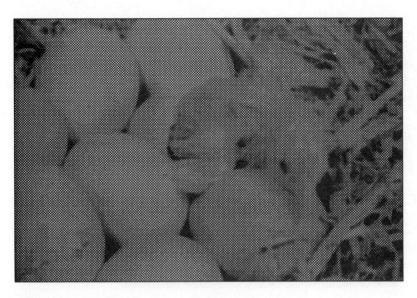

FIGURE 4. A digitized image of a bird's egg hatching.
[Oxford Scientific Films, Oxford, England]

Rate at which Time Passes

Another method of controlling time with images is to control the rate at which time passes. This is one of the most interesting ways to alter our point of view. It enables us to compress and expand time into manageable slices so that we can see things that are impossible to see from within our usual time frame. For example, in our normal world if we wanted to watch a community of starfish devour a fish carcass, we would have to sit and watch for over 24 hours (underwater, no less)—and even then the movement of the starfish would be so slow that they would seem not to be moving at all. However, by compressing time through time-lapse photography, we can speed up the action and in a few seconds watch starfish quickly move along the ocean floor in an amazingly humanlike fashion to consume the dead fish. (See Figure 5 on the following page.)

By adding interactive control to such a piece of footage, we could view the movement of the starfish at any rate we choose and could look for patterns in their motion or for similarities between the way they move and the way other animals move. Compressing time can also enable us to move through space at impossible speeds or to watch a full year's weather patterns in merely a few minutes or to see plants grow. Time compression helps us to obtain a more global view than we can obtain within the normal rate at which time passes.

FIGURE 5. (a) Starfish before feeding. [Sea Studios, Monterey, California]

(b) Starfish after feeding. [Sea Studios, Monterey, California]

FIGURE 6. (a) Two cars just before the collision. [Kansas State University, Department of Physics]

(b) Two cars after the collision. [Kansas State University, Department of Physics]

We can also control time by expanding it so that the action slows down. Motion images can be viewed frame by frame and thereby studied more closely. With the use of high-speed photography, it is possible to shoot an instantaneous event (such as the flick of a chameleon's tongue) and then slow it down to a reasonable viewing speed, slow it down further, stop it, or play it backward, to more clearly understand what is happening.

This technique allows us to see how a hummingbird's wings move, to watch a kernel of popcorn pop, or to study a two-car collision. (See Figure 6 on the previous page.) Expanding time in this fashion gives us a more detailed point of view and allows us to view events that pass too quickly to perceive in our usual time frame.

A final way to control time is to reverse it altogether and watch an action backward. This gives rather surprising results. For example, seeing a ball bounce in reverse offers new insights into the path the ball takes. Watching a scrambled egg being prepared in reverse creates a humorous awareness of the visual expectations that have built up over lifetime of experiencing time in the forward direction only. As we become more accustomed to manipulating time in a variety of ways, we'll surely uncover many interesting mysteries that we were unable to see in the everyday passing of time.

Conclusion

The growth and popularity of multimedia systems using HyperCard and videodiscs will bring countless visual images to the educational arena. The images will provide examples that illustrate teachers' and students' ideas. They will become the basis for understanding concepts that were previously relegated to complex verbal descriptions. These images will also alter our relationship to information in the information age as they become the key element in helping us take in and understand more information more quickly.

Developing systems using these images will help us become acquainted with the nuances of how images enhance the viewer's understanding of complex ideas. As we come to better understand this medium, we will learn what kinds of images and what kinds of interactions will lead to the richest educational experience. Although it might take a while to learn how to use and manipulate images as fluently as we do words, we can say that some of the most valuable images are ones that allow users to alter their point of view— and that one of the most interesting ways to do this is to use interactive images to control different aspects of space and time. As teachers and students begin to use this technology, they will become accustomed to looking for and finding new patterns and relationships. Their broadened perspective will give them an advantage in finding clues to solve the complex problems of the twenty-first century.

Hypermedia and Visual Literacy

Michael Liebhold

MICHAEL LIEBHOLD

Mike Liebhold is manager of media tools and applications in the Advanced Technology Group (ATG) of Apple Computer, Inc. The focus of this group's work is hypermedia and broadband network environments in the 1990s. Previously, he managed various groups and projects in ATG that focused on hypermedia, interactive multimedia, and strategic partnerships, as well as on CD-ROM and video hardware and software systems.

Before joining Apple, he was responsible for advanced-concept development at ByVideo, Inc. At the Atari Division, Warner Communications, he was administrative director of the Strategic Systems Research Laboratory and was responsible for its work on optical and network information systems.

He studied film and video at the University of Oregon and at Simon Fraser University, British Columbia, Canada. He is married to Bonnie Bird, who teaches film and computer-animation. His two daughters, Jenny (18) and Amy (14), are award-winning animators.

Hypertext: Linked, nonlinear text...

Englebart or Nelson

Literacy: The ability to read and write...

Webster's New World Dictionary

Hypermedia: A linked, nonlinear knowledge structure with multiple data types—text, graphics, sound, animation, video.

Anonymous

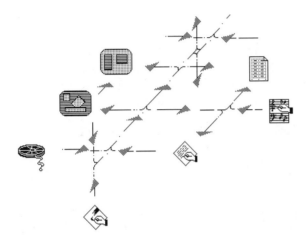

Introduction

In the first grade, children are taught to use a few visual tools such as blocks, crayons, and finger paint. Soon the artistic and tactile media are dropped in favor of verbal and linear instruction in reading and writing text. Occasionally, a social-studies or science assignment will require the students to draw a diagram or map, but by the third grade, art has largely disappeared from the curriculum.

This paper is a discussion of why visual arts should be a continuing, integral part of the new electronic curriculum.

The Vision of Hypermedia

The shining future of the 1990s and the twenty-first century is filled with promises of personal media networks built on broadband fiber optics, erasable optical discs, personal supercomputers, picturephones, electronic books, and interactive cinema.

Teachers and students have a lot of new media technology to absorb—computers, telecommunications, and video and optical discs. We are, nonetheless, experiencing a period of profound excitement surrounding the birth of interactive multimedia and educational hypermedia—a curricular synthesis and combination of the new technologies.

The full instructional potential of hypermedia requires highly refined media technology and software, and *interactive media–literate* teachers, students, domain experts, and producers.

Classroom Uses of Hypermedia

Before we consider the new skills that are challenged by the promise of hypermedia, here is a brief review of a few educational applications:

Exploratory Learning Environments

A computer with video is used to present a real or simulated *space* for teachers and students to explore. Margo Nanny has created a virtual classroom on the computer screen, in which students can explore Mathemagic with Donald Duck. Kathy Wilson and her colleagues at Bank Street College and Sarnoff Labs have created a digital video map of a Mayan ruin, where students can take a private exploratory expedition.

The MIT Architecture Machine Group built the first movie maps a decade ago. The most famous, of course, is a video movie map of Aspen, Colorado.

Interactive Fiction

Text adventures are the most familiar: "You are in a castle. The Wizard hands you a golden chalice." Inigo, the cat created by Amanda Goodenough, represents a new graphic-style interactive fiction, in which children can follow the cat on a day of adventure by clicking on pictures.

Classroom Presentations

Videodiscs of large image collections are beginning to be used for classroom lesson presentations by students and teachers. Optical Data Corp.'s *Living Textbooks*™, the Videodiscovery, Inc.'s Bio-Sci disks, and the Apple Multimedia Lab's Visual Almanac™ are all excellent examples. Using HyperCard software, each student or teacher may create a personal composition from the thousands of available slides or video segments.

Iconic Programming

Computer programming does not necessarily mean being fluent in and typing a computer language. Thousands of children worldwide have begun to learn programming by cutting and pasting buttons and icons, using Apple's popular HyperCard program.

Graphic Navigation

Children are beginning to use hypermedia to navigate complex nonlinear "hyperspace" by clicking on pictures in a "stackmap." Maps and diagrams of traditional taxonomy can be browsed. The branches of government, families of organisms, and the table of elements can now be learned graphically, interactively.

Animated Simulations ("soft laboratories")

Hypermedia provides potentially valuable lab experience that is otherwise too complex, too dangerous, too expensive, or too messy. The old linear film strips, 16 millimeter films, and videotapes provide *no* opportunities for interaction or experimentation.

New Creative Skills

Effective hypermedia requires both new visual creative skills and new visual thinking skills—so that kids can eventually create more elegant and compelling interactions. Teachers and kids might find it easier to acquire these new skills than to learn about computers. The new hypermedia is, in many cases, more similar to movies or TV. (Clearly, skills and understanding of sound effects, dialog, and music are also important but are not discussed in depth here.)

A few of the creative skills that could be constructively reintroduced into the curriculum are discussed on the following pages.

Drawing and Painting

Images are more than mere lines. Effective visual communication requires both an understanding of and skill in using surface, shade, shape, and value.

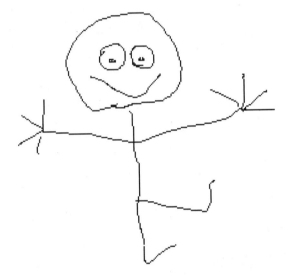

Quantitative Graphics

Diagrams and numeric visualization are often taught as part of science and mathematics, but frequently as *only a minor part of the curriculum.*

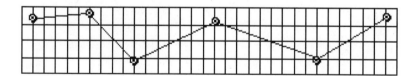

Interactive Graphic Visualization

Interactive graphic visualization is a powerful new scientific tool enabling close-hand observation and manipulation of things that are too small (a quark), too big (a galaxy), too slow (an eon), too quick (a picosecond), and too complex (a metamorphosis).

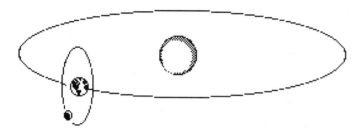

Visualization can be used to demonstrate the structure and relationship of knowledge objects.

Mapping—More Than a Graphic Skill

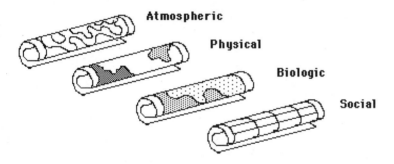

Geography is a *metaknowledge*. Biology, politics, physical sciences, and business statistics all use maps to communicate complex relationships in space and time. The science and art of cartography includes a rich vocabulary of graphic icons and data overlay.

Animation

The world is *not* static. Visual rendition of motion over time is as important a skill as writing a literary narrative. We need to take cartoons more seriously!

Storyboards

Storyboards are a combination of literature and graphics used to plan a hypermedia composition.

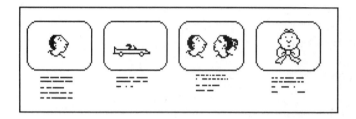

For practice, kids could easily create a comic strip and then a *timed* storyboard depicting their summer vacation!

Video

Hypermedia production, video camera work, and editing are complex skills requiring the synthesis of other training in story, visuals, and sound. In addition, effective manipulation of VCRs, computer editors, and cameras requires lots of practice.

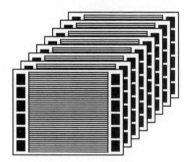

New Thinking Skills

Humans are so bombarded by media that it becomes necessary to be *critical* of the media in order to evaluate the flood of information. The number of hours that kids spend watching TV is staggering: *How many sugar candy and cereal commercials? How many murders?* The media is powerful! How do we decide if television is telling us the truth?

Production knowledge is a potent armor: *If kids understand how media is produced, they are more prepared to deal effectively with its persuasive power.*

What are dramatic structure, tension, and release? What is real? What is fantasy? What is "suspension of disbelief"?

We can enjoy a media fantasy while still fully understanding the unreality of the show!

Here are some of the new thinking skills implied by "Media literacy":

Visual Semantics, Iconics, and Symbolism

What on earth do these pictures mean???

Some cultural phenomena are arbitrary: Does + mean church, hospital, or plus? Or is it merely an intersection of two lines? Both cartographic and mathematic conventions are in use. Visual context is also important—on maps or in formulae, as well as in literature.

Trash

Why does this trashcan mean "delete file"? We need to develop an understanding of the difference between concrete and abstract expression.

Color and Pseudocolor

The difference between color and pseudocolor is a major topic when scientific visualization is discussed. Does red mean "Hot" or "Danger"? Why blue for the ocean, green for vegetation? The answer is not always intuitive!

Perspective

Perspective implies both visual and dramatic issues. Kids have a hard time developing visual-perspective skills, but it's really just two simple concepts—horizon and vanishing point.

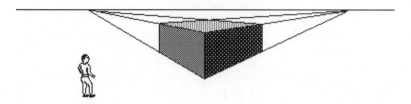

Point of View

Point of view (POV) implies both camera position and author's voice.

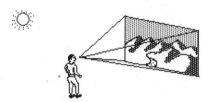

Image Composition

Image-composition and page-layout skills are valuable for use with electronic books as well as for papers.

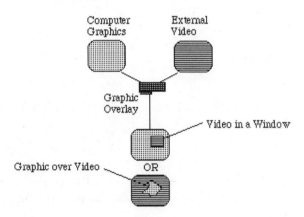

Montage: The Sequencing of Images

Now that we've begun integrating videodisc images into the curriculum, we are handing children the power of traditional cinematic assemblage. Skillful montage and animation both implies and demands a new sense of time and timebase for pacing of action, timing of cuts, and continuity. Computer data is becoming temporal!

Also, interactive media requires a new cinematic aesthetic. Ordinarily, a director has the dramatic luxury of shooting a long-range (establishing) wide-angle shot, a medium-range shot, and finally a close-up shot of the action. An interactive artist often has to crop the action closely in order to preserve precious data space on a CD, videodisc, or floppy disk.

Animation

Animation demands an understanding of physics and of constraints such as squash, stretch, bounce, shatter, and splash, as well as of the timebase of physical phenomena.

Interaction

Interaction is perhaps the most difficult new medium to master. We're flying past flat two-dimensional representation, past cinematic linear representation, to full interactive navigation and manipulation of virtual cinematic realities.

Anything can happen when we click the mouse button. Identify, interact, jump!

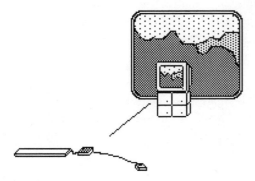

Hypermedia and visual literacy is a great challenge—and great fun.

Revitalize the fine arts!

Initiate new interactive arts!

Multimedia Technology: Tools for Early Learning

Yolanda Jenkins

YOLANDA JENKINS

Yolanda Jenkins has practical and research experience in the education of young children, with a specific focus on the use of technology for early learning.

She was a teacher and a researcher for the Head Start program and a supervisor for the national evaluation of the Follow-Through program. She earned a Ph.D. from the University of California at Berkeley, where she specialized in educational research, early childhood education, and cognitive development. Her dissertation examined creativity in Head Start children.

She has been involved in educational technology for over seven years. She was the manager of research and evaluation and the acting director for the Atari Institute. She was also a manager in the educational product development group for Atari, Inc. She has worked at Apple Computer, Inc. for five years as an education market analyst and is currently the manager of the Preschool Education program. She has given numerous presentations at national education conferences on the role of technology in early learning.

...A new breed of developmental theory is likely to arise....Its central technical concern will be how to create in the young an appreciation of the fact that many worlds are possible, that meaning and reality are created and not discovered, that negotiation is the art of constructing new meanings by which individuals can regulate their relations with each other.

(Jerome Bruner Actual Minds, Possible Worlds)

Introduction

Technology is shrinking the world into a global society, into a new society built on a knowledge-based economy. The advent of this new era will demand new educational requirements—for development of higher-order thinking skills to effectively utilize the technological tools of the twenty-first century. In effect, we will have to educate a population to think creatively, productively, and prolifically. To adequately prepare a generation for this technology-based information age, we must foster a positive predisposition toward learning. The best entry point for beginning this technological education is with the young child.

During the early years, the young child experiences the joy of learning because play is the primary activity for learning. This positive attitude toward learning must be supported and sustained. One way of doing this is through effective applications of technology.

Research Findings on Technology and Young Children

Today, a great deal of attention is focused on developmentally appropriate curriculum for young children, which promotes active, creative, child-centered, open-ended, discovery learning. This type of curriculum is cited as being the most appropriate learning environment for the developmental stage of the young child. The same criteria can be applied to technology. Technology—specifically, multimedia technology—can be designed to be a developmentally appropriate, transformational learning environment for the young child. A review of the research on the effects of technology on young children provides some clear examples of technology's appropriateness.

The computer has been described as a "chameleon" (Sheingold 1983) because it takes on many guises and functions. Because of the multifaceted dimensions of computer technology, the research on the use of technology with young children has identified a variety of positive outcomes.

In a review of the research, Clements (1987) and Davidson (1988) cite a wide range of effects of technology on young children. Some of the findings regarding the effects of technology are:

- Increases social interaction and cooperative learning
- No gender differences during the preschool years in the amount and type of computer use
- Increases self-esteem and self-mastery
- Increases thinking, reasoning, and problem-solving skills
- Facilitates language development and language usage
- Facilitates concept development
- Stimulates young children's symbolic play

In an empirical study, Haugland (1989) found that when computers and developmentally appropriate software were integrated into the preschool environment and reinforced with concrete activities, a number of significant results occurred. Overall, preschool children exposed to computers with developmental software had significant gains in general intelligence, verbal skills, nonverbal skills, problem solving, abstraction, conceptualization, structural knowledge, long-term memory, complex manual dexterity, and self-esteem.

These research findings suggest the tremendous potential of technology for early learning and development. In the early years, children can enjoy learning about technology and with technology through playful interaction (Bowman 1988). Through the proper use of technology we can prepare young children for the requisite intellectual skills necessary to succeed in the twenty-first century. According to Bowman (1988), computers are revolutionizing how people think about the world.

A Conceptual Framework for Understanding Multimedia and Early Learning

The work of Jean Piaget and Maria Montessori has significantly influenced early childhood education and the content and context of early childhood programs. Both Piaget and Montessori understood that young children learn through their senses. Piaget, however, focused on the internal development of a child's cognitive growth whereas Montessori emphasized the importance of a stimulating, structured learning environment for cognitive development. The work of these two pioneers provides a basic foundation for examining the relationship of multimedia environments to young children's learning. However, the work of other cognitive theorists—such as Bruner, Vygotsky, Papert, Gardner, and Sternberg—amplifies the basic principles of Piaget's and Montessori's theories to create a more comprehensive conceptual framework for understanding the role of multimedia technology in early learning and development. We will explore some of these theories to provide a conceptual framework to discuss a multimedia application for preschool children.

Piaget has had a profound influence on early childhood educators regarding the understanding of intellectual growth and development of young children. Piaget's scientific background strongly influenced his theory of cognitive development in that he studied the internal mechanisms of cognition. Piaget labeled the early years—ages two to seven—the stage of preoperational thinking. During this period children are action oriented, learn by doing, and "externalize" their knowing by acting upon the environment. Symbolic play is the primary activity the young child engages in to express thought. According to Piaget, cognitive activity initiates play, and play—specifically, symbolic play—reinforces cognitive activity. Although Piaget was a pioneer in cognitive developmental theory, his theories emphasize the development of logical thinking and minimize the influence of context and environment on cognitive development.

Montessori, on the other hand, stressed the importance of a stimulating, sensory-rich, and reinforcing learning environment for the development of young children's thinking. Montessori believed that young children progress through sensitive periods of development. According to Montessori, this sensitivity and the absorbent nature of the young child's mind require a prepared learning environment that fosters repetition through multisensory materials.

The work of both Piaget and Montessori provides the cornerstones for what today is called "developmentally appropriate" curriculum. As the world becomes more complex and as we acquire new knowledge and tools, we must continue to build upon this curriculum and our understanding of young children's thinking and early learning.

For example, what if we found that other theories of cognition are more inclusive than Piaget's and that a much richer, broader environment than that described by Montessori is accessible? The work of contemporary cognitive scientists and the proliferation of technology might provide us with new frameworks within which to explore the various domains of young children's thinking. In this paper, we will look specifically at the application of new cognitive theories in relation to the influence of multimedia technology on early learning.

The Role of Multimedia Technology in Early Learning

Technology has developmental stages (as do children). As computer technology is becoming more powerful and sophisticated, we are witnessing the development of a new form of computer technology called computer-controlled multimedia. This form of multimedia integrates text, audio, and video with a computer. Multimedia becomes, therefore, a "technology-based medium for thinking, learning, and communication" (Ambron 1988). Because young children learn through their senses—that is, multisensory learning—a compatibility exists between multimedia technology and early learning.

According to Hooper (1988), technology-based multimedia stimulates the active involvement of the young child, which should enhance learning. Multimedia will also allow cognitive scientists "to study multisensory and interactive learning in ways that have been prevented in the past" (Hooper 1988). Thus, the multisensory learning of the young child that occurs in the preschool environment offers a rich laboratory for exploration.

Additionally, recent trends in cognitive theories have particular relevance to understanding the congruency between multimedia and early learning. The work of both Gardner and Sternberg stresses the differentiation of intelligence—that is, the existence of different types of intelligence. These theories challenge the definition of intelligence as a unitary construct. However, they are very helpful in examining the relevance of multimedia to the young child's learning process.

Gardner (1983) defines multiple "intelligences" within an individual, one or more of which are dominant. The intelligences Gardner defined are: logical–mathematical, linguistic, bodily–kinesthetic, musical, spatial, and interpersonal. These intelligences, according to Gardner's theory, are autonomous but can combine in a multiplicity of ways, varying with the adaptation of the individual within the culture to which he or she belongs. Multimedia technology, through the incorporation of a variety of media, has the potential to tap and stimulate each of these intelligences.

Sternberg (1988) conceptualizes the triarchic mind as consisting of three components: metacomponents or executive processes (such as planning, monitoring, and evaluating phenomena), performance components (that is, lower-order processes necessary to carry out the metacomponents' demands), and knowledge-acquisition components (for learning how to solve problems). These components are highly interactive and carry out three primary functions within the environment: selection, adaptation, and shaping. Essentially, Sternberg describes intelligence as the interaction between internal components, experience, and the environment. He defines intelligence as "the purposive adaptation to, selection of, and shaping of real-world environments relevant to one's life and abilities" (p. 65).

Using both Sternberg's and Gardner's theories, multimedia applications could be used to create "microworlds" (Papert 1980) in which we could systematically observe young children's strategies and dominant modalities (or "intelligences") for adapting, selecting, and shaping these "microworlds." We could use these theories to begin building a conceptual framework appropriate for understanding the influence of multimedia technology on young children's thinking and learning.

An important factor to discuss regarding the use of multimedia with young children is interactive multimedia's unique advantages over traditional multimedia forms in the preschool environment (such as blocks, crayons, paints, and so on). Some of the attributes of multimedia are:

- Multimedia can extend the sensory *content* of the preschool learning environment through sound, music, video, animation and graphics.
- Multimedia can provide multiple, multisensory *learning contexts* (for example, observing the transformation of a caterpillar into a butterfly or composing the music for songs with graphics).
- Multimedia offers a *safe* environment for risk taking, experimentation, exploration, and problem solving.

In essence, multimedia exposes the young child to multiple content and contexts as well as stimulates a variety of cognitive processes. I believe that future research will show a positive correlation between multimedia environments and the multisensory learning of the young child.

The Magic Classroom: A Preschool Design Example

In the spring and summer of 1988, Apple Computer's Multimedia Lab developed a preschool design example to demonstrate how multimedia technology can be used and integrated into a preschool environment. In the initial stages of the project, a team of software designers, video technicians, cognitive psychologists, and early childhood educators met to create the content and format of the preschool design example. The result was a multimedia application using HyperCard (a software platform) as the controller and as the graphical user interface on a Macintosh computer, plus a videodisc and a videodisc player.

The first screen the child sees on the computer is a picture of a little girl in a "magic preschool classroom." (See Figure 1.) The child accesses a variety of learning activities by clicking on the unshaded objects in the young girl's Magic Classroom.

By clicking the mouse on an object, the child can enter new worlds. For example, the child can explore the world of transformations to see the growth of mushrooms, the metamorphosis of a caterpillar into a butterfly, or the birth of a chick. Alternatively, the preschooler can make new friends by taking an electronic field trip on the Magic Bus to the homes of children from various ethnic backgrounds. (See Figure 2.) This activity allows the child to visit different neighborhoods and get a sense of the cultural diversity within the world. Moreoever, "anticipating that telecommunications technologies should soon be available that will let preschool classrooms—which are often isolated and quite homogeneous—communicate with other preschool classrooms, we focused this activity on children presenting their worlds to each other" (Hooper 1988, p. 53).

An activity that promotes creative expression is Musical Animals (see Figure 3), a musical tool that allows children to compose and record their own songs. When the child clicks on some part of the animal in the picture, the computer makes an animal sound and the pitch is controlled by the musical staff notation. In this activity, the child learns about different animal sounds and music composition.

FIGURE 1. The preschooler activates a learning situation by clicking on an unshaded object in the Magic Classroom.

FIGURE 2. *The preschooler visits the homes of children from various neighborhoods by riding the Magic Bus.*

FIGURE 3. *The preschooler activates an animal sound by clicking on an animal in the Musical Animals activity.*

One activity that clearly exemplifies the unique attributes of multimedia technology is Dancing Stories. (See Figure 4.) This activity relates directly to Gardner's musical and bodily-kinesthetic intelligences. Dancing Stories also shows how technology can be used for large-group, large-movement learning activities. In this activity, the child can choose different environments to visit (the beach, the moon, or the zoo). After a setting is selected, the child or children can choose either to go on a magical trip or to select the order of animals or characters they want to see. After they have made their choices, the video-disc is activated and the children begin to dance along with the video on the screen.

Other activities in the Magic Classroom example complement the preschool curriculum—for example, pictures that can be printed, such as an activities calendar, a world map, and a clock that says the time.

What has been created with this preschool design example is a highly interactive, multi-modal, multidisciplinary learning environment. This design example can also be used by teachers as an instructional, planning, or diagnostic tool.

FIGURE 4. The preschooler chooses an environment in Dancing Stories and then selects from additional options; then the children dance along with the video on the screen.

The Magic Classroom:
An Instructional, Planning, and Diagnostic Tool

As an instructional tool, the teacher can use the Magic Classroom to develop a variety of learning activities. For example, the preschool design example has a Guess Who? game that shows the child different parts of an animal, and the child has to guess the animal. The teacher can extend this activity into the preschool environment by cutting up pictures of different objects, pulling pieces of the picture out of an envelope or folder, and having the children guess what the object is.

The teacher can also talk to the children about the texture of the different animal parts shown—such as the roughness of the elephant's hide or the furriness of the kitten—and then provide different materials that represent different textures to create a set of tactile activities. Additionally, teachers can develop science and language-development activities, art, music and dance projects, math games, and so on. The range of activities is determined by the creativity and resourcefulness of the teachers.

Through the use of the Magic Classroom preschool design example and correlated preschool activities, a broad set of concepts and skills can be learned, including:

- Basic concepts (colors, numbers, letters)
- Language development
- Problem solving
- Creativity and creative expression
- Observation and focused attention

As a planning tool, a teacher resource section is included in the preschool design example; it allows the teacher to plan daily and monthly classroom activities and to record pertinent parent information, keep track of staff schedules, and so on.

As a diagnostic tool, the teacher can use the Magic Classroom as an observation tool, recording and assessing children's levels of development in the cognitive, motor, and social–affective domains. Through careful, systematic observation, the teacher can also identify a child's dominant learning modalities, activity preferences, and interests.

Summary

Multimedia technology can provide rich, interactive learning environments in early childhood education to promote exploration, understanding, and mastery. Multimedia can create both the context and content for learning.

In the preschool design example, a wealth of learning activities is available to the young child, and the theme of transformation is prevalent throughout. Children create transformations through play, imagination, observation, and movement.

Multimedia is a versatile tool for the preschool teacher because it can be used for learning, instruction, planning, diagnosis, and assessment.

Multimedia technology offers limitless opportunities for young children by providing dynamic landscapes for learning.

References

Ambron, S., and K. Hooper. *Interactive Multimedia.* Redmond, WA: Microsoft Press, 1988.

Bowman, B. "Technology in Early Childhood Education." Paper presented at the Early Childhood Mini-Conference for the Association for Supervision and Curriculum Development. Alexandria, VA. December, 1988.

Bruner, J. *Actual Minds, Possible Worlds.* Cambridge, MA: Harvard University Press, 1986.

Clements, D. "Computers and Young Children: A Review of Research." *Young Children.* November, 1987, Vol. 43, no. 1, 34–43.

Davidson, J. *Children and Computers Together in the Early Childhood Classroom.* Albany, NY: Delmar Publishers Inc., 1989.

Gardner, H. *Frames of Mind: The Theory of Multiple Intelligences.* New York, NY: Basic Books, Inc., Publishers, 1983.

Ginsburg, H., and S. Opper. *Piaget's Theory of Intellectual Development.* Englewood Cliffs, NJ: Prentice-Hall, Inc., 1969.

Haugland, S. "The Effect of Developmental and Non-Developmental Software on Preschool Children's Intelligence, Creativity, and Self-Esteem." Unpublished manuscript. Southeast Missouri State University, 1989.

Hooper, K. *Interactive Multimedia Design 1988.* Technical Report #13. Cupertino, CA: Apple Computer, Inc., 1988.

Montessori, M. *The Secret of Childhood.* New York, NY: Ballantine Books, 1966.

Papert, S. *Mindstorms.* New York, NY: Basic Books, Inc., Publishers, 1980.

Piaget, J. *Six Psychological Studies.* New York, NY: Vintage Books, 1968.

Shade, D., et al. "Microcomputers and Preschoolers: Working Together in a Classroom Setting." *Computers in the Schools.* Vol. 3(2), Summer 1986, 53–61.

Sheingold, K. "Issues Related to the Implementation of Computer Technology in the Education of Young Children." Paper presented at the Thirteenth Annual Early Childhood Conference. College Park, MD. March, 1983.

Sternberg, R. *The Triarchic Mind: A New Theory of Human Intelligence.* New York, NY: Viking Penguin Inc., 1988.

Cognitive Load in Hypermedia: Designing for the Exploratory Learner

Tim Oren

TIM OREN

Tim Oren is manager of the Information Access and Architecture (IAA) group with Apple Computer's Advanced Technology Group (ATG). The IAA group investigates issues related to information retrieval and hypertext architectures, including portable hypertext representations, statistical and connectionist retrieval methods, and agent functionality and portrayal.

Prior to joining ATG, he was a member of the AppleCD project team and created HyperCard applications for CD-ROM and multimedia. He was project manager and principal designer for the Apple Learning Disc CD-ROM, a collection of HyperCard educational applications, including the Electronic Whole Earth Catalog™ and the Apple/Grolier American History projects, of which he was also primary designer.

Before coming to Apple, he was affiliated with KnowledgeSet Corp., where he participated in the implementation of the original Grolier Electronic Encyclopedia CD-ROM. He also designed and implemented a graphic hypertext interface for representing and browsing through dependencies between stored documents, which has since been released as part of KnowledgeSet's Graphic Knowledge Retrieval System for CD-ROM.

He earned a B.S. and an M.S. from Michigan State University. His professional affiliations include the IEEE Computer Society and ACM SIGIR and SIGCHI.

HyperCard and Exploratory Learning

In projects presented in this book and elsewhere (Chignell 1988, Crane 1988), HyperCard has been applied to education as a tool for exploratory learning. This is a direct consequence of its strengths and weaknesses. Because HyperCard integrates multiple media—text, graphics, sound, animation, and video—it is a good presentation tool. Because it lacks the overviews and fluid interface of programs such as More™, it works poorly as a "thinker's tool" for composition. It also lacks the mechanisms to support drill-and-practice-style CAI (computer-aided instruction). Although these tools can be added at some cost, HyperCard seems better suited to exploratory browsing in a database in which the author's expertise is rendered in presentational form. Indeed, Bill Atkinson, Hyper-Card's author, saw it as a means of liberation from the "school bus of the curriculum" into a world where students would explore on their own (Atkinson 1987).

Exploratory Learning and Cognitive Load

Exploratory learning offers increased freedom and motivation to the student. It bears a cost of *cognitive load,* mental burdens imposed by the task of digesting and organizing information, which might be partially understood when it is first encountered. A curriculum or textbook usually provides an apparatus for organizing material and measuring progress through it, and takes measures to minimize the number of partially understood concepts at any one point, staging and testing its material. Exploratory learners are often on their own when it comes to controlling complexity. A failure to control complexity can lead to cognitive overload and failure to learn. A fair question to ask about any electronic learning environment is how well it supports or hinders the task. If we take the physical world of index cards, libraries, and notebooks as a benchmark, how does hypermedia technology in general and HyperCard in particular compare?

Cognitive Load and Hypermedia

Hypermedia systems generally impose their own additional cognitive load in the form of so-called "navigation." The fundamental issues are orientation—"Where am I in the data?"—and affordance—"How and where do I go from here?" (Conklin 1987). The difficulty is compounded by the tendency of card-based hypermedia systems to promote writing in many small, interconnected chunks. How acute the cognitive load becomes depends on the quality of orientational cues in the database and the number of choices offered at one time. Dealing with these problems of exploratory learning and hypermedia is one of the central challenges facing designers of educational content in HyperCard.

To partially deal with the orientation issue, HyperCard offers the "go back" (Back) and "recent card" (Recent) options. However, compared with other hypermedia systems, HyperCard has several limits that can act to further *increase* cognitive load. HyperCard presents only one screen image at a time. This makes it more difficult to relate pieces of information in the system, because only one external representation can be viewed: All other relevant information must be kept in the student's memory. This is often noted as a problem in using HyperCard's own Help stacks, where the exact nature of a problem might be forgotten before getting to the appropriate documentation, or where the way to fix it might be lost before returning to the point of difficulty. The one-screen system also makes it difficult to construct and display overviews of the information, similar to outlines of a text. Although these can be built into a stack, again the current location must be left and kept in memory in order to reach the overview information.

Marginalia, note taking, and bookmarking are important means of externalizing mental loads in physical systems. HyperCard in its basic form affords few facilities for annotation and marking of its contained data. Although cut and paste is still effective, no facility exists for joining the extracted data with its source in the hypermedia database.

Methods for Reducing Cognitive Load

Many known and proposed methods exist for ameliorating cognitive load in hypermedia systems. This discussion begins with proven techniques, pointing to existing HyperCard-based implementations, and moves toward methods that are derived from current research and are thus more speculative. Figures and references to current work should allow the potential educational designer to become familiar with these techniques.

A popular method is information hiding, reducing the choices visible to the user by hiding less-used options in the form of a menu. This lowers the number of choices toward the well-known "seven plus or minus two" figure considered optimal for the user. The screen in Figure 1, from the Electronic Whole Earth Catalog, shows its pull-down menu exposed. Items on the menu (normally hidden) are used for long-range navigation. The controls that are exposed are the more commonly used short-range navigation options.

As noted above, the concrete nature of physical systems allows their use for externalizing information. Designing features analogous to bookmarks and annotations back into electronic systems allows the learner to save parts of mental states for later reference. For instance, the Perseus Greek Classics project (Crane 1988) has implemented "paths" that allow the user to save and modify a personal trail through the information. (See Figure 2.) The notebook stack from the Project Jefferson freshman-writing database

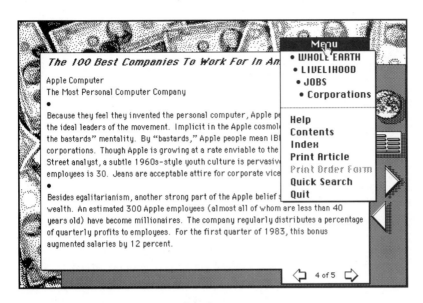

FIGURE 1. Article card from the Electronic Whole Earth Catalog, with the navigation pull-down menu exposed.

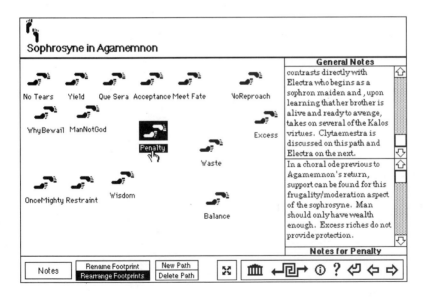

FIGURE 2. Path card from Perseus Greek Classic database. [Copyright © 1989 by President and Fellows of Harvard University and the Annenberg/CPB, Cambridge, Massachusetts. Used with permission.]

(Chignell 1988) allows the student to take "snapshots" of cards and collect them in a personal, modifiable data space. (See Figure 3.)

A simple but often overlooked method of reducing the load on the user is to reduce the number of hypermedia links emanating from any particular card or data node. This requires parsimony and editorial restraint but can yield big benefits in clarity. An overabundance of confusing links can become as useless as no links at all.

Strong visual cues at each card can orient the user within a database structure. If well designed, nonintrusive cues are a nearly subliminal confidence builder. Figure 4, another card design from the Electronic Whole Earth Catalog, exemplifies both approaches. The background graphic provides a cue for the overall topic. The specific card layout shows the location in the generally hierarchical database structure. The design limits the branching factor at the card and leaves each potential target clearly legible.

Another approach to navigation is to provide a "safety net" for *re*orientation when failure occurs. The well-known HyperCard Home button is the ultimate escape for the lost. In the Whole Earth screen of Figure 4, the globe icon provides a quick return to the table of contents. A system of clear landmarks to which the current position can be related is an underused technique in current design.

Related to the notion of landmarks are maps, overview nodes that show the connectivity of the database in the form of icons and interconnecting traces. (See Figure 5.)

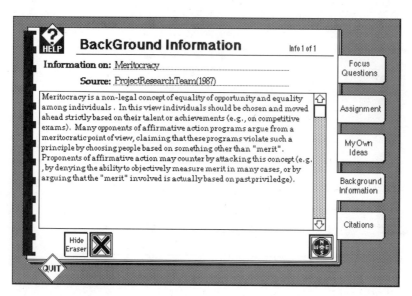

FIGURE 3. *Notebook card from Project Jefferson stacks.*

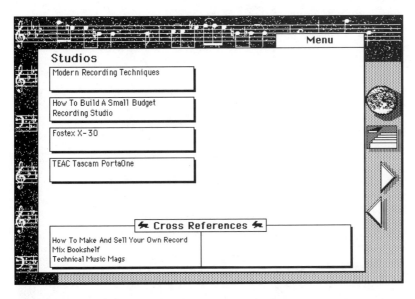

FIGURE 4. Cluster map card from the Electronic Whole Earth Catalog.
Boxed titles are hierarchical links. Cross-references branch sideways in
the Catalog. Background indicates the general topic area: Music.

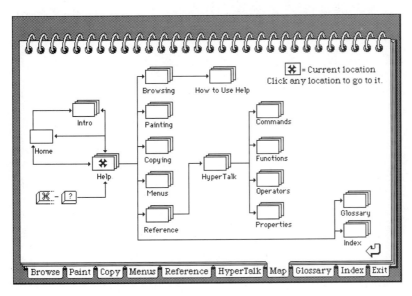

FIGURE 5. Map card from the HyperCard Help stack.

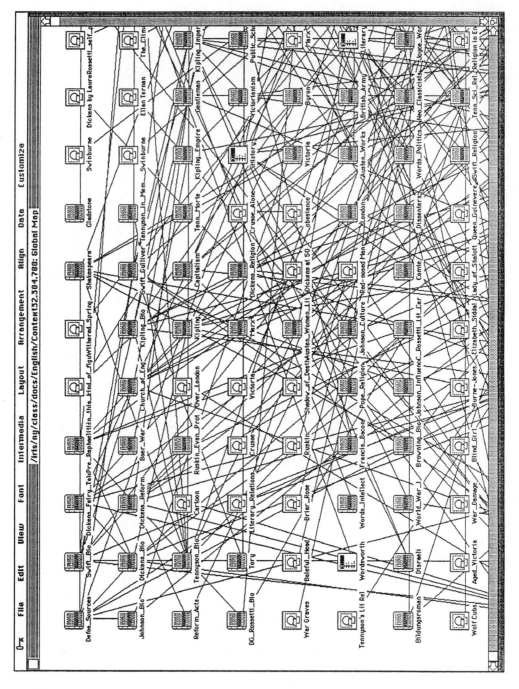

FIGURE 6. Overview map of a complex Intermedia document web. [Copyright © 1987 by Brown University, Providence, Rhode Island. Used with permission.]

Alan Kay has suggested that maps are essential if a user is browsing through more than a few hundred unfamiliar nodes, which is the situation facing the exploratory learner (Kay 1987). However, unless the topology of node interconnection is restricted, it is generally more than a two-dimensional layout problem. This leads to complex displays resembling a spiderweb more than anything else and having doubtful value in reducing navigational load. (See Figure 6.) As a result, designers are now turning to systems of local-point-of-view maps when dealing with very large hypermedia databases (Utting 1989).

The presence of dynamic elements in hypermedia allows inclusion of active presentations within the database. Some of these presentations might take the learner on a "guided tour," providing a preplanned introduction to a portion of the information. A number of approaches can be used to create guided tours. Work at Xerox PARC (Zollweger 1989) and at the University of Maryland (Furuta 1989) has enhanced simple path mechanisms with programming formalisms or created a succession of "tabletops" with commented collections of nodes (Marshall 1989). At Apple, we have designed audiovisual tours (see Figure 7) that contain links to related nodes within the overall database (Salomon 1989).

FIGURE 7. Tour card from the Apple/Grolier American History project. VCR-like buttons allow the user to control the tour's progress. The icon in the lower left corner links to a related node within the underlying database.

A step beyond canned tours is attempting to provide a "dynamic tour guide," which will adapt to the interests of the user while providing a simplifying "next move" utility to the user. Another feature of the Apple/Grolier American History project is "guides," personified guidance functions that deliver navigation information in the form of preference lists as well as content related to their point of view. (See Figure 8.) We have found that users are able to intuitively associate the guide images with a probable character and set of preferences for information (Oren 1990, Laurel 1990).

Another approach to adaptivity is dynamically altering the appearance of the database. Existing experiments, restricted as yet to textual databases, allow the user to express interests as keywords or by rating viewed articles as acceptable or not interesting (Frisse 1988, Frisse 1989). User testing of a similar system has shown that users find the adaptive textual structure more effective in answering questions (Egan 1989). Experiments at Apple with trace data from a public kiosk suggest that it might be possible to infer the emergence of goals and their nature by monitoring user behavior, without the need for explicitly requested feedback (Husic 1989).

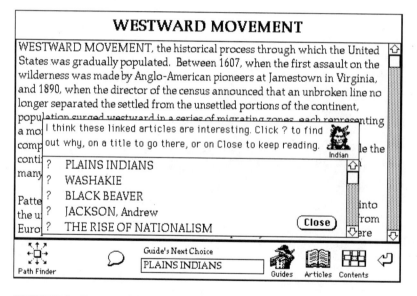

FIGURE 8. Text card from the Apple/Grolier American History project. The Indian-guide figure presents a restricted and reordered list of available next moves.

Summary

A dominant use of HyperCard in education is exploratory learning, where students are free to browse through a topically related database of material, learning at their own pace and guided by their own interests. This freedom comes at a cost of cognitive load, imposed by the learner's need to find a way through an environment in which no instructor or CAI program doles out the next bit of information. The cognitive load of way finding might be antagonistic to the mental effort required to integrate the information in a database. This discussion has surveyed the hypertext and human-interface literature to point out ways in which this problem might be ameliorated.

References

Atkinson, Bill. Transcript of Whole Earth Catalog design meeting. January, 1987.

Chignell, Mark H., and Richard M. Lacy. "Project Jefferson: Integrating Research and Instruction." *Academic Computing,* September, 1988, 12–44.

Conklin, Jeff. "Hypertext: An Introduction and Survey." *IEEE Computer.* September, 1987, 17–41.

Crane, Gregory, and Elli Mylonas. "The Perseus Project: An Interactive Curriculum on Classical Greek Civilization." *Educational Technology.* November, 1988, 25–32.

Frisse, Mark E. "Searching for Information in a Hypertext Medical Handbook." *Communications of the ACM.* 31: 880–86.

Frisse, Mark E. "Information Retrieval from Hypertext: Update on the Dynamic Medical Handbook Project," *Proc. Hypertext '89,* November 5–8, 1989, Pittsburgh, Pennsylvania, 199–212.

Furuta, Richard, and P. David Stotts. "Programmable Browsing Semantics in Trellis." *Proc. Hypertext '89,* November 5–8, 1989, Pittsburgh, Pennsylvania, 27–42.

Husic, Freda, and Anne Nicol. "Analysis of CHI '89 Kiosk Data." Apple Computer Technical Report, 1989 (forthcoming).

Kay, Alan C. Transcript of Whole Earth Catalog design meeting. January, 1987.

Laurel, Brenda, Tim Oren, and Abbe Don. "Issues in Multimedia Interface Design: Media Integration and Interface Agents." *Proc. of CHI '90,* Association for Computing Machinery (forthcoming).

Marshall, Catherine C., and Peggy M. Irish. "Guided Tours and On-Line Presentations: How Authors Make Existing Hypertext Intelligible for Readers." *Proc. Hypertext '89,* November 5–8, 1989, Pittsburgh, Pennsylvania, 15–26.

Oren, Tim, Gitta Salomon, Kristee Kreitman, and Abbe Don. "Guides: Characterizing the Interface." In Laurel, B., ed., *The Art of Human-Computer Interface Design,* Addison-Wesley (forthcoming).

Salomon, Gitta, Tim Oren, and Kristee Kreitman. "Using Guides to Explore Multimedia Databases." *Proc. 22nd Hawaii International Conference on System Sciences,* January 3–6, 1989, Kailua-Kona, Hawaii, 3–12.

Utting, Kenneth, and Nicole Yankelovich, "Context and Orientation in Hypermedia Networks." ACM Transactions on Information Systems, 7 (1), 58–84, January 1989.

Zellweger, Polle T. "Scripted Documents: A Hypermedia Path Mechanism." *Proc. Hypertext '89,* November 5–8, 1989, Pittsburgh, Pennsylvania, 1–14.

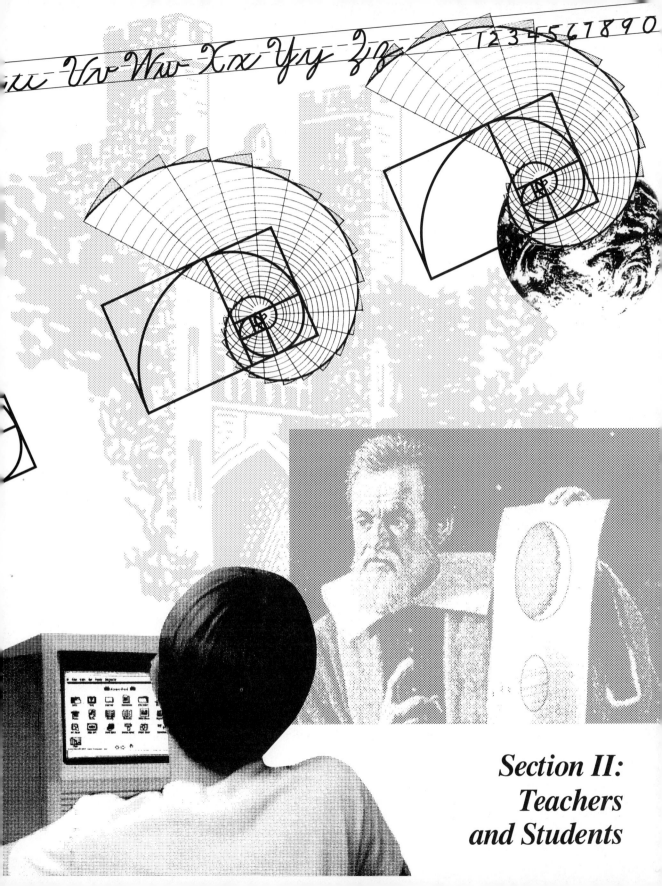

**Section II:
Teachers
and Students**

HyperCard has been in the hands of teachers and students in a few elementary, high-school, and university settings for two years. This section of the book includes essays that describe what children, teachers, and university professors are doing with Hyper-Card. Also included are general comments about the use of multimedia tools in schools.

Currently, children and teachers are using HyperCard in classrooms around the country. Anne Nicol, from Apple's Human Interface Group, observed and interviewed children and teachers at two schools about their experiences. She was looking both for features of HyperCard that distinguish it from more conventional media and for ways that the interface could enhance learning. She raises some broader research questions that should be addressed as multimedia authoring tools are introduced into classrooms.

David Mintz is a former classroom teacher who is teaching teachers how to use technology. He provides insights on ways to learn and ways to teach HyperCard. He feels the key to learning how to program with HyperCard is to allow the learner to participate in the learning.

James Lengel and Sue Collins approach questions about multimedia in schools from two practical perspectives—that of educators who have been in the classroom and that of technology consultants who know what is possible. Their paper focuses on HyperCard, but their advice also pertains to other multimedia tools.

Joseph Hofmeister, a forward-thinking educator, envisions school as the "place where knowledge is integrated, synthesized, and tested instead of a place where knowledge is transmitted from those who know to those who don't." He describes the use of Hyper-Card and other multimedia tools at the Cincinnati Country Day School as a step in the direction of realizing a new kind of learning environment in a school.

Barry Stebbins, a science teacher, explains how HyperCard was used to create a community of learners at West High School in Columbus, Ohio. He describes several applications of HyperCard developed by students and teachers. He feels that people who use HyperCard must learn to think in logical sequences, program in HyperTalk, and solve programming problems. Although the end-user must invest significant time to be able to use HyperCard, Stebbins thinks the rewards justify the effort.

Robert Campbell, a librarian, and Patricia Hanlon, an English teacher, worked together on Grapevine. Grapevine is a multimedia database and tool environment for teachers and students to learn about John Steinbeck's *The Grapes of Wrath* and about the Depression. Campbell and Hanlon share their experiences of using multimedia material in their classrooms. Is the incorporation of multimedia into the learning process worth the trouble? Their answer is "Yes."

Jan Biros has initiated and supported HyperCard development projects at Drexel University. Biros describes HyperCard applications in neuropsychology and literacy development at Drexel. She also discusses the importance of support for faculty and students using HyperCard in universities.

Peter Olivieri, a faculty member in computer science from Boston College, explains that the most important aspect of HyperCard in an academic community is that it fosters sharing and learning from others. He says it has helped to make everyone a teacher. He offers several suggestions for ways to merge the power and potential of tools such as HyperCard with the power and potential of teachers, and he encourages educators with the observation that educational uses of technology will only get better.

Children Using HyperCard

Anne Nicol

ANNE NICOL

Anne Nicol, who earned a Ph.D. in educational psychology from Stanford University, was a university professor for over a decade, teaching courses in research design and educational technology. Her research interests center around computer learning environments. She worked on the first CAI systems at Stanford, studied children using Logo, and recently initiated a project at Apple Computer called "Interfaces for Learning," which makes interface design recommendations based on classroom observations and interviews with children.

She heads the User Studies Team in the Advanced Technology Group at Apple. This team is conducting research on advanced, interactive help systems and on collaborative work. They also consult with other development teams to help them incorporate user research into the design process.

The way that we think and act is shaped by the media with which we choose to work. Children working with HyperCard will be using a new medium—one that has no simple metaphor in their real world. No easy analogies come to mind between HyperCard and other creative media, computer-based or not. Also, because HyperCard is still in a formative stage, attempts at categorizing it in terms that we know from past experience in education are likely to fail. For those of us interested in fostering, observing, and studying children's cognitive processes, HyperCard in the classroom presents a serious and exciting new challenge.

My purpose in conducting research and writing about HyperCard is to analyze those features of HyperCard that distinguish it from other, more conventional media and tools and to suggest ways the interface might be enhanced for educational purposes. My "data" come from observations, discussions, and interviews I've conducted with children and teachers who are using HyperCard in the classroom.[1] To conclude, I will raise some broader research questions that I think need to be addressed as HyperCard and other multimedia authoring tools are introduced into classrooms.

Distinguishing Features of HyperCard

One thing that HyperCard clearly *is* is an "interface builder." Almost every new HyperCard stack has a new interface. The general classes of interface features are determined by HyperCard and by the Macintosh itself, but stack authors have extraordinary creative license within these classes—with regard not only to appearance but also to functionality of all the stack features. Because the interface, be it the HyperCard authoring environment or a stack created by a teacher, is the medium for the child-user, the focus here will be on the interface and on features of the resulting child-computer interaction. In this section, three HyperCard features are described briefly: buttons, graphics and sound tools, and links. In later sections, I discuss how children use these features and raise some questions for research.

Buttons

A HyperCard button can be an extremely complex object. Its major components are its appearance on the card (form) and its script (function). A button can take on a full range

---

[1] At the Open School/Vivarium Project in Los Angeles and at Sacred Hearts School in San Francisco, children were observed and interviewed, and discussions were held with teachers. Unless otherwise noted, the examples from children's stacks and their comments quoted in this paper come from my visits at those two schools. Many thanks to the teachers, administrators, and children who shared their time and experiences with me.

of looks—from a standard Macintosh button to any graphic a child-designer can imagine. In fact, a button is simply a "hot" area on the screen which, when it is clicked with the mouse (or receives certain other "stimuli"), initiates an associated script. The user can create a standard button using the New Button dialog, an icon button by referring to icons stored as resources with the stack, or a custom button by specifying the location and size of the "hot" area on the card and placing a graphic on that area. Buttons can be invisible too, in the case where the designer creates a button that has no corresponding graphic.

Buttons are complex because:

- Only incidental standards exist that relate appearance to functionality.
- Button scripts are initiated by any or all these common events: moving the pointer over the button, pressing the mouse button, or releasing the mouse button.
- The range of actions that can be associated with the button script is enormous (and ever-expanding).

For example, clicking on a button can move the user to another card, cause a sound to be played, show a visual effect, bring up a dialog, and/or execute an external command to initiate some activity outside of the HyperCard program (such as display video, launch another application, access a CD-ROM, and so forth). This list of actions is presented from the script writer's point of view. However, from the user's perspective, the categories of button actions are quite different and do not correspond directly with the programmer's view. Animation effects, for example, can be produced by programming a button to switch quickly back and forth between two cards; the programmer in this case would have a different concept of the button's function than the user.

Graphics and Sound Tools

Children have had opportunities to create computer graphics and sound prior to the release of HyperCard, but not in a mixed environment and not with the range of tools available now. They can use Paint tools to draw their own graphics, or they can cut and paste from other sources; they can generate music by writing scripts that use HyperCard sounds or MacinTalk or by using tools that were designed to work with HyperCard such as MacRecorder.[2] Some children are also able to incorporate videotape and videodisc images, depending on the availability of equipment.

---

[2] MacRecorder is distributed by Farallon Computing of Berkeley, California.

Links

Links between bits of information can be built in a number of ways in HyperCard, depending on the format of the information and the design of the stack. A simple link can be created that takes the user from one card to the next; a more complicated link can be created that shows a video clip on another monitor when the user gets to a certain point in the stack; and finally, very complex algorithms can be written in such a way that the links are more dynamic and dependent on sequences of the user's actions.

The HyperCard mechanism for creating links supports a bottom-up process. Users build links one at a time, in the context of the background or card they are working on. Support does not exist for defining the network and its nodes first, automatically generating the linked stack to fit the network. Furthermore, although links can be programmed to be two-way, they are inherently one-way connections. Although HyperCard itself has a mechanism for letting users work back, one at a time, through the nodes that have been visited, it is not easy to build a backtracking capability into a stack or database.

A Continuum of HyperCard Uses in Classrooms

Children in classrooms will be using HyperCard in widely different ways. I think it might be useful to look at these along a continuum, which is a function of how much control the children have over the creation, organization, and presentation of HyperCard material. (See Figure 1.) At one end of the continuum, the children might be viewing a HyperCard slide show for which they simply click on arrows or buttons to progress on a linear path through the stack. At the other end, children are HyperCard authors, with all the HyperCard tools and resources at hand. This continuum is also useful for labeling classes of HyperCard interfaces, for categorizing possible focuses for research, and for examining educational objectives.

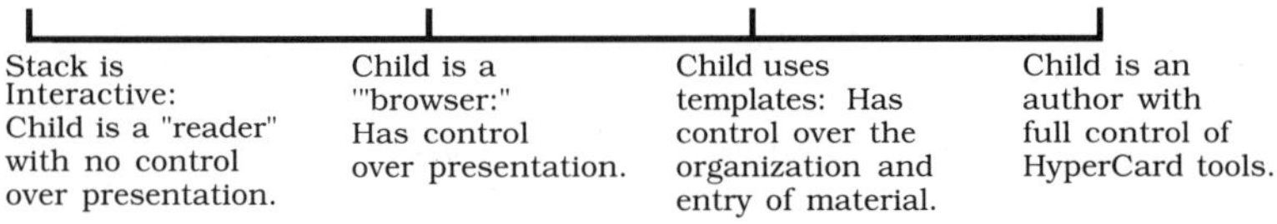

| Stack is Interactive: Child is a "reader" with no control over presentation. | Child is a '"browser:" Has control over presentation. | Child uses templates: Has control over the organization and entry of material. | Child is an author with full control of HyperCard tools. |

FIGURE 1. A continuum of HyperCard uses in classrooms.

Giving Children Control over the Presentation of Material

Stack designers can give users control in different ways. In the lovely HyperCard stories by Amanda Goodenough,[3] children help tell the story by clicking on places in the drawings to show what they think might happen next. (See Figure 2.) Stacks that allow the user to explore by choosing among options are letting the user customize the presentation of the information; different users can view the information in different sequences. In other stacks, the same general topic might be presented in video segments, audio tracks, graphics, or text. Users can choose as many ways as they want to "look" at the material; different users can view the information in different formats and media. Fabrice Florin's WorldView[4] is an elaborate example of this type of design.

FIGURE 2. A child-user helps "narrate" the story by clicking on a part of the illustration. "Inigo Gets Out" by Amanda Goodenough

Giving Children Control over the Organization and Entry of Material

At this point, children begin to become HyperCard authors—but they might not know it. When children use templates to create stacks and databases, and when they use the Find and the Sort commands and buttons, they are making decisions about the organization

---

[3] AmandaStories of Santa Cruz, California.
[4] See "Information Landscapes" in Section I.

and retrieval of information. The clever animation and storytelling templates created by teachers at the Open School/Vivarium Project fit this category and are mentioned later in this paper.

Giving Children Control over the Creation of HyperCard Material

This is the point along the continuum that we know the least about from observations and research in other media. Trying to make predictions about the creative behavior of children in a new medium is a risky business. A much more fruitful approach is to begin by watching carefully what children do as they learn to use the new authoring tools. After we begin to see which concepts they adopt readily and which ones give them trouble, we will be in a better position to develop hypotheses and conduct more systematic research.

In my work, I have concentrated on the two latter points of the continuum. The children I observed and talked with were either adding information to template stacks created by a teacher or other adult, or they were creating their own stacks. One example of a template stack is a "flip book," which consists of a stack of cards with existing buttons. The children create the animations by using Paint tools on successive cards. (See Figure 3.) Another example is a storybook template the children use both to write and illustrate their stories. (See Figure 4 on the following page.)

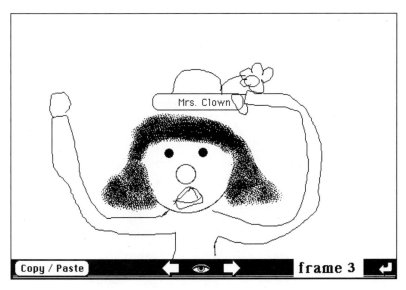

FIGURE 3. A child drew this picture for an animation using Paint tools.

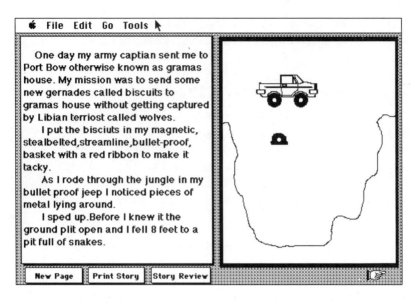

FIGURE 4. *A child wrote this (unedited) story using the storybook template.*

Fourth-grade and fifth-grade children with whom I spoke were doing research projects on animals. They created their stacks completely from scratch. Although certain types of information were to be included (where the animal lives, what it eats, and so on), the design and format was left up to the children. (See Figure 5.) At another school, the children were designing HyperCard stacks to present information about particular Civil War battles. This type of project falls at the "high" end of the continuum with regard to the amount of control children have over the design of the stacks.

Some of the children I observed had used HyperCard for over a year, since its early stages of development; others had only recently been introduced to it. A number of the children at the Open School/Vivarium Project were using HyperCard daily for a wide range of school-related activities, some had HyperCard at home, and some had taken advantage of HyperCard experts at the school to introduce features into their stacks that are more sophisticated than many adult users could imagine. Clearly, what I saw is not representative of the way that HyperCard will initially be used in more typical class-rooms. However, the opportunity to see and talk with these children provided rich data about the basic issues of using HyperCard as an integral tool in learning.

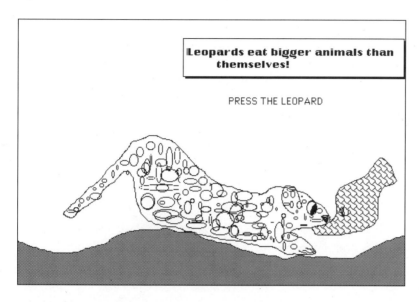

FIGURE 5. A card from a stack, designed and formatted by a child.

Initial Observations

My approach to exploring children's use of HyperCard is to look for obstacles: What features seem to get in their way when they try to accomplish their goals? At the same time, I try to look at the features that are most attractive to them, with the ultimate goal of enhancing HyperCard in ways that will make it more exciting and useful as an educational tool. My observations are for the purpose of improving product and interface design rather than to add to the scientific literature on children and child development. But in the process, I have identified a number of related research issues that could be explored further, shedding light on some intriguing questions about the way children think and work in multimedia environments.

Buttons: What Are They? Where Are They? and Where Do They Take Me?

In describing HyperCard buttons earlier, I mentioned how complex a button can be. I suspect children develop and build a concept of "button" over time and in parallel with their understanding of scripting and of abstractions in general. Looking at children's use of buttons would probably be a good way to track their general development as Hyper-Card authors. At first they use them in their simplest form—to move from one card to the next. They are thinking of buttons simply as links to the next card. They then begin to add visual effects and sound. At this point they are beginning to think more about audience and of using media to capture attention and convey information. Later, they learn to modify scripts so that buttons can be used as counters, to play animations, to bring up hidden text fields, and so forth. As an example, one sophisticated sixth-grade author has created a game in which clicking the Fight button results in looking in an inventory to see if the player has the right weapon. If the weapon is missing, the outcome of "Fight" is dramatically different than if the weapon is present; in fact, "you die."

Another child, in discussing a situation where the user chooses one of three buttons, said, "That's decision making. Decision making is very popular in our class." Not knowing quite what he meant by the term, I explored with him a little further. It turns out that the distinction he was making was between choice situations where only one choice, or button, is "correct" (as defined by the designer), and choices where there is not really a right or wrong consideration. In the "decision making" situation, the child truly gets to choose one of the alternatives and then deals with the consequences. But there is probably more sense of control no matter what the outcome than in the case where buttons are seen as being right and wrong.

As children move beyond the simple use of buttons to get from one card to the next, they use buttons to create levels of information on a single card by bringing up fields of text. The concept is relatively simple: Click on this object and you obtain some textual information about it. The script to carry it out is simple, too. The hard part is connecting the button to the field. One child I observed changed context eight times and took more than 15 steps to complete the task. From talking with teachers and seeing what students are doing with HyperCard in many settings, I suspect that this "definition" of a button ("give me more information") will be fundamental in their use of HyperCard. Quicker, more intuitive ways are needed to build the connections between levels of information.

A major problem with buttons is finding them. Because buttons need not have a standard appearance, they can easily be lost. Even the stack author forgets where the buttons are, as evidenced when several of our young designers showed off their stacks. This issue comes up with regard to other hypertext and hypermedia systems as well as with other age groups. In earlier tests with adults, we found that at first they tended not to realize that nonstandard buttons could be clicked on. After they got the idea, they tended to "overgeneralize" and began clicking on everything. It was difficult to establish a working theory about where to click because there tended not to be much consistency from stack to stack. The system provides an easy solution by giving command-key access to see all the buttons on a card. But users don't necessarily know about the key, and this is an external solution. It is preferable to help designers develop conventions that communicate the presence of buttons to their users.

Finding the buttons is only part of the issue; the user also needs some hint about the consequences of clicking on a given button. With adults, it might be that the disorientation they experience in hypertext systems is largely due to a mismatch between where they think they are going (on the basis of button cues) and where they actually end up. Learning how to convey this kind of relational information is critical to successful design in HyperCard and other hypermedia environments. I've had fewer reports of disorientation from children than from adults. Although I found some of their stacks difficult to navigate myself, the children claim that their classmates have no problems. This would be an interesting topic for further research. For example, do these young authors design and recognize navigational and story cues that are more obscure to adults who haven't had the same exposure to media and computer games?

A related issue concerns the expected sequence of user actions. From a design standpoint, it is desirable to avoid giving instructions and to convey the sequencing visually. This is extremely difficult in many cases, especially for young children who presumably have difficulty in taking another person's point of view into account. In quite a few of the stacks, the children have inserted instructions like "now click on the door," in order to help the user know what to do next. This probably represents a first step towards recognizing audience requirements.

True Integration of Graphics and Sound[5]

Children using HyperCard are working in an environment that lets them mix graphics, text, and sound almost simultaneously. The accessibility of the Paint tools and the ability to cut and paste images seems to result in projects in which the visual elements are much more central than they are in more traditional projects. It might be that the medium will encourage a lot more attention to the communication value of visual elements. For example, the children really like to use the visual effects[6] in creating their stacks. This is partly explained by the fact that using visual effects is a quick way to get a sense of movement and animation. It might also be that the children recognize that visual effects can convey additional information. A wipe to one side or the other can support the notion that one is moving in a linear fashion through the information, a different effect can help reinforce the concept of depth, and so forth.

---

[5] Because the children I observed were not yet using video in their creations, I do not include it or other media in the discussion. Some of the general issues raised here will surely apply as other media and tools become available to children.

[6] Visual effects can be produced by including an instruction in the script. The visual effects are animations that produce effects like "wipe left" or "iris open" as the user moves from one card to the next.

If children are to use the tools actually to draw and paint, they will require better input devices than a mouse. Although most of the children drew enthusiastically and without inhibition, several comments were made about artistic talent; the children, even in the lower grades, had identified those who "could draw." HyperCard and other graphics environments on the computer now create a place for some talented children who might not be drawn to computers otherwise. On the other hand, children who consider themselves not to be artists might be discouraged. One little girl said repeatedly as I brought her from the classroom to the lab that she wasn't good on the computer because she couldn't draw.

Producing a multimedia document naturally draws on a variety of talents. In some cases the teachers encouraged the children to form "multidisciplinary" teams to do their work, and in other cases the children had joined their talents spontaneously. However it came about, it was fairly common to see products produced by teams rather than by individuals working alone. And often the members of the team had fairly well-defined responsibilities; for example, one child is an animator while another is the sound person.

While HyperCard has a wide range of tools for drawing and painting, it does not support animation directly. Movement can be simulated, however, by moving quickly through a series of cards (similar to using a flipbook). It is also possible, as I learned from one of the fourth-graders, to use the Drag command to move an object on a single card. A number of the children in this study were experimenting with animation and, in doing so, were confronting some interesting problems regarding both timing and the passage of time. For example, on one project about energy, children were animating a scene in which an alarm clock goes off, a rooster crows, and the lights come on—simultaneously. Having actually to show the sequence in motion, as opposed to telling about it (as they would in a traditional report), required the children to think very carefully about the order and synchronicity of events. The inclusion of tools for animation or the production of animation templates and aids would add significant value to HyperCard.

HyperCard does not make it easy for children to use sound in their productions. Although one of the children claimed to have written his script for "Wipeout" by ear, others using the HyperCard tools for producing sounds were not very successful. The children at one of the schools had learned an external command for using MacinTalk, so they included quite a lot of speech in their stacks.

Sound can serve a variety of functions in an interface and can take several forms. The sound forms that appeared in the children's work were speech, music, and natural sounds. In some cases the speech and natural sounds served as entertainment or illustration; in others, the sounds carried information (for example, served as a cue or redundantly conveyed the result of some user action). Digitized sound, such as that produced by MacRecorder, takes up a lot of disk space and is thus inappropriate if the stacks are to be "portable."

Although the children were generally just playing with sound, it was clearly important enough to them to expend a lot of effort in getting the sound incorporated into their designs. It might be easier if, as one third-grader suggested, the Objects menu included an item called New Sound.

Building Links: A Bottom-up Approach to Design

One of my interests in observing and talking with the children was to learn how they approached the task of building a HyperCard stack. What kinds of planning and preparation did they do in advance? As it turned out, I did not observe or hear about any advance planning unless their teachers had required a design or plan. In these cases, the children had made lists of the ideas they wanted to portray or they had drawn paper sketches of the cards they would be making. Comments of several of the older children suggest that they recognize the need for planning and that they usually go through a prototyping process using HyperCard: "We've just been experimenting with it; we didn't really *get into it* yet." In fact, some of the more frequent HyperCard users had completed a number of stacks that they still considered to be merely experiments. Some evidence suggested that the amount of advance planning, of any type, might increase with one's familiarity and mastery of HyperCard.

Both the Paint tools and the linking mechanisms in HyperCard encourage a bottom-up approach to design. This approach has the advantage of providing a very rich and forgiving environment for prototyping. It has two disadvantages that I observed: (1) There are no tools or aids to help the designer get an overview or model of the process or product. (2) Children tend to "get lost in fat bits"—that is, the tools are so elaborate and it is so easy to work and rework one little piece of a graphic that the children often spend inordinate amounts of time on very small parts of the project.

In contrast with written or video materials, and even with more typical computer software, HyperCard stacks are "malleable." The appearance of cards can be dramatically changed by a few editing strokes; cards can be easily added and deleted at any point in a stack. A single stack can seem to be organized in very different ways depending on the route the user chooses through the stack, and a particular bit of information can be portrayed in very different ways depending on the designer's choices. Like their adult counterparts, the children will probably have to learn new ways of conveying navigational cues (and perhaps new ways of conveying the structure of the information) for this medium. For example, one child had built a menu using a book index as a model. The index items themselves were buttons that linked to the appropriate sections in his report. But cross-references in the report itself were just text references back to the index when they could have been buttons linked directly to the referenced information.

A Rich Field for Research

Countless opportunities for research emerge from the observations and interviews with children using HyperCard. In this section, I will suggest a few that I find particularly intriguing and that focus on ideas that might be unique to the multimedia environment.

First, I think we have much to learn about how children conceive of and understand "buttons." As mentioned earlier in the paper, the HyperCard button is a complex concept. Of special interest is its capacity for providing links (broadly defined) to other information. What are the most salient attributes of buttons to children of different ages or to children who use different styles of communication?

Another related issue is the extent to which children are able to design for an audience. What navigational cues do they provide as they design their stacks for others to use? And as users, are they differently equipped than previous generations for navigating in Hyper-Card? Have present-day media experiences like MTV, video games, and computer technology already provided them with new ways to understand and process multimedia, networked information?

Although children (more than adults) have always used art as a means of communication and have had opportunities in school to illustrate stories and add pictures to their reports, working with graphics has been legitimatized by the Macintosh interface and by the integration of art tools in HyperCard. To what extent will children develop visual languages for expressing and communicating their ideas and for processing information? What conventions will they adopt and what new interface features will they require to work in this realm?

Finally, one of the most pleasing observations that comes out of this study is the wonderful way in which the children collaborate and cooperate to produce their HyperCard projects. The roles they take are different from traditional group projects where children usually divided up the subject matter, each taking a piece of the content. Now they are forming multidisciplinary teams. Rotation through roles should help children develop a range of talents for working with multimedia, and the chance to choose their own roles supports individual differences and strengths. Useful research would look at the long-range effects of such early teamwork and examine the continuing behavior of these children after the novelty of the computer and HyperCard has worn off.

Launching Teachers into a HyperWorld

David Mintz

DAVID MINTZ

Dave Mintz has taught for 10 years in public elementary and secondary schools in Boston, Massachusetts; Paterson, New Jersey; and Los Angeles, California. He started using a computer with elementary-school children six years ago and has taught many teachers and children since that time. He worked with five other people to implement the first districtwide educational computer program for the Los Angeles Unified School District.

He is now a full-time Apple "Field Geek," coordinating activities for Apple Computer's Vivarium Program at the Los Angeles Open School, where he works with the teachers, children, and parents of the school.

I am not sure which is more frightening: staring at the blank screen of a word processor or being handed four HyperCard disks, an assortment of manuals and tutorials, and being told, "This is the greatest educational product ever!!!" (well, "maybe the greatest educational product to come along since the greatest one that came along a few years ago").

HyperCard is the most usable, useful tool to come along in my history. Unfortunately for the teacher who really wants to use this "construction kit" and has little computer programming experience, the sheer size of HyperCard, the number of books, manuals, and Help stacks, and the potential are simply too large, too complex, and too overwhelming to be effective. This, at least, is my experience.

Who I Am Talking To

I hope to talk to educators at all levels, who plan to use HyperCard in various educational situations. I am talking to those who wish to learn to use HyperCard for their own purposes. I am talking to people who have little or no experience with a programming language or those who will be working with people who have such experience.

I have spent the last year working with a group of teachers and administrators at the Open School in Los Angeles as part of Apple Computer's Vivarium Program. Additionally, I have spent numerous hours educating other teachers and parents in the use of HyperCard.

Uses of HyperCard in Education

For the purpose of this article I am thinking of HyperCard being used in the following ways:

- *By the teacher for the teacher*—Record keeping, generating forms, keeping personal business, having fun, learning what it is like to learn something new.
- *By the teacher for the children*—Setting up computer-learning stations, preparing demonstrations, creating record-keeping stacks for children to use, cataloging whole curriculums, teaching programming and database management, controlling laser-disc and CD-ROM players.
- *By the children for the children*—Learning to program, having fun, making tools for themselves.

■ *By the children for the teacher and the classroom*—Storytelling, creating animation, managing a database, doing presentations, gathering and sorting information for reports, developing art projects, controlling external devices (laser-disc and CD-ROM players).

What I Am Going to Propose

I am talking about educating classroom teachers in the use of HyperCard—how they can control HyperCard as they control other educational tools to meet their classroom needs. I do not believe there is one right way, but that *the right way is the one that fits the individual teacher's teaching style and methods.*

I am talking about two principal learning methods—where people learn in live sessions and where people learn individually, using materials developed by others.

HyperCard is huge. What I hope this article will do is provide some insight for ways to learn and ways to teach HyperCard. I will propose ways of breaking HyperCard into doable, understandable pieces that will empower the learner with the capacity to control HyperCard in self-determining ways.

Where I Am Coming From

My experience with computers in education goes back a number of years. I have used computers in my own elementary-school and secondary-school classrooms, spent many years on the "conference circuit" teaching hands-on lessons to small groups, taught inservice sessions in many school districts, and set up a learning center for a retail computer store. I'm currently serving as Apple's coordinator of the Vivarium Program at the Open School in Los Angeles, working directly with a small group of educators.

What HyperCard Is and Is Not

HyperCard is an incredible tool in the hands of users who are willing to understand and use it and an awe-inspiring tool for teachers who have the time, willingness, and ability to use it with and for children. However, it causes plenty of fear when not understood. The methods and suggestions related in this essay are meant to bring about understanding and remove fear.

HyperCard is not easy. HyperCard is not always logical and fun. HyperCard is not the end-all of programs. HyperCard will not solve every educational problem. HyperCard is not a complete educational package. Still, it is a step in all the right directions.

Some Facts—And What I Think Can Really Be Done

- Learn in groups of four to five people.
- Utilize a lab setting where teachers learn and share with one another.
- Use only small sections of the manual at a time.
- Create small stacks with scripts (fewer than 10 cards) that the teachers will understand.
- Provide examples of the broad range of possibilities HyperCard permits.
- Provide teachers with small stacks that contain scripts that they will understand.

Have people *do it!* I was propelled into teaching people to use computers when, after attending my first hands-on lesson at a conference, the leader spent the first 60 minutes of the 90-minute session talking about what we were about to learn. People understand *after* they have done it—and not before. I did not learn this after one lesson, though. In the first programming session in which I taught (Logo), I spent the first 30 minutes explaining in great detail the 10 most frequent errors and how to solve them. I was going to save (protect?) my teacher-students from every error I had made. In the next 90 minutes each student made many, if not all, of the errors I had talked about. Worse, when I explained and helped them to solve their errors, they all acted as if they were hearing this for the first time. In fact, they were. Though they had written down my every word and listened carefully, they did not hear and could not hear until they had *done it,* until each had hooks on which to hang the new knowledge.

Experience has taught me that the manuals and Help stacks are great—if you have a good deal of experience and know what you want to know. But teachers who are new to programming or new to computers or who have limited time and resources are not helped much. The stacks that come as examples are wonderful; unfortunately, the scripting is confusing and too complicated for new users—the stacks are too beautiful and precise to offer much assistance.

I propose that people learn HyperCard in small groups, learning from each other, gaining support, and setting up a situation where the leader of the group is not the only source of information. A lab setting might be most effective. However, because not all learning can happen in a lab, the stacks used as examples must be simple to follow and easy to understand so that teachers can learn from them. Such stacks might have audio tapes available to lead the learner through the building process. In either case, the idea is to build stacks, not merely to learn isolated skills and concepts.

I am basing this article on my work with groups of between four and thirty teachers. In each case, the sessions lasted from two to four hours. The learners left the session having built a stack that utilized various HyperCard skills and concepts and many HyperTalk commands. Each teacher experienced learning how to find help on her or his own. The examples later in this article are from those classes and show the skills and concepts that determined the specific stack the class would build. At the start of each session, the basic outline for the stack was presented, along with the basic skills, concepts, and HyperTalk commands. Later in the session, the stack was broken down so that it could be presented to the class in small, learnable pieces. Each teacher in the class had the opportunity to learn the small piece, apply it to her or his stack, and experiment with the skill. I not only try to get each student to ask many questions, but I also try to go off in directions the students feel is important, always pulling them back to the central stack. At the end of each session, the students leave with a stack and a set of "homework" suggestions.

Using this outline, I will present four such major stacks and ideas. The first stack is a "typical" introduction to HyperCard—what is this stuff, what is the vocabulary, what is important, and what people can be expected to do. The second is the first stack people created together—an animation stack. The third is a more complex, yet beginning stack, based on work others have done in teaching Logo, called Haiku. The fourth is a more complex stack used with people who have more experience and is in a bit of a game format called Car Shopper.

Learning HyperCard at an Introductory Session—What to Do First

Having stated the importance of *doing,* I believe learners must have an introductory understanding of what HyperCard is and what vocabulary and main concepts they will need to grasp HyperCard. Bill Atkinson, in demonstrating HyperCard, does a grand job of taking the user through HyperCard from level 1 to level 5 and explaining some vocabulary as he goes. This is a requirement. Teachers need to look at HyperCard, starting at level 1, to receive basic explanations; see and practice browsing; use HyperCard vocabulary (Stack, Card, Background, Button, Field, Script, Home); use Menu Items such as Help, Message, Go (Next, Prev, Back, Recent); play with Paint tools; use Copy and Paste; and play with Sort and Find. Without this background, there will be little or no understanding.

In each situation the leader of the session must continue to ask the learners how they are learning, what they are understanding, and whether they feel that the leader is presenting the material with clarity. The issue is to assist the learner with the vocabulary and awareness to provide hooks on which each teacher will hang new information.

Following this 60-minute tour, all students should make a simple stack. Each should create a New Stack, add a few New Cards, use Background and Card Level, write a simple button script, create a field, add text to the field (and delete text from the field), and then use the A tool to paint "text" and try to delete it.

A good starter stack is a simple Address Book. Any education that the teacher provides must be rich and simple. The learner must have many examples, must move around in HyperCard a great deal, and must have an opportunity to make mistakes. Let them *do it!* The leader of the class must stand aside and keep help to a minimum.

HyperCard elements: Creating New Stack, Background, Card, Copy/Paste, New Button, New Field, art tools, Sort, Find, Help, Browsing

HyperTalk commands: Sort (alphabetic, numeric, dateTime), Find, First, Last

Let the group make an address stack by copying the background from the existing HyperCard sample stack Stack Ideas. (See Figure 1 on the following page.) Have each learner give his or her stack a unique name and save the stack to an appropriate place.

Once into the new stack, learners should look at the Stack, Card, and Background Info boxes. This provides them with hooks to help themselves in the future.

I wanted to get rid of unneeded buttons and provide learners with an opportunity to use HyperCard tools. The class used the Button Tool and Cut Button (from the Menu Item) to remove the buttons at the bottom of the card. (See Figure 2 on the following page.) This provides a good opportunity to observe how the Menu Items—Cut/Copy/Paste—change, depending on which Object the user is talking to.

It is critical to let the learners talk about what they are learning. Be sure they share their "discoveries" and help each other. Let the learners teach as well as learn.

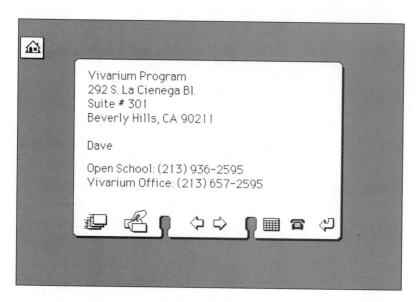

FIGURE 1. A card as copied from Stack Ideas.

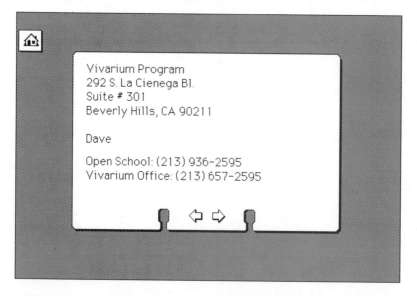

FIGURE 2. A card whose buttons have been deleted by using the Cut command from the Menu.

I had them add a few fields and give a name to each field and to the stack. I added a BirthDate field and a Number field, which contains a number designating the order in which I put the name into the stack. (See Figure 3.) This exercise provides a convenient way to introduce sorting and raise some questions later on. I ask each student to "paint" (using the "A" tool) the name of his or her field under the field for easy recognition.

After the card was built, we could add a New Card. Because I did not correct the students every time they did not make changes in the Background, the New Cards usually looked something like the card in Figure 4 on the following page.

Students who made all the alterations in the Background could work on their own while the others made the proper corrections. This is the best way to make people aware of Background and Card level. If you can set them up to make a "mistake" (learn a crucial point), then you are doing a good job.

In the typical computer class, participants are told how to do every step, and the result, at the end of the day, is a perfect program. However, when they are at home or in their classroom and make errors, panic sets in, for they have no experience correcting problems. It is important to put learners in real-life situations.

After adding a few more cards and completing the cards, we were ready to Sort. Again, I had set them up to observe some "problems" and talk about solutions. When they first

FIGURE 3. A card with BirthDate and Number fields added.

FIGURE 4. *A new card, illustrating names placed at the Card level rather than in the Background.*

sorted, all cards were sorted by first name. When the class questioned me about this, I took them immediately to the Help stack. Again, the leader of the class cannot be the only source of information. Any good teaching plan must be designed to show students how to get help on their own. It is important to guide them through finding the answers. Help is not immediately useful to people who are new to HyperCard. By using Help, they can study the Sort rules for sorting by first or last name and create appropriate buttons. (See Figure 5.) Have your students create many buttons and name them appropriately.

I then asked them to sort by BirthDate and Number. (See Figure 6.) Once again, I set them up to observe some problems. They were instructed to go back to Help and find the answers on their own. Along the way they needed to use the Next, Back, and Recent commands. They had a chance to do more scripting, to play with the mouse, and to ask questions.

If time remained, I had them use the Find command, thus using the Message box.

Toward the end of the session, I pulled the group together to discuss with me what they had learned. It is important for the learner to express as many items as possible. I listed each item on the board and then had them rate their understanding of the item on a scale of from 1 through 10. This forced them to think and reinforced what they had learned. Such feedback makes me a better teacher and provides a good model for them.

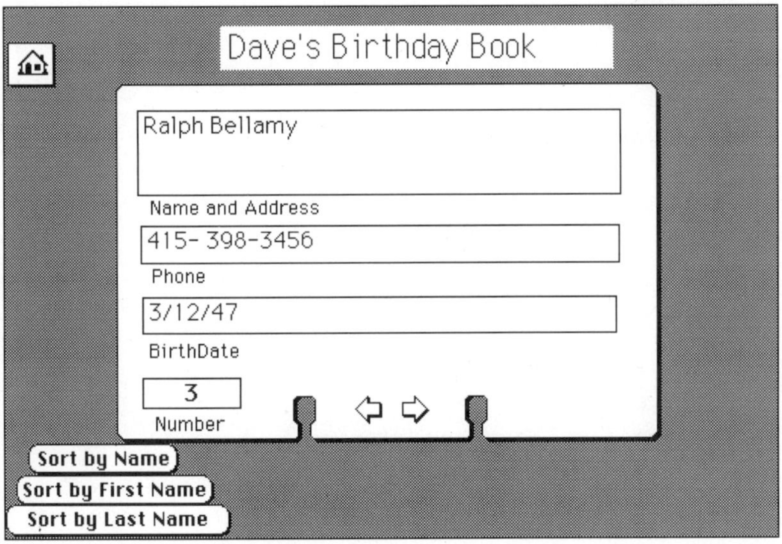

FIGURE 5. *A card properly done, with the first set of buttons added.*

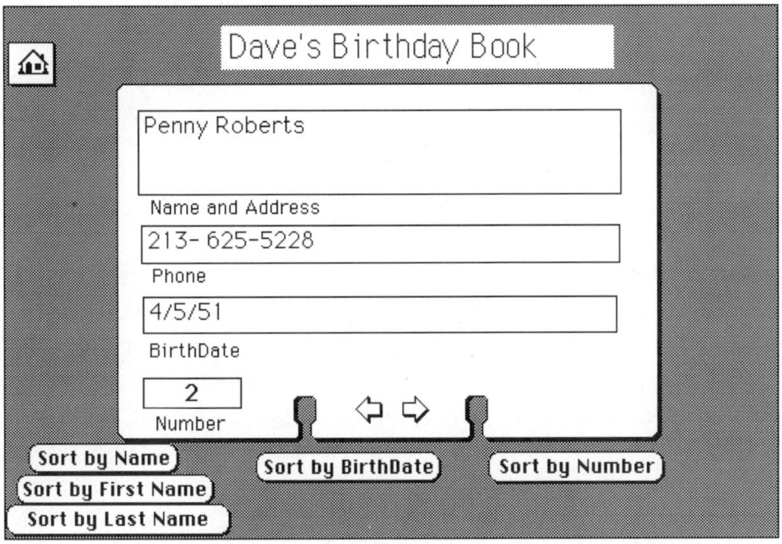

FIGURE 6. *The final version of a card, with all the buttons added.*

Scripts for Sorting Buttons Shown in Figure 6

```
-- Script of background button "Sort by Name"
on mouseUp
    sort by field "Name and Address"
end mouseUp

-- Script of background button "Sort by First Name"
on mouseUp
    sort by first word of field "Name and Address"
end mouseUp

-- Script of background button "Sort by Last Name"
on mouseUp
    sort by last word of field "Name and Address"
end mouseUp

-- Script of background button "Sort by BirthDate"
on mouseUp
    sort dateTime by field "BirthDate"
end mouseUp

-- Script of background button "Sort by Number"
on mouseUp
    sort numeric by field "Number"
end mouseUp
```

Teachers Introduce HyperCard to Their Classes

The Open School has divided the children into five clusters, each with 60 children and two teachers. Each class is a cross-age group of two grade levels, and, although Apple has loaned computers and other equipment and provided a good deal of training, it is the classroom teacher who is best equipped to decide how to use the equipment and what to teach the children. (Apple is present to learn from the children and teachers and to research the software and hardware we hope to use 10 years from now; hence, HyperCard is one step in the whole process, and it is the part we expect the teachers to take ultimate control of.) Because the computer is to be a tool in the development of the entire curriculum, each teacher chose to introduce the subject in a different way—resulting in different outcomes. I am going to focus on the upper three clusters (grades 3–6); later I will talk about their current activities.

The school was introduced to HyperCard in the summer of 1987; the teachers received much additional in-depth training in the summer of 1988.

Dolores Patton and Leslie Barclay teach third- and fourth-graders. Their classroom is a mix of a million different activities, with children working at a variety of levels. To them, all activities should relate to one another in some way. They chose two main introductory activities—"flip-book" animation and a two-card story. *Before going to the computers,* the children studied, talked about, and used little flip books (the ones you can buy at Disneyland or other amusement parks). The children told little stories and then drew—on paper—a few scenes, stapled the "pages" together, and flipped through the pages. The idea of using multiple cards and changing one or two objects to get the effect of movement was pretty clear to them before going to the computer.

A template for the flip book was prepared for the children that included a Play button for playing the animation and a Copy/Paste button for copying and pasting cards. The children were limited to eight cards so that the project could be finished, and, because they were familiar with other Apple Macintosh–computer paint programs, they learned quickly and easily to use the tools in HyperCard. The children drew a picture, pressed the Copy/Paste button, moved an object, and continued until finished. When finished, they printed eight cards to a page, laminated the page, cut each card, and stapled the cards together. During the next month or so, all the children were running around showing off their flip-book animations.

Their next project was again a template; however, this time the template incorporated a card with one field for writing and a second card for drawing. The children learned to write in a field, change its attributes, and then use the Go menu to select the Next Card to draw a picture. The result was two cards printed to a page, and again the pages were laminated—creating a wonderful combination story and illustration to hang on the wall.

B.J. Allen-Conn and Donna DiBernardo teach fourth and fifth grades. They took a similar approach to introducing HyperCard to their students. They used a template, named Story Book, to allow the children to write and illustrate stories. They discussed their stories *long before going to the computer.* Group lessons were taught showing children how to use the HyperCard tools and Menu items. The Home stack was modified to have only a few buttons—one that took them to MacWrite, another to MacPaint, and a third that would make a copy of Story Book and allow the children to rename the stack and save it in the proper place. Story Book had a card for the title page and a second card with one area for writing and another for illustrating. Buttons at the bottom of the card allowed for making New Cards, Go Next, Go Prev, and Print the Stack. In their first activity, the children were to see only a little of HyperCard and were to use their skills mainly for writing and drawing (so that they would begin to feel comfortable in the HyperCard environment).

In the fifth-grade and sixth-grade classes, Judy Zaidner and Flo Truitt used a slightly different approach. They taught some group lessons with HyperCard, showing the tools and then teaching the students to create a Go Next button. Then, *before going to the computer,* the children were given a set of 3-inch-by-5-inch index cards and were asked to draw pictures for an animated story. In groups of 10 or so, the children showed each of their cards and told their story. Then the cards were given to another member of the group, who rearranged them—and a new story was created. This went on for some time, until the students had a sense that HyperCard allows one to move the cards in many directions, link one card to another, change the links, and continue. After this introduction, the children sometimes went on to create huge animated stacks for both in-class reports ("How the Lizard Gets Food," "The Trojan War," "How to Stay Off Drugs") and many adventure games, allowing the children to learn and experiment with HyperCard elements and vocabulary.

Note: We did not encourage the use of the Link To option but rather advocated that the children name cards and write scripts to Go To a named card. We all found it impossible to follow the logic of children's stacks and to help them solve their linking problems without having simple card-name references. This also seems to fit into each teacher's desire for labeling in normal subjects such as math (word problems, area, perimeter) and having students place titles on their written stories.

In each classroom the HyperCard Help stacks are readily available, and all children are requested to use them. When a group of children learned about visual effects and asked which ones they could use, they were instructed to go to the Help stack, find the names, and then continue. This also facilitated learning Go Recent. Finally, a few of the children decided it was a good idea to print the Visual Effects cards and became the "class experts," at least until the others printed out their own copy. HyperCard books are also available, and each teacher has assembled written notes and guides for the children to use.

Animation

What can people learn quickly so that they will be able to work on their own stacks in the future, gain experience with many tools, play, and have some fun and learn? Flip-book-style animation is the answer. Consideration might be given to providing a tool for learners to review in the privacy of their home, one that supplies notes and assistance for work on their own stacks.

HyperCard elements: Background, Card level, Button (card and background), Field (card and background), Paint tools, Message box, use of Menu Items, Copy and Paste, using a programming tool to make tools for oneself, New Card, order of cards

HyperTalk commands: On MouseUp, Put, the number of, concatenation, DoMenu, Show All Cards, Repeat (variations of the theme), Wait

I decided to draw a tree that holds an apple and to animate the falling apple. (See Figure 7 and Figure 8 on the following page.) A simple tree and apple are drawn at card level.

The entire card is copied and pasted. Using the Lasso tool, the apple is moved down and the process is duplicated.

I asked people to look at the Card Info command to see where in the stack they were working. Using the Copy Card and Paste Card commands, it is easy to get lost. Often, people will actually Paste three or four cards without realizing they have done so. The idea is to provide in-class experiences that allow the learner to gain confidence and learn how to learn. We explored the difference between drawing the tree on the background and drawing the apple on the card to see what happened when New Card was chosen.

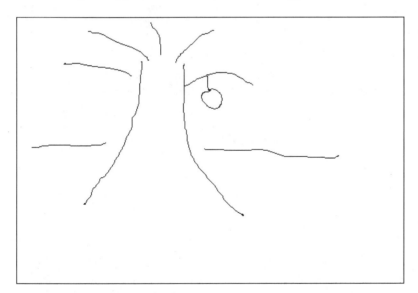

FIGURE 7. Card 1 shows a tree with an apple hanging by its stem.

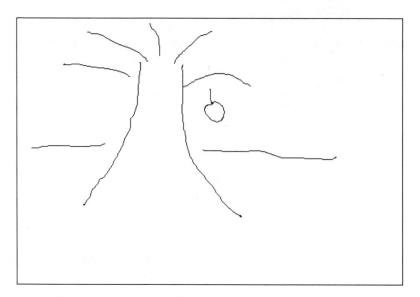

FIGURE 8. Card 2 shows the tree depicted in Figure 7, but the apple is "falling"—that is, the apple and its stem have been moved down, using the Lasso tool.

This led to the concept of asking HyperCard to respond in the Message box as to which card the student was working on. (See Figure 9.) Further, it seemed that a button could automate the whole process. Finally, they were able to control the Menu, learn concatenation, and use the Message box as a tool.

```
-- Script of button - "Copy/Paste - Show Number"
on mouseUp
    doMenu "Copy Card"
    doMenu "Paste Card"
    put the number of this card && "of" && the number of cards
end mouseUp
```

After the animation was finished, we used the Show All Cards message to flip through the stack—first typing this into the Message box and then creating a button called Play1. Usually the participants wanted to see the last card and not be returned to the first card. Additionally, they wanted to slow the animation down, which was a lead into Wait. Let them play, let them ask questions, give examples rather than giving them answers. Send them to the Help stacks, and show them how to use them. We ended up writing a variety of buttons using Wait and then using a Repeat loop, a variable, and the property of Number of Cards. (See Figure 10.)

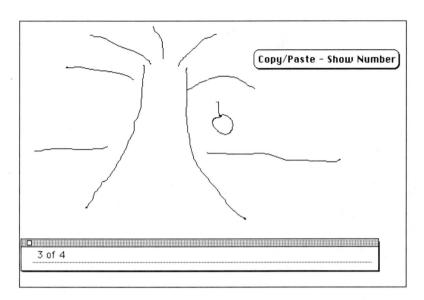

FIGURE 9. HyperCard, in the Message box, tells which card is being worked on.

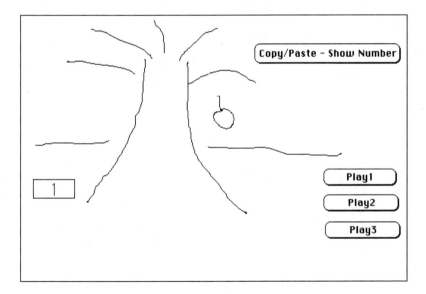

FIGURE 10. Card 1 of tree animation with three buttons. Each button provides a method of flipping through the stack.

```
-- Script of button "Play1"
on mouseUp
    show all cards
end mouseUp

-- Script of button "Play2"
on mouseUp
    repeat with A is 1 to the number of cards
        go next card
        wait 15
    end repeat
end mouseUp

-- Script of button "Play3"
on mouseUp
    repeat with A is 1 to (the number of cards -1)
        go next card
        wait 15
    end repeat
end mouseUp
```

During the classes I am never worried about the physical appearance of the stack; rather, I am interested in the programming used to complete the stack. I find that using many buttons is better than changing scripts. One should provide people with a plethora of information for review purposes. Class notes should be inside of buttons and fields; the stack itself should serve as the notes. Many little pieces of paper are no match for a working stack and examples of a variety of scripts.

Very importantly, the students need to work on a project of their own—either at home or in class—that uses the skills and enforces them.

Type of homework: Stack of animation that shows the number of the card in a background field and has an end card with the student's name and credits, which can, during the animation, be read. Possibly run the animation at various speeds.

Haiku

A really big hit was a stack to "create" Haiku poetry. I have used this type of program before in a Logo class, and it works even better in HyperCard. (I learned of this program at a conference many years ago, but I cannot give proper credit to the author, as I do not recall who it was.) The idea is to create a small, but very important and usable stack—

one that people would take home and use for information, one on which they themselves can develop skills that they can use in creating their own stacks.

HyperCard elements: Variables, Random, Card and Background fields, small buttons to build to large items, pulling items from a list or field, concatenation, controlling one button by another, Copy fields, copying field information, Text tool vs. "A" tool

HyperTalk commands: Put, the number of, Random (), item, &&, Click at, Loc of

Lesson
I presented the first card of the Haiku stack, as shown in Figure 11.

It was important to start with something or too much time would be spent making the stack, rather than programming. We started by thinking about Haiku and the other fields and words we would need. (See Figure 12 on the following page.) I proposed the name of the fields to use. The students learned to copy the attributes of a field by using the Option-click method and then changing only the name of the field, using the "A" tool to paint the name of the field under the field itself. We explored the differences in changing text fonts and painted fonts. We looked at what happens when you put information in the background or at the card level. (I had them try New Card occasionally to see what was happening.) Students added their own words to the fields.

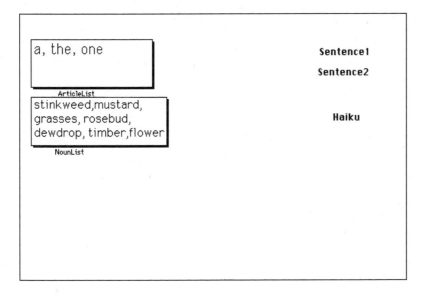

FIGURE 11. Card 1 in the Haiku stack.

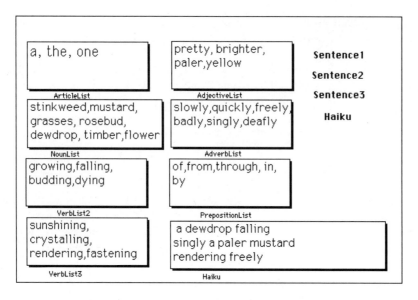

FIGURE 12. Haiku stack built by teacher and students.

Obviously, the focus here is on HyperTalk. I broke down the concepts into small pieces. I told the class that some very important concepts would be presented. However, I emphasized that the point was to create a Haiku machine and that they would have time later to play with the concepts I presented and to test their own ideas. I would teach a concept, let them practice, help with problems, and then pull the class back together to give more examples. If a concept was critical, I told them so; if it was of minor importance, I said that too. Students had time to create their own fields and to add the appropriate words. I broke the Haiku into three sentences. We wrote the script for Sentence1 together. The students wrote scripts for Sentence2 and Sentence3 on their own.

Finally, the students were to write one button to execute the entire Haiku poem. They tried and were successful with many ideas but not with any that I wanted them to learn. So I had an opportunity to show them how to use one button to control others, using Click at.

```
-- Script of background button "Sentence1"
on mouseUp
    put the number of items in field ArticleList into randomNum
    put random (randomNum) into whichOne
    put item whichOne of field ArticleList into article
    put the number of items in field NounList into randomNum
```

```
      put random (randomNum) into whichOne
      put item whichOne of field NounList into noun
      put the number of items in field VerbList2 into randomNum
      put random (randomNum) into whichOne
      put item whichOne of field VerbList2 into verb2
      put article && noun && verb2 into field Haiku
   end mouseUp

-- Script of background button "Sentence2"
on mouseUp
      put the number of items in field AdverbList into randomNum
      put random (randomNum) into whichOne
      put item whichOne of field AdverbList into adverb
      put the number of items in field ArticleList into randomNum
      put random (randomNum) into whichOne
      put item whichOne of field ArticleList into article
      put the number of items in field AdjectiveList into randomNum
      put random (randomNum) into whichOne
      put item whichOne of field AdjectiveList into adjective
      put the number of items in field NounList into randomNum
      put random (randomNum) into whichOne
      put item whichOne of field NounList into noun
      put adverb && article && adjective && noun into line 2 of field Haiku
   end mouseUp

-- Script of background button "Sentence3"
on mouseUp
      put the number of items in field VerbList3 into randomNum
      put random (randomNum) into whichOne
      put item whichOne of field VerbList3 into verb3
      put the number of items in field AdverbList into randomNum
      put random (randomNum) into whichOne
      put item whichOne of field AdverbList into adverb
      put verb3 && adverb into line 3 of field Haiku
   end mouseUp

-- Script of button "Haiku"
on mouseUp
      click at loc of bg button Sentence1
      click at loc of bg button Sentence2
      click at loc of bg button Sentence3
   end mouseUp
```

Using this example, the students wrote many poems of different styles. Everyone enjoyed lunch, as people quoted poems to one another.

Another lesson to be learned here is that the computer can spit out lots of random words, but it does not think of them on its own: The computer is a dumb machine working at the will of the intelligent user.

Part of the Haiku program required the use of Random, which students had many questions about. Together we created a quick card that taught many of the concepts of Random. It was easy to test some theories by putting answers in the Message box; however, as questions became more complicated, it was important to create button scripts and a field to hold results.

My first response to most questions is always to direct students toward the Help stack to find Random. Students need to know where to find help when the leader is not around. You have an opportunity to show them the difference between commands and functions. I was able to point to other ideas they might want to know about later—Round and Trunc.

One-card Random tool
The idea is to explore and show students how to explore. It is important to provide a method for keeping the results of their exploration.

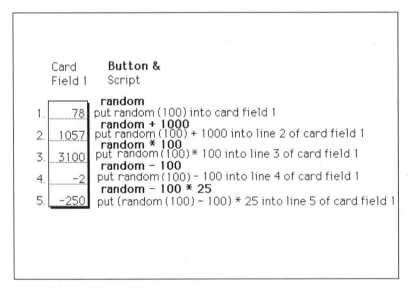

FIGURE 13. *A card displaying the use of Random. Each button is boldface, and the main line of script is displayed.*

I started by replacing the entire contents of Card field 1 each time we tested one of the Random buttons. (See Figure 13.) It became apparent that a better idea was to place each button's result in a different line, utilizing a skill they had learned in earlier sessions. Students were encouraged to try as many ideas as they thought of and share their results, be they expected or not.

Car Shopper

After teachers had had many programming experiences, I wanted to create a stack that would take a few days to build and provide teachers with a hefty assignment to do away from the class.

HyperCard elements: Script, Background scripts, collecting data in variables and fields, providing users with knowledge of their place in stack, card and background fields and buttons, conditionals (Repeat, If/Then), variables

HyperTalk commands and functions: Put, number of fields, Cards, Buttons, Set, Repeat With, Repeat Until, Repeat For, Visual Effects, If/Then, Random, use of Message box, Speak, Answer, MouseV, MouseH, MouseLoc, rect, lines of field

The teachers were presented with a two-card stack named Car Shopper. (See Figure 14 and Figure 15 on the following page.)

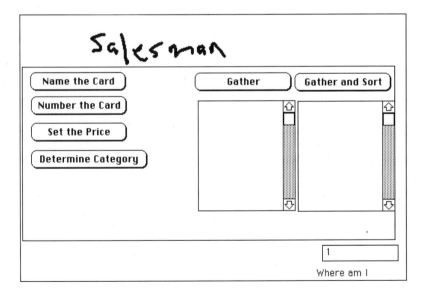

FIGURE 14. The opening card (Card 1) of the Car Shopper stack.

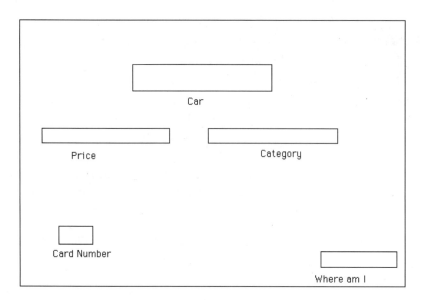

FIGURE 15. Card on which to enter information about a particular car.

The first card of the stack, shown in Figure 14, contains appropriate buttons and fields. The word *salesman* (at the top of the card) will be turned into a button later. The focus at this point is programming, not how good the stack looks.

Teachers were asked to make five or six New Cards, placing the name of the car in the Car field. (See Figures 15 and 16.) From here we went back to the main card.

At this point we talked about the game—how it would be played and what information we needed to gather. I had explicit ideas of what we needed to do, and each button expressed one of those ideas. The idea is to lead, allow for questions, and move on appropriately.

An important concept the teachers needed to learn was that programming could happen in places other than buttons. To demonstrate this, I had prepared the following Stack scripts, which provided fodder for questioning.

```
-- Script of stack
on closeStack
    hide card field "Expensive Cars"
    hide card field "Cheap Cars"
end closeStack
```

```
on openStack
    show card field "Expensive Cars"
    show card field "Cheap Cars"
end openStack
```

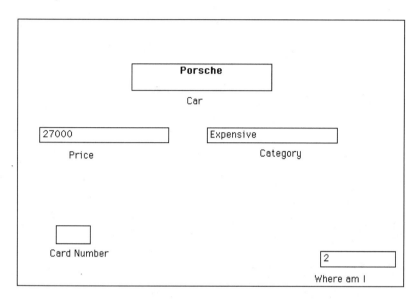

FIGURE 16. The card in Figure 15, now containing information about one car.

Another tricky concept is to put a message of a card into the script of the Background. The following script is useful because the learners want to know where they are in the stack.

```
--Background script
on openCard
    put the number of this card into field "Where am I"
end openCard
```

The method involves teaching some small, bite-sized idea, and then letting the students practice applying it to a task of their choosing, ask questions, and use those skills later.

Because I wanted to be able to call a card by its name, we chose—in the script on the following page—to set the name of the card to the name given in the Car field. The point is to learn about controlling properties in HyperCard.

```
-- Script of button "Name the Card"
on mouseUp
   --name the card the name of the vehicle in the field called Car
     repeat with cardNum is 1 to (the number of cards -1)
        go next card
        set the name of this card to bg field Car
     end repeat
     go card Salesman
end mouseUp
```

As we might later sort the cards in various ways, I wanted always to know which card
we were actually on and where it was in the stack—hence the two fields: *Card Number*
(which numbers the cards 1 through the number of cards in the stack) and *Where am I*
(which shows where the card is in the stack). It appears to be very important that this is
understood clearly as the learner creates stacks. The better students were able to understand where they were, the more they felt that they were in control and the faster we
moved.

```
-- Script of button "Number the Card"
on mouseUp
    -- put the numbers 1 through the number of cards into the Card
    -- number field
    repeat with cardNum is 1 to the number of cards
        put cardNum into bg field "Card Number"
        go next card
    end repeat
end mouseUp
```

Because the Random function and its use are important and are frequently misunderstood, I forced the issue of randomly setting the price of the cars. This is not accurate
pricing; however, in the Southern California market, this method of pricing might not
stray too far from the reality of car pricing. In any case, the idea was to use Random to
set the car prices in increments of $3,000. This allows practice. When we first did this,
the idea was to set the prices quickly—but students wanted to see what was happening
and wanted to be in control. This led, in the following script, to the *repeat until the mouse
is down* statement that lets the user have complete control. Many students went home to
rewrite this to allow them to change the random price if they wanted to.

```
-- Script of button "Set the Price"
on mouseUp
    -- Set the price of the car to be random number from 3 to 30 K
    -- in increments of 3 K
    go next card
    repeat with carPrice is 1 to (the number of cards -1)
        put random (10) * 3000 into field price
        -- this allows the user to see the price being set
        repeat until the mouse is down
        end repeat
        visual dissolve to black
        go next card
    end repeat
end mouseUp
```

After the prices had been set, it was necessary to determine if the car was Cheap or Expensive. This allowed for what appeared to be the most misunderstood concept in programming—conditional If/Then statements. The idea was to use what they already knew—creating a button that would do the work and inserting the new information—to decide if the car cost less than $20,000, and to stamp it Cheap or Expensive, depending on the price. We arrived at the following button:

```
-- Script of button "Determine the Category"
on mouseUp
    -- Place "Cheap" or "Expensive" in field category
    -- depending on car price
    -- under $20 K is cheap, $20 K and over is expensive
    go next card
    repeat with carCategory is 1 to (the number of cards -1)
        if field price < 20000 then
            put "Cheap" into field category
            visual dissolve to black
            go next card
        else
            put "Expensive" into field category
            visual dissolve to black
            go next card
        end if
    end repeat
    put "All the cars are priced now!!!"
end mouseUp
```

Now we had to gather the information in a usable manner—a field on the main card. The first task was to learn how to gather information. In this case we would gather all the cars into a variable and place it in a field. (See Figure 17.) We tried a number of approaches—finishing with this script:

```
-- Script of button "Gather"
on mouseUp
    -- first gather of cars
    -- Gather the all cars
    put empty into categoryHolder
    repeat for the number of cards
        put field category & return after categoryHolder
        go next card
    end repeat
    put categoryHolder into card field "Expensive Cars"
end mouseUp
```

After that script was written, the teachers could write one that would put Cheap cars in one field and Expensive ones in the other, as follows.

```
-- Script of button "Gather and Sort"
on mouseUp
    -- Gather the cars according to "Expensive" or "Cheap"
    put empty into expensiveHolder
    put empty into cheapHolder
    go next card
    repeat with A is 1 to (the number of cards -1)
        if field category = "Cheap" then
            put field category & return after cheapHolder
            put cheapHolder
            go next card
        else
            put field category & return after expensiveHolder
            go next card
        end if
    end repeat
    put expensiveHolder into card field "Expensive Cars"
    put cheapHolder into card field "Cheap Cars"
end mouseUp
```

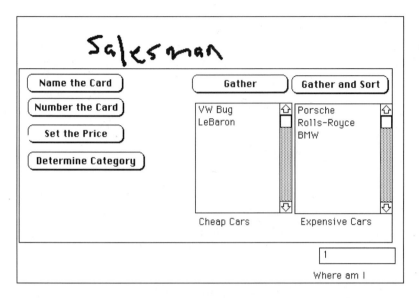

FIGURE 17. *The opening card, now containing gathered information.*

Without being given all the answers, the students built and tested their ideas, saw why this case required a variable to be declared before it was needed, and learned to move information within a variable. Each student participated in thinking of ideas and testing them. As leader of the class, I found it important to create situations where people could talk, share their ideas, and collaborate with successes and failures.

At times it became important to forget HyperTalk and talk about how they would perform an operation physically. In the case of gathering the cars by the Cheap or Expensive criterion, they decided they would use two clipboards—one for each category. (This is like "put empty" into the Cheap and Expensive car variable.) Then they would go to the first car (like Go Next Card). They would determine whether the price was less than $20,000 (the If/Then statement). Finally, they would write the answer on the first available line of the clipboard for the particular category. After that discussion, it was simple to write the HyperTalk scripts.

We also learned to use "a field as a button." The idea was to click on the name of a car in a particular field and go to its card. This led to much exploration of *x,y* coordinates. We explored what they were and how they worked in HyperCard. We explored what it meant to have a field of lineSize 16 and fontSize 12. Each student measured the size of the lines and worked to understand what a pixel is. Given the new words of MouseV and MouseH, we were able to figure out a way to determine the given line of a field, put that name into a variable, and go to the card with that given name.

```
-- Script of fields "Cheap Cars" and "Expensive Cars"
on mouseUp
    put the mouseV into vPosition
    put the textHeight of me into height
    put item 2 of the rect of me into topOfField
    put ((vPosition - (topOfField - height) + (the scroll of me)) ¬
    div height) into lineNum
    put "line" & lineNum
    -- go card lineNum +1
    put line lineNum of card field short name of me into cardName
    go to card cardName
end mouseUp
```

To take this to a more interactive level required a salesman who could ask you questions and respond properly. (See Figure 18.)

```
-- Script of button "Salesman"
on mouseUp
    speak "Which type of car do you want?" "Expensive" or "Cheap"
    answer "Which type of car do you want?" with "Expensive" or "Cheap"
    put it into whichType
    if whichType is "Expensive" then
        show card field "Expensive Cars"
    else
        show card field "Cheap Cars"
    end if
end mouseUp
```

From here many other possibilities exist: buying on credit, determining total cost, adding up license, extra features, and on and on. That is homework, but the stack is built.

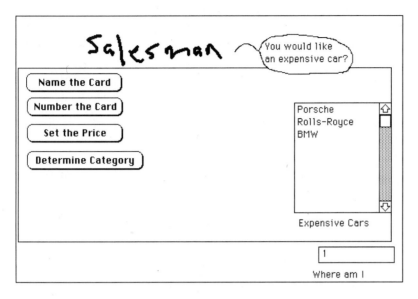

FIGURE 18. The opening card, now showing expensive cars only.

What the Teachers Are Doing Now (Fall 1988)

A number of chapters could be written about each teacher in each classroom and how each is bringing HyperCard to the students, what the results are, and how far each believes the kids can go. We are in a unique situation, given the support and number of machines; however, much of what each teacher and student is doing can be replicated.

Last year the children in the fourth and fifth grades created long (over 100 cards) stacks illustrating fish behavior they had studied during the year. Using simple flip-book animation, they created long scenes with voice, sound, and text. Drawing from this experience the teacher, B.J., decided it was time to teach more complex animations using one card. This type of animation involves creating fields to hide objects under and fields to move objects to, as well as creating buttons to gather coordinate points and buttons that will control the Paint tools to drag objects from one area to another. Each child receives instruction in a small group, receives handouts developed by the teacher, and has an opportunity to work on lessons during the week. As the year has progressed, the children have made more and more complex cards for Halloween and Thanksgiving, and comical illustrations; soon they will be moving into ocean scenes and Westward Movement scenes as part of their social-studies unit.

With their new-found skills and understanding, Dolores and Leslie are teaching their students additional HyperTalk and using fewer templates for their children. Again, they introduce a topic with which the children are familiar, teach small group lessons, provide children with handouts, and allow them to use their own creativity to develop their own stacks. The teachers have found that initially limiting the children to a specific number of cards allows the child more freedom. They are particularly interested in design and spend a good deal of time with the children discussing what the point of the stack is, how it looks, and why each object and field is in a particular place.

The older children study a whole range of topics, doing their lessons in small groups. Judy and Flo have allowed the children to learn to control laser-disc players to incorporate video into their presentations, conditional (If/Then) statements, and Repeat loops in their work. The children use all their skills and abilities to use HyperCard as a tool for solving classroom educational problems. Children use the large screen to show their work to the class, for discussions of HyperCard techniques and of the content of the stacks. Stacks documenting the Olympics, political elections, animals from around the world, drug awareness, Greek myths, and the like proliferate throughout the classroom.

Currently, the teachers feel fairly comfortable with HyperCard and are now beginning to speak at conferences and conduct training sessions for other teachers.

Summary

HyperCard is an incredible tool; however, teachers will need an adequate amount of assistance before they will be able to use it. Additional, less complicated example stacks and training methods must be provided if teachers are to use this "construction kit" in their classrooms. The example stacks that are provided with HyperCard are wonderful, but they are too complex for the nonprogrammer or teacher who has little time to spend trying to understand the scripts that make the stacks so wonderful.

In talking with developers of HyperCard stacks, it is clear that much learning took place, not only of the HyperTalk vocabulary and usage but also of the content of the stack itself (world geography, U.S. Constitution, mathematics, science) as they prepared a stack for educational use. It would be good to remember this as we prepare training materials; the stack must allow the learner the same excitement and depth of learning that the developer receives. It would be a terrible mistake to take this extraordinary tool and create stacks so beautiful, so complete, and so creative that novice users are exempted from learning to use HyperCard.

A provision must be made to introduce important concepts, skills, and vocabulary to the new user. In the future, training stacks and, potentially, audio tapes must be developed that will allow the new learner to move through the complexities of HyperCard and HyperTalk in a quick, efficient manner.

In talking with teachers and with educators who have taught teachers, it is clear that the key in learning to program is to allow the learner to participate in the learning.

Other languages have been brought to teachers with mixed results. HyperCard is the most readily usable product to enter the educational market. Hopefully, we will learn from experience, and we will present teachers with the proper tools—and thus make HyperCard an integral part of their educational program.

HyperCard in Education: Perspective from the Field

James G. Lengel and Sue Collins

JAMES G. LENGEL

James G. Lengel is Apple Computer's education technology consultant in the Northeast region of the United States. His calling is teaching. He spent 13 years at the State Education Department in Vermont, the last three as deputy commissioner of education. He is the co-author of Law in American History *and* Using Computers in the Social Studies.

SUE COLLINS

Sue Collins is Apple Computer's education technology consultant in northern California. She is a science educator who also served as the technology director for the Department of Public Instruction in the state of Washington.

HyperCard in Education: The Potential

HyperCard can change the ways we use technology in education.

- *Presentation and reporting.* In the hands of a typical student or teacher, HyperCard is a superb presentation and reporting tool. It is as easy to present a message or a series of ideas on HyperCard as it is to write them down on paper in the traditional fashion. It's more efficient. It allows links between one item and another (between a map and a text, for instance). Its Find feature is an automatic index, and its ability to scan in or clip in images adds a visual dimension to presentations. The educational process has always included presentations of some sort—lecture, book, movie—as its chief mode of interaction; HyperCard allows teachers to use this traditional mode more effectively. Just as desktop publishing lets every typist be a publisher, HyperCard has the potential to enable every teacher—and perhaps every student—to be a multimedia producer. It empowers us to do our best.

- *Widespread computerization.* In the hands of the "average Joe," HyperCard allows educators to "computerize" types of information that have never before been taught with computers. Educational databases, collections, pictures, and information of all sorts—previously too time-consuming and expensive to store electronically—can now be put "onto the machine" because of the ease of setting up and entering information into HyperCard. When this gathering activity occurs, it will increase the amount of software available to educators in all subject areas, especially in the forms of databases and information bases. The more that this kind of software is available at low cost with easy access, the more likely are educators to integrate computers into their teaching.

- *A new class of tools.* In the hands of a creative artist, HyperCard can produce a new class of tools for learning. The artist would be first a teacher, second a master of the content area, and third a person who understands the ways that the mind would like to work. HyperCard tools allow the user to find ideas in a haystack full of data and information, and then to link these ideas with many other ideas. HyperCard provides ready access to both navigation and "meaning-making" tools, so the user can find his way and be led toward the gems of meaning that lie buried in the dross of data. The ideal author of this new class of publication is one who has taught the subject to many students before and is thus aware of the typical paths they take on their journey through it. Such an author knows the chief ideas and principles he wants his students to understand. Most important, the author realizes that students do not reach the pinnacle of wisdom in a subject unless they discover it for themselves. With HyperCard, this "master teacher" can produce a tool that is powerful, elegant, and intellectually defensible.

Teachers have always used "media" in the schools. They have used the lecture, the book, the film, the TV show, the lab demonstration, the dramatic presentation. Teachers themselves are media. All these media have served us well in the classroom, but they have one serious shortcoming.

What educators have always wanted to do is to get students to *wrestle* with knowledge. The hope is that, out of this struggle, students will construct their own ideas and concepts. Teachers want them to enjoy an original relationship with data, to interact on their own with facts and history and existence, and then to invent and build their own understandings. But teachers have never been able to bring this about in schools. Media have gotten in the way. Here's how.

First, the teacher wrestles with knowledge in its original, nonstreamlined, elemental form:

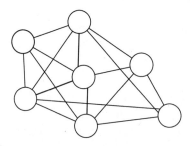

This interaction results in a representation in the teacher's mind that is similar to the original but not an exact copy. It might look like this:

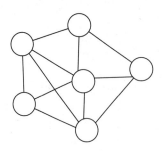

Next, the teacher takes this representation and writes it into a book or produces it as a film or records its verbalization in a lecture. By necessity, the weblike structure of the original knowledge (and of the mind's representation of it) is transformed into a *linear* layout, like this:

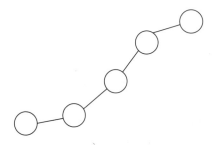

Most of the original elements are there, but they cannot relate to each other in the original ways. Finally, students read the book or watch the film or listen to the lecture. From this they reconstruct the knowledge in their minds. The chances of the students' conceptions matching the original form are slim. Such conceptions probably look something like this:

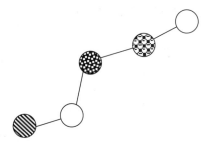

The media—the teacher and the product—got in the way. By forcing weblike, parallel knowledge into linear, serial media, teachers have limited education.

While HyperCard cannot guarantee that every student has the ability to wrestle directly with knowledge in its original form, it can come closer to that ideal than has been possible with the media that teachers have used in the past. It can organize knowledge into weblike relationships and links. It lets students find their own pathways through knowledge. It can present reality through pictures, graphs, and sound as well as through words. With HyperCard, students are more likely to construct in their own minds a rich and complex representation of the subject at hand.

Why is This New?

Hasn't education enjoyed computers for more than a decade? What makes HyperCard different?

HyperCard allows us to move up the educational pyramid. The pyramid looks like this:

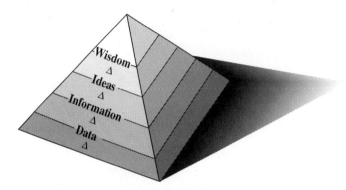

What education is supposed to do is to get students to see *data* (facts) in such as way as to inform themselves. The data in their minds are combined into *information*. Information is then related to other information to produce *ideas* in the students' minds—concepts that help explain the world. Some students combine these ideas (we wish more of them would) to produce a *wisdom* that understands the whys and wherefores of life and truth. The aim of education is to move up the pyramid.

Educational computing has been relegated to the bottom of the pyramid, dealing with data for the most part, sometimes getting students to draw information from the data, but seldom reaching beyond. Few educators employ computers to help students develop collections of information into ideas. School computers do not often contain meaningful pictures or graphics and almost never are employed to achieve wisdom.

This data-driven approach contrasts with "great teachers" such as Socrates, who hang around the top of the pyramid and cajole students to wrestle with and see connections between ideas. It contrasts with the arts (the oldest forms of education), which use visual and aural devices to express ideas directly without words.

The connections we make in our minds are wide-ranging, quick, often nonlinear, mostly visual, and seldom verbal. Great teachers and great writers and great artists exploit this facet of our intelligence.

HyperCard promises to allow educational computing to use the techniques of the great artist and the great teacher. HyperCard makes it easy to see and make connections between data, information, and ideas. It gives us the freedom to associate. (*"The mind works by association,"* says the flyer, *"so why not computers?"*) We in education have never had this capability before.

The potential is great. HyperCard promises to give educators a hand in climbing up the pyramid.

HyperCard in Education: The Reality

How are schools today using HyperCard?

In the schools actively using HyperCard, we see it most often employed as a *presentation and reporting tool* for teachers and students. HyperCard enhances delivery of a lecture or presentation of a term paper. A computer novice can use HyperCard in these ways after an hour's introduction.

HyperCard is also used as a simple *index/database tool*. Students and teachers find that they can organize, store, and use all their information easily without the "records/fields" restrictions of a typical computer database. Most schools index their most commonly used information first.

HyperCard is also used for *instructional programs*. That's what schools had used their Apple II computers for, so it's natural to do the same, faster and more efficiently, with HyperCard. We see two types of instructional uses at the moment: home-brewed adaptations of other people's stacks and commercial ports of drill and practice exercises.

These are hardly the most advanced uses of the medium. Why do we see this pattern of use in the schools? Why haven't the schools gone directly to the "power" uses of HyperCard?

- *Lack of applications*. Few powerful "new class of tools" applications of HyperCard are commercially available in the marketplace. Those few that exist seldom address traditional school subjects.
- *The structure of schools*. We must remember that schools move slowly in adopting computer technology. Schools go through a common series of developmental stages in their use of technology:
  - ☐ **The P stage:** Schools teach **P**rogramming and treat the computer as an object of instruction. At this stage, the computer is a **P**eculiar item in the school, usually a **P**ersonal item "belonging" to the one or two teachers who brought it into the school.

- ☐ **The D stage:** Schools use computers for **D**rill and practice in the regular curricular **D**isciplines, especially in math and reading. Computers are **D**iffused throughout the school. **D**isappointment often results when the promised "computer revolution" fails to materialize.

- ☐ **The T stage:** Schools use computers as productivity **T**ools, **T**ailored to the needs of students, **T**eachers, and the curriculum. Schools move away from direct instruction with computers and toward the use of general tools such as word processing, databases, spreadsheets, and **T**elecommunications.

Most schools today are at the **D** stage, while some advanced schools are entering the **T** stage. We predict that the next two stages will be:

- ☐ **The T² Stage:** Schools use the "new class of tools" (such as multimedia), large on-line or CD-ROM databases, laptop word processors, and so forth, throughout their curriculum and operations.

- ☐ **The U stage:** Computers are **U**biquitous in the school, **U**sed for everything. They are as commonplace as a pencil or a book. Computing is **U**nobtrusive and **U**neventful, part of the **U**sual and customary school day.

Apple's recent survey of 3,200 schools in the Northeast confirms that most schools are in the **D** stage. A school that's using computers at the **D** stage will naturally take a new tool, such as HyperCard, and use it to perform the same functions. Teachers in such a school assimilate HyperCard into their current ways of doing things, so they use it for presentations and direct instruction. Most educators are not accustomed to using computers as general tools for learning; they do not expect that from computers because they've never seen computers do that. They must move up the rank of stages before they jump up to the more powerful potentials of HyperCard.

- ■ *The "installed base."* Only a minority of the microcomputers in K–12 schools are Apple Macintosh computers; not all of these Macintoshes can use HyperCard. Schools own the Apple II computer in great numbers, and so they are not as likely to interest themselves in an Apple Macintosh–computer-only product such as HyperCard. Publishers cannot develop a commercially viable product for such a small potential market.

- ■ *What schools are really for.* Socrates could not have educated Plato as he did if he had had 29 other students, six periods a day, and recess duty and if the students had had football on Saturdays and TVs at home. Schools discovered many years ago that under these conditions it is virtually impossible to make "wrestling with ideas" and "aiming for wisdom" educational goals for all students. So schools have set their sights lower. They have been satisfied to teach the data and some information, but they have not taken it upon themselves (except for a precious few) to scale the pyramid.

Now comes a tool such as HyperCard that can help schools scale the pyramid. Before we can expect HyperCard and powerful linking and idea-processing software to take hold, we need to raise the expectations of schools. How do we raise educational expectations? We must demonstrate how technology can help change schools and how technology empowers learners and teachers. Technology can indeed be the spark that lights some new fires and restores loftier educational goals to the schools.

Suggestions for the Future

If we—those of us committed to use of interactive multimedia—want HyperCard to realize its potential in K–12 schools, we must recognize what functions schools serve and where they stand developmentally. As we work to provide tools for education, we might be wise to follow these precepts:

- Start where the schools are at. Use familiar metaphors to get students and teachers into the software—book, museum, map, picture, document. Teach traditional subject areas and course titles.

- Allow users to link one idea to another directly, to find a link that's been programmed in or to discover links on their own. The links should be visual and direct whenever possible. Remember that a topical index is not a link. Indexing and categorizing cards and images by topic, while important, is *not* the same as linking the ideas and meanings in them.

- Explain things along the way. Allow users to find out *why* you led them here from there, *why* you linked this to that. Keep these explanations in the background (but easily accessible).

- Aim at wisdom. Do not develop a product that does not aim at powerful ideas about life and truth. Let wise experts in the field devise a conceptual framework. Ideas should form the core of the product.

As we bring HyperCard to education, we should:

- Focus on familiar, traditional subjects first—on topics that are related not to the computer but to the curriculum.

- Realize that the Apple Macintosh computer is an appropriate machine for schools—for all grade levels and for curricular as well as administrative purposes. Apple II computers forever—but not for everything.

- Proliferate stacks with sample ideas (buttons, scripts, fields) using traditional subject matter (history, literature, science). Distribute them through CD-ROM, telecommunications, and other channels. Show schools the software is available. Design the product so that it's easy for educators to get their fingers into HyperCard.

- Show off HyperCard to K–12 schools. Show prototypes, commercial products, and home-grown stacks. Let educators know HyperCard exists, and show them how easy it is to use.

And if all these strategies fail...

- Go for the coaches. The most powerful and influential person in many schools is the football coach. Coaches, especially the successful ones, are traditionally conservative in the use of technology, but they have easy access to the resources necessary to purchase an Apple Macintosh computer. If we show that the coach can do it, the rest of the school will follow. You see, HyperCard is the perfect tool for designing football plays:

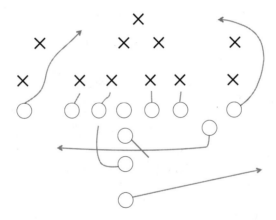

With HyperCard, the coach can show, repeat, and modify both offensive and defensive maneuvers. He can show backs in motion, split ends, and pass patterns. A good coach will quickly assimilate HyperCard into the football program. And it won't be very long before the coach will accommodate himself—and perhaps the entire school—to the fuller and liberating uses of technology.

The Birth of HyperSchool

Joseph F. Hofmeister

JOSEPH F. HOFMEISTER

Joe Hofmeister has been teaching in high schools for 30 years. For the last 20 years he has been at Cincinnati Country Day School, an independent school in southwestern Ohio known for its strong academic program. He is a regrooved math teacher, having assumed leadership of his school's computer program in 1980. His school has become known as the HyperSchool because of the faculty's innovative and broad-based curricular use of HyperCard.

He is married to Frances, a psychologist, and has two sons—Scott, a computer science–math major at Oberlin College, and Craig, an eleventh-grader whose March 1988 freshman term-paper stack named "Hannibal" has received wide recognition.

Some people don't like computers now any more than they did 10 years ago when precious few of them were around. While the installed base of microcomputers in schools is now between 2.25 million and 2.5 million, the integration of computers into the warp and woof of secondary education has remained minimal.

When the computer "goes down" in today's banks and insurance companies, business comes to a standstill. However, when the computers go off in a school, you hardly notice. An occasional programming class might be interrupted, but the majority of the "readin', 'ritin', and 'rithmetic" goes on without missing a beat. Obviously, the computer is not part and parcel of what is going on in the classrooms. If you remove or render unusable the dominant technology in schools, the technology that has been pervasive in classrooms for the last 100 years—blackboard and chalk—then you might have a problem.

One teacher said to me, "Well, we don't *want* everything to come to a halt just because the computers aren't working." Of course we don't! Banks and insurance companies aren't fond of it either. The point is: In a school where information is being processed, compared, tested, and integrated, students should have available to them—at "knowledge stations"—the most powerful mind tools available. We don't like it when the electricity or water supplies go off either, but the students go home when that happens. Should we not be so dependent on heat, light, and water? Hardly.

Thoreau put his finger on the issue, I feel, when he gave his reason for not liking all these modern inventions. (He was referring to the telegraph.) He said that many of them seemed like an "improved means to an unimproved end." Concerning computers, had he lived to see them, he might have asked how we have improved the end, now that we have this powerful new means. I'm afraid the answer would be, "Not much." Unless we are using computers to do things that we couldn't do without them—improving the ends— we aren't meeting the challenge. Some teachers haven't done much with blackboards either, although that technology has been around for quite a while. It is *not* rare to find a teacher using a blackboard almost exclusively to transcribe the textbook (or some other book), or notes, or outlines. Imagine what classrooms must have been like before the advent of blackboards, with students using individual pieces of paper. Then came individual slates, followed by large blackboards that filled the walls. Great teachers discovered how to use these blackboards to achieve new dimensions in learning. As a graphic, multiuser, color-capable, user-friendly technology, they represented a significant step forward, and some teachers made good use of them. They improved ends by allowing teachers to do things with the blackboard that they couldn't do before.

Let's be specific here. The majority of drill and practice programs for computers don't represent anything new, although they are a useful means. Many teachers have found that drill and practice using computers, which are inherently "patient," has helped develop skill levels more quickly. Lots of it, however, is just electronic "seat work"—an improved means. Writing labs that use computers with word-processing programs are a great improvement for teaching students how to write. They are hardly the innovative development to which I'm referring. What's surprising about writing labs is that they are seen as new. They should have been installed eight years ago, when they *could* have been. When writing things out in longhand is compared with typing them on a computer keyboard, keyboard work wins hands down. If a student's writing rate can be improved by 300 to 500 percent, to say nothing of the editing power available, how is it possible that keyboarding and word processing weren't immediately accepted? Why hasn't this technology impacted our concern about small motor development in elementary grades where children's handwriting skills get as much attention as the ideas they are trying to express? Money hasn't been holding us back. I know of school districts that didn't even unpack their computers because they didn't know what to do with them. Changes in the way things are done in school are implemented only with difficulty. It is even more difficult when the change involves doing something never done before.

At Cincinnati Country Day School, Apple's first HyperSchool, we are finding that HyperCard is making the improvement of ends a distinct possibility. We've been involved with educational computing for a long time. (See Figure 1.) By 1974 we were one of a very few secondary schools that had its own minicomputer, an HP2000, with 15 terminals throughout the school; several schools in the city were using us as a base for their time-sharing operations.

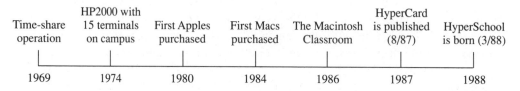

Time-share operation	HP2000 with 15 terminals on campus	First Apples purchased	First Macs purchased	The Macintosh Classroom	HyperCard is published (8/87)	HyperSchool is born (3/88)
1969	1974	1980	1984	1986	1987	1988

FIGURE 1. *History of computer use at Cincinnati Country Day School.*

We bought our first Apple Macintosh 128-KB computers in 1984 and worked with them for several years in various pilot programs. The most informative of these was a fifth-grade class with an extraordinary teacher, Frank Laurence, a Ph.D. in American literature and an international expert on Hemingway who had given up college teaching to join our staff. Upset by what seemed to him a general lack of writing skills in college students, he decided to take a teaching position in grade school, where students are taking their first steps as writers.

In 1986, with an Apple loan of six Macintosh computers, we built a program that Frank Laurence called "The Macintosh Classroom." (See Figure 2 on the following page.) What happened was, in my opinion, altogether new—an improved end. Students were accomplishing tasks in all disciplines that they couldn't have accomplished without the Apple Macintosh computer. Algebraic equations were being solved using a MacPaint exercise that Laurence called "Boxes and Clinkers." Sentences were being diagrammed electronically, with each word being labeled as a part of speech. The particular part of speech—noun, verb, object, and so on—was drawn from a group of "wells" at the top of the page, using the MacPaint duplicate option. Maps were drawn and redrawn and edited using the shrink, enlarge, and rotate options from the menus.

The students took no computer classes or programming classes. They were given just enough instruction to start a project. "Educational software or courseware" was not available. We were using MacWrite and MacPaint, programs that came free with the Apple Macintosh computers. Students were doing new things in history, English, and math, and the Macintosh was invisible. It became a tool. I remember distinctly how exciting it was. I brought my camera to school every day because I was afraid I was going to miss some major discovery. Eventually we begged and borrowed video equipment and recorded the story on tape. We sent copies all over the country, mostly to Apple people, but a group of our parents were excited enough about it to come up with the money we needed to buy our own machines and continue the project. For us, however, it was the precursor of HyperSchool, because it showed us that an innovative teacher, *who knew nothing about programming*, could integrate the computer into all academic disciplines.

Some people at Apple were excited about this development; however, they were individuals, people ahead of their time (even at Apple). Fortunately, our local support people at Apple's Cincinnati office, Cheryl Burt and Craig Wolverton, were among the people who understood what had happened and thereafter provided us a voice at Apple. In 1986 Macintosh wasn't exactly a dirty word at corporate headquarters, but almost. The Apple II family of computers was widely viewed as the computer of choice for the school environment. It was a cash cow, and no one was interested in putting that cow out to pasture.

We had 50 or 60 Apple IIs on our campus at the time, but we had only about 12 Macintosh computers, six of which were on loan from our Apple representatives. Nevertheless, our experience with Macintoshes in Frank Laurence's classroom made an indelible mark on some of us: We became committed to this new machine with a passion, because we saw the entry level for new technology drop to levels attainable by everyone, and because we saw students becoming involved with their own learning in a new way. (The "we" of this essay is a handful of teachers who unabashedly have supported the use of computers in our school.)

FIGURE 2. Frank Laurence and the Apple Macintosh computer classroom.

Our teachers as a body were not so very different from others in their acceptance of the new technology—that is, we couldn't claim widespread acceptance. We had a science teacher who had integrated the computer into his biology course, but he was one of the best programmers on campus and what he was doing with students involved programming in BASIC. The reaction of many of our teachers was typical of the way teachers often respond to the need for new-skill acquisition: "I think I'll have to get into a course about that next summer—or sometime." In Cincinnati, as in many other cities, computer courses available in the summer vary from irrelevant to absurd. However, if teachers could leapfrog over the programming hurdle by using Apple Macintosh computers as Frank Laurence had done, then they could become involved without costly in-service programs or coursework. They could learn "on the job."

"Sure," you say, teachers are going to jump right on this and take off with it, learning as they go. And pigs will fly. The issue of teacher training and acceptance of new technology is a major factor in what happened at our school but I will discuss it later, after HyperCard comes to center stage.

HyperCard hit the streets in August 1987, just before the start of another school year, and like many other teachers familiar with the Macintosh, we were wondering how we could make use of it. More accurately perhaps, we wondered what in the world it was. The magazines were teeming with HyperCard articles; Atkinson and Goodman were in the process of becoming household words (at least in some households). Teachers were beginning to ask me what all the fuss was about. In October, I volunteered to give a talk on HyperCard at a local conference to be held the following February—a ploy I used to force myself to learn the program. Over the next few months, I spent a lot of time reading about it, playing with it, and talking to friends who knew a lot more about it than I did. Giving the talk at the conference, and getting feedback from teachers about Hyper-Card, began to give me an inkling that it might be important in our classrooms. The concept of an electronic stack of cards that could be linked together in many different ways seemed to have some definite possibilities for classroom uses. Even the most elementary use of HyperCard as a synthesizing, organizational tool seemed to promise enough uses in a school to justify the trouble and time required to learn it.

In March, during our two-week spring break, I suggested to my ninth-grade son, Craig, that he ought to do a HyperCard stack instead of the standard six- to eight-page term paper he had been assigned. (See Figure 3 on the following page.) He took me up on it, despite his misgivings about how his noncomputer-using history teacher might feel about it. The subject of the paper was to be Hannibal's crossing of the Alps with elephants. He spent his entire vacation working on the stack, quickly surpassing me in his ability to use HyperTalk, the scripting language of HyperCard. He worked probably five times harder and five times longer than he would have had he done a standard term paper, but he had a great time working on the term paper and learned a lot about Hannibal.

As he began to construct his project, it was clear that his "paper" was emerging as a different breed of cat altogether. (See Figure 4 on page 207.) Ordinary term papers consist of a body of text that one reads through in a linear fashion. Graphics, if used at all, are inserted after the part of the text that they are meant to illustrate. Occasionally, a picture or drawing is meant to illustrate a whole section of text that precedes it. While looking at the picture, you might want to page back through the text you have read and refer to various items that the picture ties together.

The use of HyperCard transformed the Hannibal project into almost the inverse of the ordinary term paper. "Hannibal" is a series of graphics that can be examined in greater detail by clicking on parts of the picture. The text of the paper is tied together by the pictures (instead of the other way around) and can be read in any order or as many times as a user desires. Furthermore, the information can be linked in many different ways. Not only is unlimited cross-referencing possible, it is easy. In addition to having text

FIGURE 3. Craig Hofmeister, author of "Hannibal."

available from various parts of the graphics, animation becomes possible. Hannibal's path through the Alps is shown by a thick line that begins in southern France and works its way across the mountains into Italy. (See Figure 5.) Because historians disagree as to the exact path followed by Hannibal, a second picture shows a "minority-opinion path," also animated. The animated path stops at several places to highlight events of special significance that occurred at these positions, the details of which can be read by simply pushing buttons placed at those spots.

When it became clear to Craig that his project was becoming "truly awesome," he added a final touch by downloading digitized sounds from local bulletin boards and installing them in his stack. The final product was now far beyond anything I had anticipated. Papers I had done as a student had almost always included some rudimentary graphics, but they were 95-percent text. HyperCard had looked to me like it might be an easier way to handle these "normal" ingredients—"an improved means" for putting a standard paper together. My son had no preconceptions about standards for a term paper. As a ninth-grader, he had done only a few projects of this size before, and never in this formal context. He had no ambition to reinvent the term paper.

FIGURE 4. The first screen of "Hannibal," a HyperCard "term paper."

FIGURE 5. A thick, dark line shows Hannibal's path through the Alps.

In retrospect the Hannibal project seems like a worthwhile endeavor, perhaps even a mission! Lining up all the term papers done in any one school year in the secondary schools of this country would probably make a stack of paper several miles high—a mountain of agony. Students dread doing them; teachers hate correcting them. Has anything ever needed reinventing as much as the standard term paper?

Furthermore, watching a ninth-grader working his way through this project was an eye-opening experience. When he asked me how I thought he should do footnotes, I naturally suggested a separate card at the back of the stack to hold all the footnotes, my version of a "modern" approach to doing footnotes. This card would be viewed whenever someone clicked on a superscripted numeral in the text. However, unencumbered as he was by my experiences of term papers and now immersed in the HyperCard environment, the foot-note problem was simple—and for him the solution was obvious. When you click on the superscripted numeral, up comes the reference in a pop-up field, right at that spot in the text, on the same card with the text needing the reference. (See Figure 6.) Footnotes no longer had to be notes at the foot of a paper. In the Hannibal stack, all "footnotes" are right where you need and want them. They are next to the text but invisible and out of the way, until you want to see them.

The Hannibal stack made a big impression on the many people who saw it, even on my son's noncomputer-using teacher. Teachers across the country reacted very positively to it. The concept was so obvious and interesting that it made people say, "Of course. Why didn't we think of this sooner? It's so simple."

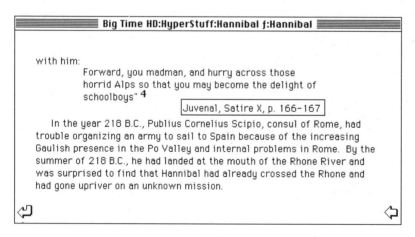

FIGURE 6. When the user clicks on a superscripted numeral in the text of "Hannibal," a reference appears in a pop-up field.

The next chapter in the story of HyperSchool's birth centers around another teacher. Nancy Fogelson, a history teacher, had returned to teaching after raising her children. Love of the profession and a desire to contribute were the overriding considerations that brought her back into the classroom. A self-professed noncomputer person, her interest in the Apple Macintosh computer was piqued by the ease of drawing and illustrating maps in MacPaint. (See Figure 7.) Leaning heavily on Frank Laurence's earlier work with MacPaint in his fifth-grade history classes and on Fogelson's own avowal that "there is no teaching of history without teaching geography," we showed her some of the things that could be done with MacPaint using scanned maps as the basis for student lab work. Delighted with the prospect, she put the students in her Modern European History class to work several days a week in the Apple Macintosh computer lab. Students shaded in the countries of the African continent with different MacPaint patterns to show European influence in Africa in the mid-nineteenth century. Natural resources were drawn and inserted with the standard MacPaint tools. Maps were printed out on the LaserWriter. The result: Students who "couldn't draw a straight line" were proud of their work.

FIGURE 7. Nancy Fogelson in the computer lab.

Comparing these new maps with what they had been able to do before, they felt like *National Geographic* authors! Most important of all, juniors and seniors were excited about their required history courses.

The hook was set. Is anything as compelling for the good teacher as seeing students excited about what they ought to be learning? No matter the extra time involved to rethink the course or the frustration of dealing with this new technology. For good teachers, student enthusiasm is the pearl of great price and an elixir to ban all thoughts of burnout. The students come to school each morning after late-night hours of preparation, dragging their books behind them as they head for their classrooms, but their eyes are glowing!

That was the way it was for Fogelson using MacPaint. The next step—to HyperCard— was an easy seduction. Using the Hannibal stack as an example and introducing Hyper-Card as "kind of a fancy MacPaint that includes MacWrite" started an explosion of ideas and projects that shook our campus and caused ripples all the way to Cupertino. Fogelson might have had a little less respect for the computer staff the morning after, as she found herself suddenly up to her hips in computers, system folders, and floppy disks. Fear and trembling were as present as the excitement of people learning as she went into her new laboratory classroom several times a week with students who were not only computer novices but openly frightened of the technology. No one will write any poems about it, but any teacher can empathize with the situation: "I don't know about these Macintoshes; I don't know much about MacPaint; I don't understand this HyperCard program; but my students are excited and making the kind of historical connections now that they weren't making before."

One of the most remarkable aspects of Fogelson's work was the fact that she started from zero at the end of March, knowing nothing about even the Apple Macintosh computer, and had her students producing exciting, interesting HyperCard stacks by the beginning of May, with her only training being on the job. She was accused of organic connections to Danny Goodman's 700-page opus, *The Complete HyperCard Handbook,* which she carried everywhere. She was quick to admit that the students had much less trouble dealing with HyperCard than she did and that in the lab, students were more likely to be able to solve a computer problem than she was.

She understood well the basically simple concept of stacks of related cards on which HyperCard is built. She prepared lab assignments that followed her understanding of the HyperCard structure before she was able to prepare such stacks herself. This is a critical point. She couldn't manage the technology very well but she could still integrate it into her work. She knew what she wanted the stacks to contain, and what the fundamental linkages would be—these concepts she was able to explain to her students and to summarize in assignment sheets. Creating cards and buttons, navigating through stacks, importing MacPaint images to various cards, and duplicating various features were less than perfectly clear to her during those first weeks.

HyperCard made her classroom as exciting for her as it was for her students because not only were they able to handle the mechanics of HyperCard, but they also began to be more interested in history, making connections that she hadn't expected. They began to develop a taste for having the correct information. Standard reference books took on a new meaning. Her students discovered that she was a most enthusiastic, genuinely appreciative audience of their work. Her admiration for their ease with the machinery fueled their efforts. She was constantly corralling other faculty members to have them see what her students were doing, showing them off to the school. The fact that her students were not in the honors sections underlined the achievements. Her obvious pride in their accomplishments gave these students a new perspective on their own work.

The excitement surrounding the work with HyperCard was infectious at Cincinnati Country Day School. Apple's interest was now obvious as visitors streamed through the school to see what was happening. Another major step in faculty interest and involvement occurred when the head of the English department, Bill Briggeman, joined the effort. (See Figure 8 on the following page.) As the newly appointed head of a department that traditionally saw itself as nontechnical, he was a key person in moving toward what Sue Collins, Apple educational technology consultant, has called "a critical mass" in faculty development. Sparks from lead teachers are not uncommon in schools; however, what we were looking for, what we wanted to happen, was a conflagration.

Briggeman had personally been a computer user for some time. He owned an Apple IIC and had used it for word processing for several years. We spent an hour with him one afternoon explaining what Fogelson was doing and demonstrating HyperCard. A week later he came back and described a stack idea he had worked on and showed his plans to reorient his senior English class, placing HyperCard on center stage.

The simplicity of the HyperCard concept had been clear to him, as it was to Fogelson, even though he had never used the program. His design employed T.S. Eliot's poem "The Hollow Men," a relatively short, but difficult poem that he had taught in the eleventh-grade American literature course. (See Figure 9 on page 213.) Using a copy of the poem, whose lines continue from one card to another, he had designed a stack that used various typefaces to alert the reader that an explanatory note was "behind" the word and could be reached by clicking on the word. His intent was to build a stack that would do a very thorough analysis of this poem, with cards that explained Eliot's rich

FIGURE 8. Bill Briggeman in the computer lab.

imagery and allusions, and then to explain the references to other cards signaled by font changes in the references themselves. If Eliot's reference was to Dante's *Divine Comedy,* for example, an excerpt would be available on a separate card to help the reader understand the allusion. If the reference from the *Divine Comedy* included a reference of its own, perhaps some scriptural allusion, then students could get the quotation from the Bible by clicking on the word in the *Divine Comedy*. Briggeman's aim, in his words, was "to build an abstract pyramid, with the text of 'The Hollow Men' written across the top, and a wealth of references and allusions hanging down and spreading out the further down you went."

With this model to show his students, he intended to assign each student or group of students a poem, story, or project; they would use HyperCard to construct a similar "pyramid" for their poem, story, or project. There is an interesting footnote to this story. Briggeman wrote to Harcourt Brace Jovanovich (the publishing company that owns the rights to Eliot's works) for permission to use the poem and references in his stack,

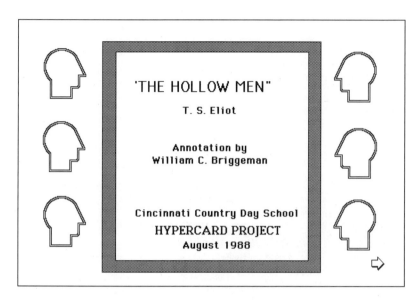

FIGURE 9. The first screen of a HyperCard stack designed
for "The Hollow Men."

although he was reasonably certain that such personal use of the material was not a viola-
tion of copyright. To his surprise, he was refused on the grounds that they felt that once
the texts were on a floppy disk, no control over distribution would be possible. Though
perhaps understandable, the objection reminds us not to look to publishing companies for
help in reinventing schools.

Briggeman's presence among the teachers using HyperCard was extremely important
because he represented a major curriculum area coming on board. History and English
programs are not the traditional places to expect the new technology to blossom with
"improved means to improved ends." Therefore, their use of HyperCard caught the eye
not only of Apple, but of administrators, parents, and trustees.

In the computer science department, we had been teaching BASIC and Pascal, a software
studies course, and Advanced Placement (AP) computer science classes. The program
was typical of a school with a strong computer science program but atypical in that we
used Apple Macintosh computers for the program. One of our graduates, Jeffrey A. Spain,
M.D., an anesthesiologist and Macintosh aficionado, had written several stacks for my
AP class, notably one to help demonstrate the Towers of Hanoi recursion problem. (See
Figure 10 on the following page.) With his urging, I decided to substitute HyperCard's
scripting language for BASIC in a semester course I was teaching to ninth-graders.

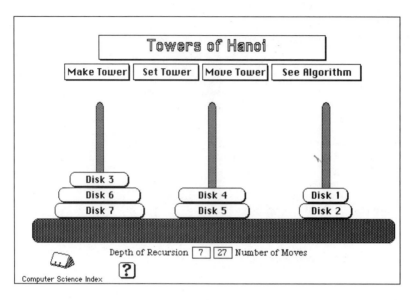

*FIGURE 10. A screen from Dr. Jeffrey Spain's HyperCard stack
designed for the Towers of Hanoi recursion problem.*

During the first half of the course, from January to mid-March, I had been using the
Apple Macintosh computer version of True BASIC, so my students were already familiar
with the Mac. To my students I described this pilot program that would occupy us for the
final half of the semester as part of a general HyperCard-centered experiment going on
in our school. They accepted the new language with enthusiasm; for pizzazz, it left True
BASIC at the gate. They suddenly found themselves "experts" in something everyone
was talking about.

We started the program at the end of March and by the end of the course in the second
week of May, meeting each day for a 40-minute class, students were able to do a selection sort. The Random function filled 10 fields on a card. (See Figure 11.) After pushing
the Sort button, the numbers rearranged themselves in 10 other fields, in order, on the
same card. Doing standard sorting exercises using BASIC represented a skill level we
had come to associate with a semester's course in programming. With HyperTalk, the
class was able to reach the same programming level in half the time. The easy access to
graphics using HyperCard adds a rich, visual dimension to an otherwise abstract skill.

Because of the success of this class in elementary programming using scripting instead
of BASIC, we decided to drop BASIC as our standard first computer language and use

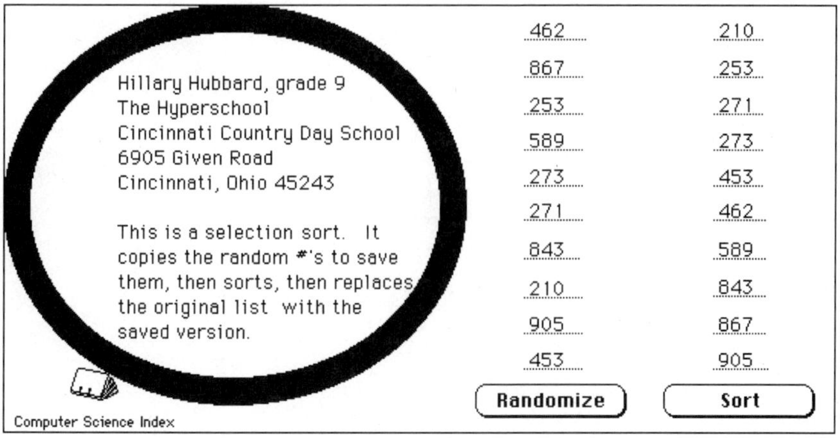

Hillary Hubbard, grade 9
The Hyperschool
Cincinnati Country Day School
6905 Given Road
Cincinnati, Ohio 45243

This is a selection sort. It
copies the random #'s to save
them, then sorts, then replaces
the original list with the
saved version.

Computer Science Index

462	210
867	253
253	271
589	273
273	453
271	462
843	589
210	843
905	867
453	905

(Randomize)   (Sort)

FIGURE 11. A screen from a selection sort.

HyperTalk in its place. Although HyperTalk might not reverse the present national trend in secondary schools away from programming classes, it has increased enrollment in ours. Learning programming with HyperCard has a different flavor than the standard programming class, especially when the student's teacher wants it used in another class. It becomes immediately practical. Students who know HyperCard find themselves able to do things that only serious hackers would have attempted previously.

In a different arena, our elementary-school coordinator and my partner in the computer department, Joyce Rudowski, was working with a third-grade teacher, Bobbie Menter, who was anxious to give her students a chance to try HyperCard. Several sessions were scheduled for the third-graders in the high-school computer lab, and Rudowski met with Menter to discuss what was happening in third grade. A Macintosh computer artist in her own right, Rudowski prepared several "template stacks" dealing with Egyptian tombs and the pyramids. (See Figure 12 on the following page.) Cards were prepared that laid out diagrams of the tomb of a king, for example, and open fields were put next to objects; each third-grader filled in the names of the objects in the blank fields, using her or his textbook to look things up or to check spelling. Part of the stack that the third-graders liked best was a room (card) in which they were expected to make their own drawings on the walls and to build objects that might have been left in the tomb by the king's family. Students ended up with stacks that were uniquely their own, each one on a separate disk—Rudowski having simply duplicated her template for each student. They were delighted with their own work and Menter was delighted with the unusual interest level that had been created in their study of Egypt.

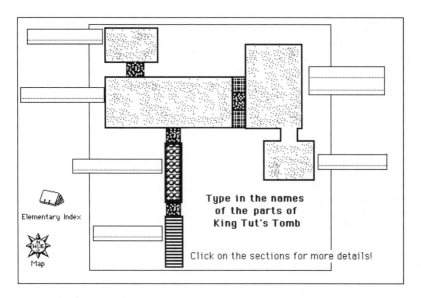

FIGURE 12. *A screen from a HyperCard "template" stack dealing with Egyptian tombs and pyramids.*

Rudowski's insight into HyperCard as an interactive environment opened up what seemed to be endless vistas for its use in the classroom. Her applications in third grade underscored for us what we were discovering about HyperCard:

- HyperCard was suggesting customized, unique applications for teachers who were nonprogrammers. These applications matched what the teacher was doing, rather than vice versa.

- HyperCard allowed students to "create their own knowledge," rather than being limited by someone else's presentations. Our classrooms were becoming more and more centered on learning instead of on teaching.

We have been amazed at how difficult it is to communicate these ideas to fellow educators. We are continually correcting the impression that we are using HyperCard as a new, improved *presentation tool* for the teacher. Though HyperCard can definitely be used in this way, we feel that the real secret of what is happening at Cincinnati Country Day School, the gold, is the opposite of what happens with a great presentation tool. What we have working in our classes is a *construction tool*. Students are using Hyper-Card to make their own connections between various aspects of the subject matter. They are designing and preparing their own stacks, relating and integrating the information as they work. HyperCard is far from being merely a bigger and better presentation tool or one more opportunity for the teacher to try to compete with "Sesame Street" and "The Electric Company." Rather, HyperCard turns things around in the standard classroom: The teacher-centered classroom now becomes student-centered.

The classic model of the teacher standing, book in hand, lecturing to students seated on the ground around the "master" has popularized the school where the teacher is in front of the classroom, performing, doing presentations, delivering more or less exciting lectures as students sit passively—the more passively the better—receiving information as it comes from the teacher. This is school seen as the place where knowledge is transmitted from the people who have it, the teachers, to the people who don't, the students. Education becomes a process of transmission. We feel that this is an unfortunate and counterproductive view of what schools and education are about. As respectable a publication as *Time* magazine said, in a cover story* on teachers, "The teacher's primary task [is] to convey knowledge." The article states very clearly that the teacher is simply a presenter, or better, a performer, putting on "five shows a day" and usually burning out in the process.

At the HyperSchool we feel that we are working on a different paradigm of education— a concept that has been called the *constructivist paradigm.* Donald Blais, in his article "Constructivism—A Theoretical Revolution for Algebra" in *Mathematics Teacher* for November 1988, summarized his view of knowledge:

> *Constructivism does not say that knowledge is something that learners* ought *to construct for and by themselves. Rather it says that knowledge is something that learners* must *construct for and by themselves. There is no alternative. Discovery, reinvention, or active reconstruction is necessary.*

This is the model that HyperCard is helping us to develop. Empowering students is something we have talked about for a long time. Real empowerment of students, however, is pretty hard to do and examples are difficult to find. Using HyperCard on the Macintosh will not cure every wart that education has, but we are finding that its use causes a significant difference in what is happening at our school. The impact has been on a systemic level—with lots of stops and starts, ups and downs. But when the pieces fit together, you look at it and see something revolutionary.

---

* *Time* (November 14, 1988): 59.

If you have been lucky enough to see the video *Grapevine,* you will have a good example of the model. Pat Hanlon, English teacher, and Bob Campbell, librarian, formed a team at Lowell High School, San Francisco, that directed the study of John Steinbeck's *The Grapes of Wrath.* (See "HyperCard: A New Deal in the Classroom," later in this section.) One of the most striking parts of the video shows a classroom with students in the front of the room, presenting the results of their research on some aspect of Steinbeck's novel, using multimedia tools. The teacher, Pat Hanlon, is in the back of the room, behind the students, following the presentation. The students are in teams presenting various aspects of their research to the rest of the class. Their pleasure and the satisfaction of their teachers, Hanlon and Campbell, are obvious. Most importantly, students form, from this kind of experience, a more positive attitude toward the course than they do from being on the receiving end of a series of lectures. Today, seniors in high schools with good English programs are asked to read challenging works, such as *The Grapes of Wrath, Heart of Darkness,* and T.S. Eliot's "The Hollow Men." Too many of them graduate with an absolute distaste for these serious works of literature.

Changing the emphasis of the classroom from teachers to students led to certain insights. The concept of HyperSchool, for example, arose from the experience we were having. Some in our administration felt that the term was too similar to the term "hyperactive" to be used. HyperSchool, however, like HyperCard, came from the notion of nonlinearity and was prompted by what happened between our history and English departments. Briggeman, working on "The Hollow Men," a poem about World War I, found his work dovetailing with Fogelson's Modern European History course. Fogelson was already bringing into her class the literature surrounding World War I and realized, hearing Briggeman talk about what he was doing, that students would obviously see the connections between the stacks. It was not planned or anticipated, but traditional department lines were blurring as we all began using the same tools. Chris Hayward, our art teacher, already very involved with the Apple Macintosh computer, saw an obvious opportunity for students to pursue their study of art in the context of the history and literature of the times. More connections were possible than any of us had predicted. Fogelson began conversations with the mathematics department chairman, Sam Tumolo, about a business course she had in mind. She thought her students' HyperCard stacks would be a good place for his statistics students to acquire some practical experience. There had been no interdisciplinary in-service days to prompt all this. It happened because HyperCard opened up new opportunities. We began to think about what schools might be like in the future, when students would all have access to multimedia tools and would know how to use them.

Perhaps the most important thing we discovered was the interrelationship between the constructivist model of the school, HyperCard, and the ordinary teacher standing like "a steel door, blocking entrance of new technology into the classroom" (Monica Bradsher of the National Geographic Society). Our experience, limited though it has been, seems to point to a way around the "black hole" for money, time, and goodwill that in-service computer programs for teachers seem to be. We think that the millions of dollars and thousands of hours that teachers have spent in these in-service programs over the last eight years might have been largely wasted.

What we have learned from our experience is that when you move a computer into a teacher-centered classroom, you meet with strong resistance, perhaps even total rejection. (See Figure 13.) We shouldn't be terribly shocked about that. Reflection on the model offers a simple explanation. When the classroom is seen as being almost totally an environment where the teacher is "telling" or transmitting knowledge to the student, the computer is seen by the teachers as another thing *they* must do. Furthermore, in order to bring the presentation, using a computer, up to passable levels, the teacher must learn a fair amount about computers, and this doesn't sit well with our technophobic career teachers. Perhaps an apt comparison would be to discover that, for some reason, teachers could improve their presentations greatly if they spoke in Spanish. Now all you would have to do is talk all teachers into becoming fluent in Spanish. Naturally, they would rebel. "I'm already busier and working harder than I'm comfortable with. Don't load any more on me!" And they *do* rebel at the notion that they now must turn into computer hackers. You try to hand the teacher this tool, and the teacher finds that, although perhaps impressive, it is complex and demanding. Teachers aren't fond of getting up in

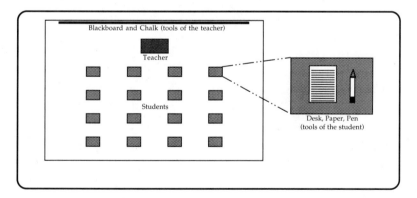

FIGURE 13. A typical classroom layout based on attitudes prevalent during the Industrial Age.

front of their students and being unsure of themselves with the tools of presentation. They like to have everything under control. They especially don't like to make fools of themselves. This is understandable.

In the contructivist (student-centered) model of the classroom, however, the teacher and the student are engaged together in learning. (See Figure 14.) The teacher is not an expert in the sense of being omniscient but rather is an experienced fellow learner. Put a computer in this kind of classroom, and the teacher and the student begin to use it immediately. The computer, used as a mind tool, becomes another way to gather, organize, present, analyze, and edit. Now all the information can be related, through HyperCard for example, and perhaps be better understood. In this kind of classroom no one is overly concerned about committing mistakes. The work, the learning, and the genuine discoveries are what is important to both teacher and student.

Blaming teachers for blocking the way is an easy tack to take, and surely plenty of blame exists to go around. If the model that they are working in puts all the pressure on the teacher, a new and tricky-to-use tool is not going to receive a big welcome. Most teachers are hardworking, committed, interested people doing the best they can. The monolithic structure of education forms a steel door, imprisoning children in their own passivity.

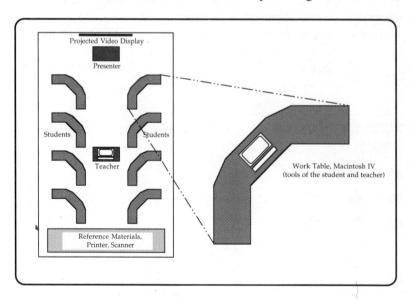

FIGURE 14. A typical classroom layout based on the constructivist model of the Information Age.

At Cincinnati Country Day School, Apple's first HyperSchool, we think we have begun to build the school of the future. (See Figure 15.) Much work remains to be done; however, programs such as HyperCard are helping us envision a school where lectures are the exception rather than the rule. We think that students will replace lectures with multimedia presentations that they will review in their own homes with a computer and a modem. School will be the place where students come *after* they have had excellent presentations and where they will, with their teachers, investigate the meaning, implications, and relationships of these presentations. School will be the place where knowledge is integrated, synthesized, and tested instead of a place where knowledge is transmitted from those who know to those who don't.

FIGURE 15. *Students and teachers from Cincinnati Country Day School, Apple Computer's first HyperSchool. [Photo: Copyright © February 19, 1988, by Apple Computer, Inc.]*

Using HyperCard
in Apple Classrooms
of Tomorrow

Barry Stebbins

BARRY STEBBINS

Barry Stebbins is a science teacher in the Apple Classrooms of Tomorrow^{SM} (ACOT^{SM}) project at West High School in Columbus, Ohio. After earning a B.S. in science education from Ohio State University in 1971, he began his career at Roosevelt Junior High School teaching general science. By 1976, he had earned an M.A. in environmental science from O.S.U. In 1978, he began teaching in a vocational work-study program (O.W.A.) for dropout-prone students and moved to Wedgewood Junior High School in Columbus. As the city schools made the transition from junior highs to middle schools, he moved to West High School in 1979 and continued as a vocational coordinator for seven years. In his role as coordinator of the O.W.A. program, he was one of the first coordinators to acquire and use computers with dropout-prone students. By teaching programming as well as applications such as word processors, databases, and spreadsheets, he saw his students improve in the areas of reading, writing, and mathematical computation.

In 1986, he joined the ACOT project as a science teacher. In 1987, biology, his area of primary interest, was added to the ACOT classroom. During the summer of 1987, he also received training at Apple Computer, Inc., in Apple's newest application, HyperCard.

Let me begin by giving you a little insight into an experimental classroom that Apple Computer, Inc., has allowed to develop.* About four years ago, someone at Apple Computer asked a very simple question: What would happen if students had access to computers all the time? To find the answer to this question, Apple created a division that became known as ACOT℠ (Apple Classrooms of Tomorrow℠); Apple then went looking for a few schools that might like to participate in this research endeavor. (See Figure 1.) Fortunately, for myself and my nine fellow teachers, Apple chose West High School in Columbus, Ohio, as one of the schools to participate in this project. We became the only high-school ACOT site and started down an exciting road during the summer of 1986. We also have an additional distinction from the elementary sites: We have Apple Macintosh computers instead of the standard Apple IIE, which is found widely throughout schools in America.

FIGURE 1. A view of the ACOT classroom at West High School in Columbus, Ohio, during a discussion.

* This essay appears in a slightly different version in the journal *Computers in the Schools*. Copyright ©1990 by The Haworth Press, Inc., New York, NY.

To qualify as an ACOT site, our school and Apple Computer had to agree on many, many details. One significant detail is that each of our students is allowed to take home an Apple Macintosh computer for the entire school year and also has another Macintosh to use at school. While schools are afraid to lend students two textbooks, one for home use and one for use at school, we have a project that allows students to have access to two computers. When you consider that in many classrooms, you might see three students (or more) watching one student use a piece of equipment, the ACOT concept is extremely far ahead of its time.

To add to the ACOT concept, the Columbus city school system is also allowing 9 teachers to teach 90 students. (In our fourth year, this number will increase to 120.) At each high-school grade level, 5 teachers instruct 30 students using a team-teaching approach. Team teaching is something that also has never been tried to this extent, and our approach to team teaching is quite different from most. English and social studies compose one facet while math and science make up the other. Because two teachers are always present in the classroom, teachers meet regularly to coordinate lessons for each grade level. We try to show our students that each subject complements the others in such a way that each subject becomes far more important than its mere content area. Our students realize that all their subjects are being taught, but they will tell you that they are taking ACOT—not math, science, English, and social studies.

When we began, we defined several goals that we wanted our students to achieve. We thought that our students should retain a certain amount of knowledge and that learning should be a pleasant experience for the student. We hoped that our students would "learn how to learn." We also wanted our students to become "lifelong learners" and hoped a few might even become "experts" in particular areas. We most wanted to develop the idea that learning could best be accomplished by a "community of learners."

The one weakness that we had to overcome was that no "educational" software existed for the Apple Macintosh computer. We had to turn to various business-software programs available for the Macintosh—basically, word processing, database, spreadsheet, art or graphic software, and desktop publishing. We found that being forced to use business software caused our students (and the teachers) to use the computer as a tool—exactly as it is used in business. We now claim this "weakness" to be one of our strong points.

In the fall of 1987, Apple released one of the most powerful pieces of software ever to be considered by the education community—HyperCard. Suddenly, students and teachers had a piece of software that allowed them to present ideas, to create ways of explaining tough concepts, and to retrieve information with amazing speed. The software would function as an elaborate art tool allowing students to explore ideas in a free and creative manner. This software could "grow" with the student, so bigger and better projects could be created. Finally, with HyperCard, education was going to be able to take some giant steps forward.

I'd like to introduce you to our ACOT staff at West High. I teach ninth-grade general science and tenth-grade biology. Paula Fistick teaches tenth-grade geometry and a new (and somewhat experimental) fourth-year precalculus class. (See Figure 2 on the following page.) Carolyn Kennedy is in charge of the ninth-grade algebra-one class and the eleventh-grade algebra-two class. The three of us team teach the ninth-grade and tenth-grade math–science blocks. Richard Tracy and Sheila Cantlebary make up another part of the ninth-grade and tenth-grade team. Richard teaches ninth-grade life skills and keyboarding and tenth-grade world history; Sheila is in charge of ninth-grade and tenth-grade English. Bob Howard, who is our ACOT building coordinator, contributes to this team by teaching a computer-applications class that is taken by all tenth-graders.

Sue Misiak teaches eleventh-grade English and teams with Dwayne Marshall, who teaches American history. Paula and Carolyn also team with John Hopper, our chemistry teacher. Next year these five teachers will also be responsible for adding the twelfth-grade math–science block and the English–social studies block to the program.

From our downtown administration offices, we are given extra support from people such as Dr. Tim Best, a multimedia specialist; Larry Koslap, a video specialist; Dr. Bob Carpenter, a music specialist working with our students in the use of the MIDI interface; James Bailey, our building principal; and Dr. Howard Merriman, our assistant superintendent whose dream of what could be has helped cause ACOT to become a reality in Columbus. Jane Pratt, who is the technology supervisor for our school district, serves as our link to Apple Computer by being our site coordinator. Jane is the first person to whom we turn to solve the little problems and provide the many extra items we need to have a smoothly running program. Without all the extra kinds of help these people provide, the nine teachers in this program would probably have to live at West High to make this program work.

Often all the team members for a particular grade level are in the room at the same time, but each grade level is divided into a math–science block and an English–social studies block. With quite a few afternoon meetings, lessons are coordinated across all subject areas for a particular grade level and sometimes even throughout the entire ACOT family. The success of our project is due to the long hours of hard work and cooperation of many fine professionals.

Paula Fistick   Carolyn Kennedy   Richard Tracy

Sheila Cantlebary   Bob Howard   Sue Misiak

Dwayne Marshall   John Hopper   Jane Pratt

FIGURE 2. ACOT staff at West High School.

Prior to the introduction of HyperCard, students were able to display their work in a one-dimensional mode, usually on a sheet of paper. A few teachers had taken the "risk" of allowing students to venture out into multidimensional formats such as videotape, but such formats were not something that all students were able to "get their hands on." Also, those few who dared to try these "different directions" often found them to be very time-consuming because the materials were very difficult to use. However, with HyperCard and a Macintosh, students now compose, illustrate, highlight, animate, and even add sound to their reports. Suddenly, students have a tool that allows them to expand the horizons of the conventional classroom. Students are now required to think on multiple levels and link ideas together. Visual impact becomes very important to their *presentations*. (I can no longer use the word "report" to describe the students' work, as it does not convey a strong enough *message*.) Students quickly evolved from the "written paper" reports to actual visual presentations, and this was relatively easy to accomplish.

The limitations of the classroom began to disappear. Students can pursue the style and manner of presentation they desire. Each presentation is limited only to a given student's imagination and creativity. Finally, an easy-to-use tool is available to every student and the "reins of control" are now in the hands of the student doing the presentation.

By watching the presentations of their classmates, the students were able to conceive of how they, too, might do a better presentation. With these increased capabilities in their hands, students raced to put together presentations that were outstanding. For the first time, students actually began suggesting to their teachers how an assignment should be done. HyperCard allowed the students to venture off and explore possibilities that hadn't been thought of by their teachers. Students also built on each other's experiences, and their projects became better and better. The ACOT team at West High feels that Hyper-Card is the tool that not only changes the ways students use the classroom computer but also dramatically changes how students learn. (As I explain how we have used Hyper-Card and describe some of our students' projects, this dramatic change in learning will become evident.)

HyperCard is also the tool that moved us much closer to our goal of creating a "community of learners." Students have been allowed to work in groups for various projects and then to present their project to the entire class. Some examples from a DNA project and a Mitosis project are shown in Figure 3 on the following page and in Figure 4 on page 231.

Students share various techniques with each other, and the group's project often has been improved through the help of a multitude of "outsiders." Most teachers realize that they actually had to teach in order to fully learn many things for themselves. Using the idea

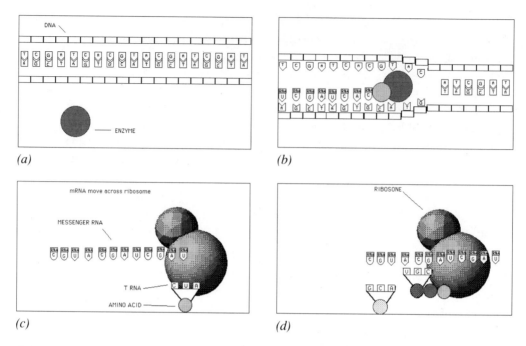

FIGURE 3. A DNA stack: (a) Card 5, (b) Card 16, (c) Card 34, and (d) Card 39.

that "the best way to learn is to teach someone else," we have often put our students in charge of teaching various sections of the text in the various content areas. This caused those students who worked on a specific area to become the "experts" in that area.

One of the things I learned by using HyperCard was that students were able to develop ways of explaining very complex concepts (that were new to them) to other students. Suddenly, my classroom was being transformed from the old, standard classroom of "one teacher with thirty students" to one of "thirty teachers with one student (me)." I was no longer the only "purveyor" of knowledge in my classroom. Yes, I was still needed at times to help explain a tough concept (due to my "expertness" in the field of science), but my students were rapidly gaining on me.

I also began to question the importance of each and every student learning each and every concept in the science book. For example, do I need to remember all that stuff I learned in college physics? Probably not, because I use it very seldom. But I do need to know how to find information when I need it and to understand it. I think this is one of the key questions that education doesn't address. How do we get to what we need? In creating their presentations for their classmates, my students were able to learn the

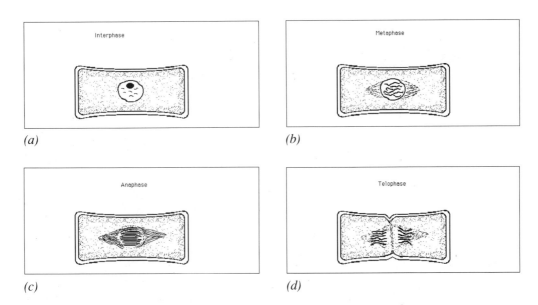

(a)   *(b)*

(c)   *(d)*

FIGURE 4. A Mitosis stack: (a) Card 2, (b) Card 12, (c) Card 16, and (d) Card 20.

processes that enable them to learn anything they need to know. HyperCard became the tool that allows the students to organize material in a manner that makes sense to them.

HyperCard is also an ideal piece of software for problem-solving–oriented curricula. The other teachers on the team and I asked students to demonstrate the best way to explain something that was causing problems for other students. The students often came up with tremendous ideas and took part in "teaching" the class. This exchange of ideas has become a very commonplace activity in ACOT.

The feature of HyperCard that most allows it to serve as an idea tool in education is a capability of fitting any user. This is true for all users regardless of age—from the elementary students at the Vivarium project in Los Angeles to the high-school students at West High's ACOT project and even to medical students in college. HyperCard's flexibility allows the user to decide what to do and how to do it. When my students create a project or presentation using HyperCard, they are able to "do it their way."

In our ninth-grade algebra class, Paula Fistick asked our ACOT students to design a stack that would show someone how to solve various algebraic equations. She assigned each student several equations. Matt Tardino, a ninth-grader, created a stack using an animation technique to simplify three equations. (See Figure 5 on the following page.) In his first example, 7 cards are used to create a 7-step animation that shows how to add two

FIGURE 5. *Matt Tardino's Algebra stack, opening card.*

polynomials to get one answer. (See Figure 6.) He had to carefully time each step so that it does not go too fast for the person viewing his stack. In his second example, 19 cards are used, but this time he created a short cartoon, showing a man writing out the equation in a book before showing the user the actual equation being solved. (See Figure 7 on page 234.) In his third example, he uses a painter who "paints" out the 12 steps required to simplify this polynomial equation. (See Figure 8 on page 234.)

Jason Wren, another ninth-grader, created a 35-card animation, in which "bombs" are used to rearrange and simplify another equation. (See Figure 9 on page 235.) Jason also explored the Resource Editor tool to add sound effects to his stack. Each time a bomb rearranges or simplifies part of the equation, the user hears an explosion. When the final answer is reached, the theme music from "Twilight Zone" is played. Jason very successfully created a video-game-type presentation that not only correctly solves the equation but holds the user's attention throughout the entire process.

Solving, simplifying, and rearranging algebraic equations is an important skill that is often used in science classes. Therefore, what is taught in algebra class also affects how well a student will do in science. Because Paula and I team teach these two classes, it becomes very easy to coordinate and integrate our lessons so that both subjects complement each other.

When Paula gave our "math" students the assignment on solving algebraic equations, I simply tossed in a few of the formulas that were being used in the science class. In Figure 10 on page 236, you see two stacks in which a student shows, algebraically, how to rearrange the area and velocity formulas that were being used in science. In the first stack, 24 cards are used to show two other possible arrangements of the area formula. On the first card, you see the basic formula and are given two choices: One choice will show

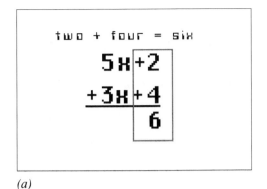

(a)

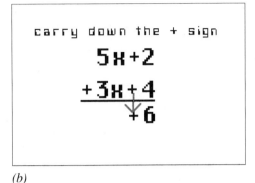

(b)

(c)

FIGURE 6. Matt Tardino's Algebra stack, Example #1: (a) Card 3, (b) Card 4, and (c) Card 7.

how to rearrange the formula to solve for length, and the other will show how to rearrange the formula to solve for width. In the second stack, 23 cards are used to show you the same concept, but for the velocity formula.

For years I often wondered why it was so hard for my science students to cope with the math formulas when we did various activities in science. By team teaching with a math teacher, I discovered the answer. First of all, the concepts that deal with rearranging algebraic formulas are not taught until about midyear in most algebra classes. Second, because any three-variable equation has three possible arrangements, I was requiring my students to memorize three separate equations without ever learning the relevant algebraic techniques. (I also looked in my college notebooks and saw that I had had many professors who also attempted to teach each variation when they introduced a new formula.) Thirdly, during the first half of the year, my science students were being

FIGURE 7. Matt Tardino's Algebra stack, Example #2: (a) Card 12, (b) Card 14, (c) Card 18, and (d) Card 19.

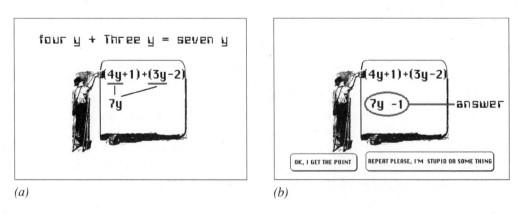

FIGURE 8. Matt Tardino's Algebra stack, Example #3: (a) Card 8 and (b) Card 12.

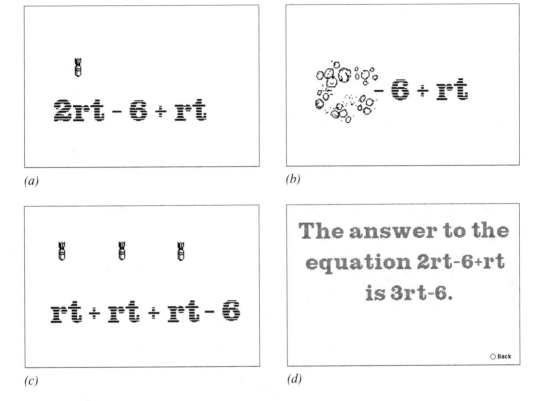

FIGURE 9. Jason Wren's Algebra stack: (a) Card 3, (b) Card 8, (c) Card 25, and (d) Card 35.

introduced to about 40 formulas, each of which contained three variables—so I was requiring them to memorize 120 different formulas.

Paula told me that she never really understood why all the science teachers were always complaining about students who didn't understand math. Through team teaching, we were able to solve this problem by rearranging the curriculum in both algebra and science so that our students were able to understand and use all those formulas in their science classes. (By the way, they also did better in algebra.) HyperCard was the ideal tool to teach this concept to "math" students because it allowed our students to create animated presentations that required step-by-step thinking.

In creating these algebra animations, our students were required to show each step of the process. In a sense, we caused them to slow down the thinking process so that each and

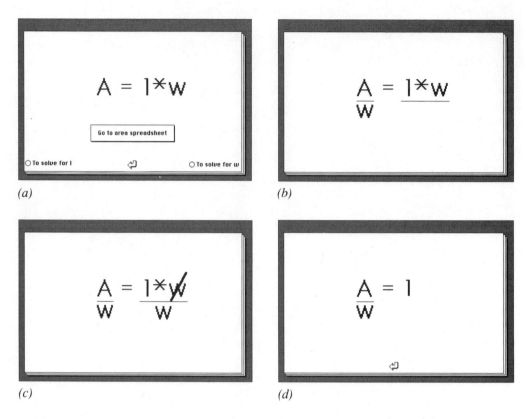

FIGURE 10. Area stack: (a) Card 1, (b) Card 8, (c) Card 11, and (d) Card 14.

every detail was thought out completely. In other words, the complete algebraic process had to be understood to create each stack. Team teaching again helped this process tremendously. Paula came up with the idea for the math project, based on what she had observed students doing with HyperCard in their science class. I was then able to teach them a little more about HyperCard. In the process, while we reinforced their algebra skills and the HyperCard techniques, we also improved their work in science: Not only were they able to understand and use those "hard" science formulas after they completed this assignment, but they also had learned some problem-solving skills that would be put to use in their next project.

As our students became more proficient with HyperCard, we also saw that HyperCard began finding its way into their other classes. In the English–life-skills class, a unit on the family contains a project that requires students to create a family tree. One of our students, Viengsack Koulapdara, created a stack for her family tree. (See Figure 11.)

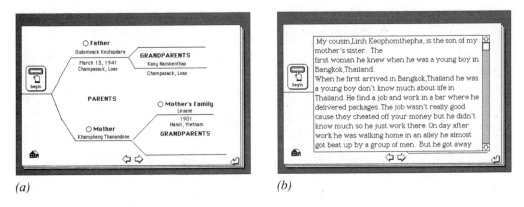

(a)   *(b)*

FIGURE 11. Viengsack Koulapdara's Tree stack: (a) Card 2 and (b) Card 3.

When her stack opens, you see a picture that she created for an earlier assignment using the MacVision–MacPaint software. (Richard and Sheila introduce our ninth-graders to MacPaint as one of their first Macintosh computer programs, so the students come to HyperCard with a pretty good understanding of MacPaint.) If you click on her picture, a text field appears, which describes Viengsack. When you click on the Right arrow button, you are taken to a card that shows Viengsack's family tree. By clicking on one of her parents' names, you get yet another pop-up text field to tell you about that parent. The text was imported from a MacWrite assignment that had been done earlier as an English assignment.

For a unit on the Middle Ages, Jason Martin, another ninth-grader, created a 7-card stack. (See Figure 12 on the following page.) On the first card, he introduces the unit. On the second card, he shows the basic layout of a medieval castle. When you click on various parts of the castle, a pop-up text field appears that describes that part. By clicking on the doorway to the central structure, you are taken into the castle. If you click on any object in the main hall, more pop-up text fields appear. When you click on the door to the courtyard, you are again shown the exterior view of the castle. The door to the armory takes you to a card showing a medieval horseman. Again, when you click on a piece of armor, up pops a text field that gives the name of that piece. Jason has also included a Show Definitions button to take you to a card containing the various descriptions and uses for each piece of armor.

In a biology class, students used HyperCard to create a stack that explains the lytic cycle of a bacteriophage. (See Figure 13 on page 239.) On the first card, you can learn the names of the various parts of a bacteriophage and their functions. On the second card, an animated sequence begins that shows a bacteriophage as it attaches to a bacteria and

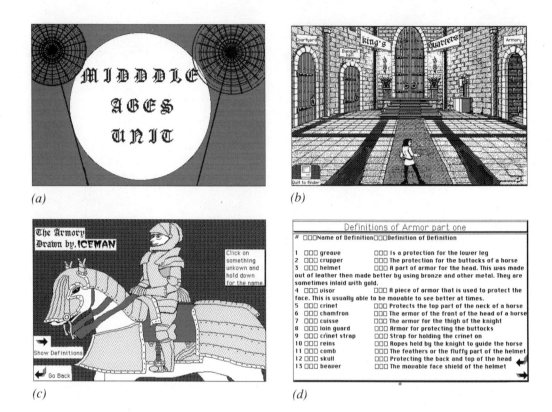

FIGURE 12. Jason Martin's Middle Ages stack: (a) Card 1, (b) Card 2, (c) Card 3, and (d) Card 5. [The image in (b) and other images in the stack are from Dark Castle, copyright © 1987 by Three-Sixty, Inc., Campbell, California.]

reproduces. Our biology book describes this process, but when my students created this animation, the process came to life for them. This is but one of many examples of how a perfectly timed animation sequence done in HyperCard has greatly enhanced my students' understanding of many biology concepts.

Another biology-class use of HyperCard was for the students to create "teaching" units. The students were divided into groups of two, and each group was assigned a particular chapter from the biology book. For this assignment, each chapter covered a phylum of the animal kingdom. As each group created a stack about their specific phylum, they all learned something about taxonomy systems used in biology. The students were told that their projects would be shared with the entire class and that they would present it when their chapter was being covered. The groups were given three weeks to create their "teaching" stacks.

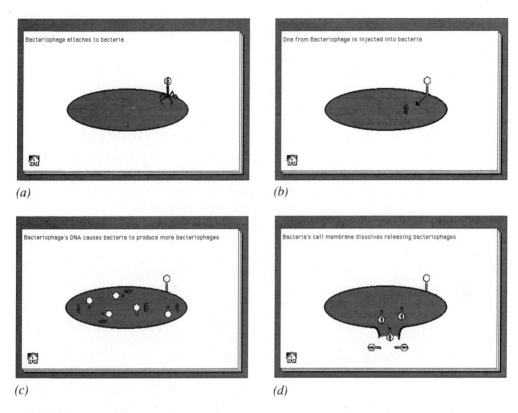

FIGURE 13. Virus stack: (a) Card 3, (b) Card 4, (c) Card 5, and (d) Card 7.

During the same time period, Bob Howard was enhancing students' HyperCard skills during his computer-applications class. They learned more about creating buttons and text fields. They learned how to import material both from databases and from word-processing files. They learned more about stack design. Bob also taught them how to control a laser video player so that real photos and movies could be added to their projects. Again, the "double effect" of team teaching combined to produce some outstanding projects. As an additional incentive, the students were told that the group with the best stack would get a day away from school to present their project at a special HyperCard gathering being sponsored by Apple Computer, involving teachers from three other area high schools, and, of course, Apple would be buying lunch.

When the judgment day finally rolled around, 15 fantastic projects had been produced. The students in each group had become the class experts on their particular chapter. For 90 minutes, my students showed their projects to the judges: the other ACOT teachers, researchers from Ohio State University, support personnel from our central administrative offices, and representatives from Apple Computer. It was very difficult to pick just one winner, so we decided to settle for the two best.

What had really been accomplished? Each group of two had learned how to assemble a unit that would be used to teach others about a given phylum. Each group had gone through the same process of evaluating material to be presented and then organizing the material so that it exhibited a logical sequence for learning that particular chapter. Each group had, in a sense, become an expert on a specific phylum of the animal kingdom. It was interesting to see the two students from each group take charge of the class when their particular unit was being presented. For example, when I had the students do a dissection lab on the earthworm, Rolanda Warren, who had done the worm chapter (see Figure 14), took over the lab and taught her fellow students all about the various organs found inside an earthworm.

By creating a "teaching" stack and eventually teaching a chapter, the students gained both a lot of self-confidence and the respect of the other students because of what they had done: They were in charge of and responsible for what they were learning. They had done it all by themselves, and now they knew they could do it again—to learn about anything they wanted to learn. I had a unique opportunity to go to Apple Fest® in Boston and take five of my biology students with me. While in Boston, we went to the New England Aquarium and the students proceeded to teach me about the various coelenterates, arthropods, and ostiechthyes that were housed at the aquarium. These were chapters that we were going to cover when we got back to school. By putting my students in charge of their biology class, they probably learned more biology than if I had been in charge.

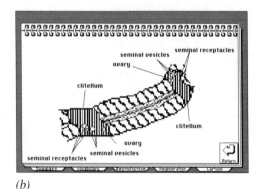

(a)   *(b)*

FIGURE 14. *Rolanda Warren's Worm stack: (a) summary of important facts and (b) reproduction in earthworms.*

The pictures in Figure 15 on the following page are from a stack that Lewis Austin created for the chapter on amphibians. The information included does a good job of covering the chapter from the book; the users can learn most of the important points they need to know about amphibians. However, the stack contains a minor error—in dealing with the process of reproduction in frogs. (Although the students who did this chapter did read the textbook, the textbook does not do a very good job explaining the entire reproductive process.) The students first show you a female frog laying eggs and then show you a male frog fertilizing the eggs—but this is incorrect. (See Figures 15a and 15b.) In reality, the male frog wraps his front legs around the female, clasping her abdomen, and then uses his large thumb pads to press down on the female. This process forces the eggs from the female's cloaca into the water, at which time the eggs are fertilized. The process of forcing the eggs from the female is called amplexus. With the aid of a laser videodisc, this process was clarified in a matter of seconds.

An excellent section in this stack shows a quick animation of the development of a frog inside a fertilized egg. (See Figures 15c and 15d.) When the student's version is compared to actual laser video photography of the development of a fertilized frog egg, you can see that the student fully understood the developmental processes—from fertilized egg through the actual hatching of a tadpole and then on to the metamorphosis into an adult frog. This demonstrates that students can learn and understand many concepts if given the chance to explore the topic on their own.

By doing, instead of listening, the student took responsibility for what was learned. This is active learning compared to the "normal," passive type of learning that goes on in many classrooms—learning controlled by the student, not the teacher. Remember, the teacher is not the only source of knowledge in a classroom. The teacher's job is to teach the students how to learn, encourage them to investigate different ideas, and then get out of their way by putting the responsibility for learning into their hands. When learning involves the students actively, they will better understand the lesson and retain its content.

The use of laser videodiscs (such as those being distributed by Optical Data Corp. and Videodiscovery, Inc.) has greatly added to my students' knowledge of biology. Using HyperCard as a video controller, students can easily add video-quality pictures to their units or presentations. As the class started to assemble all their stacks into one "package," they added pictures from various laser videodiscs. For example, in the World of ACOT Biology (see Figure 16a on page 243), when you click on the Tree button (branches of life), you are taken to a card showing an example of the five kingdoms studied in our biology text. By clicking on the amoeba (see Figure 16b), you enter the

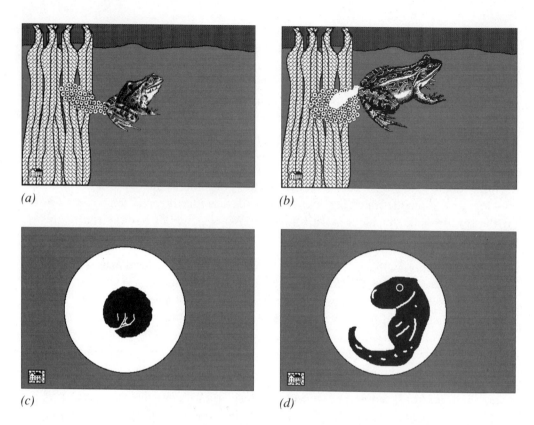

(a)   *(b)*

(c)   *(d)*

FIGURE 15. *Lewis Austin's Amphibian stack: (a) Card 22, showing female frog laying eggs, (b) Card 27, showing male frog fertilizing eggs, (c) early developmental stage of frog inside a fertilized egg, and (d) slightly later developmental stage of frog inside a fertilized egg.*

kingdom called Protista. There you will be able to study the various one-celled protozoans and algae that can be found in freshwater. As you click on any particular example (see Figure 16c), the laser video player will show you an excellent color "slide" or movie about that particular organism. You will also get a pop-up text field to show you more information about that particular member of the kingdom Protista.

The students also thought up a navigational system for this stack that is clearly unique. A picture is always in the bottom left side of the card. Behind this picture is a button that will take you back to the previous card. The picture is always of the previous card, so the path back to the starting point is always clear to the user.

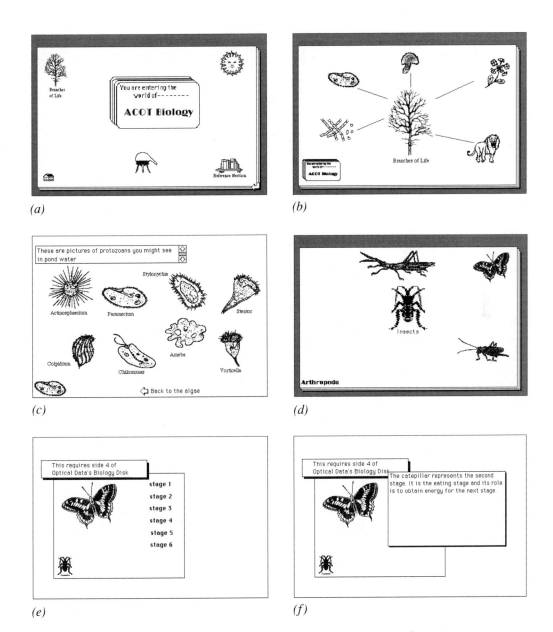

(a)

(b)

(c)

(d)

(e)

(f)

FIGURE 16. *Biology stack: (a) Card 1, opening card of World of ACOT Biology, (b) Card 2, showing a tree and the branches of life, (c) Card 19, showing the kingdom Protista and a pop-up text field, (d) Card 6, the first* Insects *card, (e) Card 21, the first card in a sequence showing the metamorphosis of the monarch butterfly, (f) Card 21, this time with a pop-up text field, (g) Card 7, the first* Vertebrates *card, and (h) Card 8, a listing of movies that show vertebrate behavior. (continued on the following page)*

continued

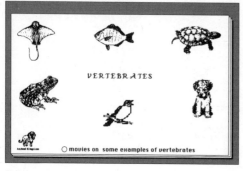

(g)

Various movies of vertebrates on side 4 of Optical Data's Biology Disk
○ Manta Ray
○ Shark agonistic behavior
○ Puffer fish
○ Komodo dragon lizard
○ Crocodile maternal care
○ Newts mating
○ Hummingbird
○ Ptarmigan
○ Ostrich and young
○ Kangaroo
○ Bat grooming and flight
○ Humpback whale sounds
○ Humpback whale maternal behavior
○ Narwhal
○ Porpoise swimming ability   ○ to vertebrate card

(h)

From the Branches of Life card (Figure 16b), if you go in the direction of the Animal kingdom by clicking on the picture of the lion in Figure 16b, you can explore all the various phyla. A section on Insects (see Figure 16d) will show the stages of development (metamorphosis) in the monarch butterfly, beginning with the card shown in Figure 16e. Each stage has a laser video picture or short movie that complements the text contained within pop-up fields on each card. If you choose to look at Vertebrates, a certain card will show you examples of the six major classes of vertebrates (see Figure 16g), followed by a card listing movies that show a particular type of vertebrate behavior (see Figure 16h). With these stacks linked together to form a complete package and tied to a laser video player, each student has instant access to a great deal of information. Also, with this technology in the classroom at all times, students can always "re-view" at any time material covered during class. Students who are absent the day the class covers a particular lesson can go to the HyperCard–laser video workstation and make up what they missed. Also, unlike the movies, which teachers check out from the local library, students can look at the material over and over again, and, more importantly, the students control the pace of the lesson. (Again, the students control the learning, not the teacher.)

Three of my students, Jason Martin, Jason Wren, and Boonluan Thanasack, were able to complete a class project on the insect collection much earlier than the rest of the class. These three students had nothing to do while others in the class were still working on their insect projects. This could have been a real problem. Instead of allowing them to remain idle while their classmates finished their projects, I convinced these three students to "finish" my HyperCard stack based on *Peterson's Field Guide to Insects*. I was going to speak at the National Science Teachers Association convention in two weeks and was preparing something new to demonstrate.

These students used an optic scanner to "scan in" the pictures that they would need to put on the various cards. They had to link the various conditions from Peterson's dichotomous insect key. They also had to tie the key to a laser videodisc and have the project completed two days prior to my talk. (See Figure 17 for a few examples.) They worked on it each class period while their classmates worked to complete the original assignment. They also came back during lunchtime every day to work on this project. They even came in for many hours after school, almost every day. All this work for just a few extra points on their insect projects.

They were required to select for the video examples only insects that could be found in Ohio. Frequently, they referred to the insect collections being prepared by their classmates to see if a particular insect had been found. They used over 130 examples in their

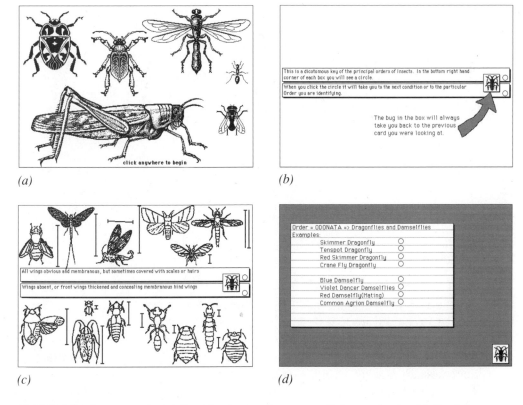

FIGURE 17. Insect stack: (a) Card 1, showing insects to click on to begin, (b) Card 4, providing instructions, (c) Card 5, describing wings, and (d) Card 47, listing dragonflies and damselflies.

stack to provide viewers with an excellent color photograph of a particular insect as they attempted to go through the key. The "little bug in a box" on the cards is the navigational tool that always allows users to back up if an incorrect path has been taken. Also, behind some of the key terms in the description of each condition is a hidden button that will show users a picture to better understand what they should be seeing when they make that choice.

This is an excellent example of "extra" learning that can go on in the classroom when students are given the chance. I would estimate that these students probably spent more time on this "extra" assignment than they did on the original one. They had to decide which pictures were best to use and how best to design the stack for others to use. The result is a wonderful presentation that can be used by their classmates at any time.

By being able to claim "ownership" of this project, these three students achieved both a sense of accomplishment and pride. They gained a little more knowledge about Hyper-Card and videodiscs than the rest of the class. Who do you think will help me teach this material to the rest of the class at some time in the future? This was a pretty sneaky way to add three teachers to my classroom and reduce my student–teacher ratio from 30 to 1 to about 8 to 1. (When all the students learn how to use the laser video player to add to their presentations, I am going to need more laser video players.)

HyperCard has been a great tool to give to students for the purposes of creating their own style of presentations. (See Figure 18.) However, HyperCard also has uses that make my job easier and that make the teaching of important concepts many times better. This year I am trying a HyperCard-based electronic notebook in my science classes. I designed a Notebook stack for each class. My hopes are that my students will be able to retrieve important information at any time during the year. In the past, it seems that pages have had a tendency to walk away from the notebook about six weeks after we have covered a particular subject. This made it very difficult to go back to some point that had been made earlier in the year.

I have found that there are natural links between many ideas in the biology course, but I have not had a good way to show these links to my students. I have tried "concept" maps, but these take a tremendous amount of time and, at best, are often difficult to use. But with HyperCard, my students can use the Find function of HyperCard and retrieve their prior notes very quickly when I want to discuss them again to reinforce another concept. The natural links contained in all subject matter can easily be shown using HyperCard.

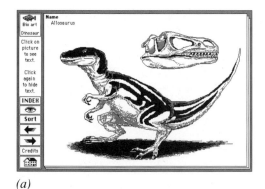

(a)   *(b)*

FIGURE 18. (a) An example from a 16-stack clip-art collection used by students. (b) Pop-up text field makes the art "educational."

Using my Notebook stack for biology as an example (see Figure 19a on the following page), you see what appears to be a graphic of a spiral-bound notebook. When the student clicks anywhere on the text section under Class Notes, that text field is unlocked and zooms open to cover the full screen. (See Figure 19b.) At this point, my students can use this field to take notes in the same manner that they have been doing with MacWrite (or with other word-processing software). My students type faster than they write, so most of them prefer to take notes using their computer. When they are finished, they simply click on the Click Here To Lock button at the top of the screen, and the text shrinks back to the normal size of a "notebook" page as shown in the original illustration.

If the students add illustrations to their notes, a message is placed in the text field (see Figure 19c) under the Illustrations section telling them that they created an illustration (or illustrations) to go along with the notes. These can easily be added using the Mac-Paint tools already in HyperCard, or I can give them a MacPaint graphic to import. I also, at times, give them my own copy of the notebook (as I did during the discussion of organic chemistry), which upgrades their notes and allows me to give them a prepro-duced animation such as the one I use to show chemical reactions.

This notebook was a way for me to show them various chemical reactions in a manner that brought them to life. (I could remember what it was like to take notes in a class as a professor went through the steps of a particular process and then, when I got home, to try to make sense of my notes.) In the illustration pages on organic chemistry, there are tex-tual descriptions which have hidden scripts that actually show how the reaction takes place. For example, in the illustration on 11/4/88 showing the hydrolysis of a polysac-chride (see Figures 19e–19g), when the student moves the hand (browse tool) into the

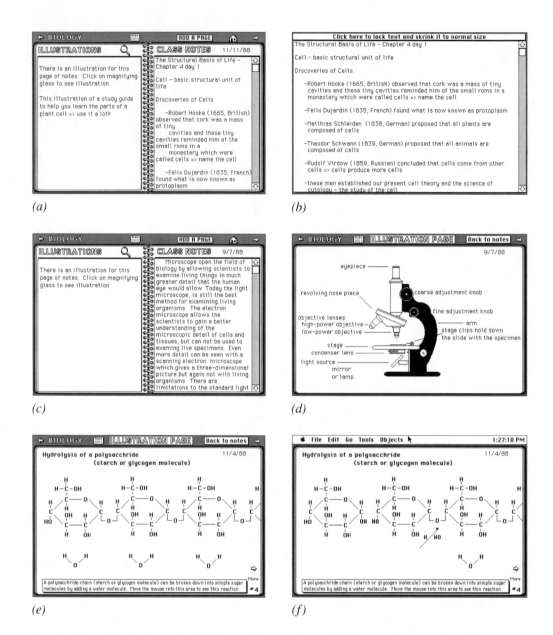

FIGURE 19. Notebook stack: (a) "normal" page view, (b) "zoomed" page view, (c) page whose text indicates a "hidden" illustration, (d) page containing illustration, (e) hydrolysis view 1, (f) hydrolysis view 7, (g) hydrolysis view 9, (h) view of a saturated fat molecule, and (i) a To Do card.

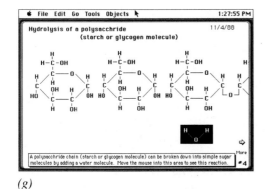

(g)

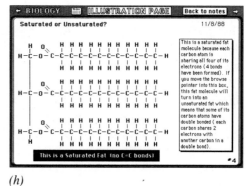

(h)

(i)

text box at the bottom of the card, a continuously running animation begins showing how water molecules enter the polysaccharide and break the oxygen bond between each glucose molecule. (This 10-step animation is done on only one card by simply hiding and showing buttons.) Finally, a notebook that can "redo" what the teacher did on the "chalkboard"! In my classroom, I use a projection panel on an overhead projector instead of drawing on the board. Now, every time I want to illustrate an important process, I can place it in their notebooks, and the animation will re-create my steps for them at home. This adds to their understanding of various processes. By giving my students a carefully animated process, I have enabled them to see the process happen, from start to finish.

They also have a one-page To Do card (see Figure 19i) that can be used to enter assignments, projects, test dates, and so on. They simply "select" the To Do(s) that they have done and type *delete* to remove them. I have also told them that they should never have more than one page because if they do, it means that they are too far behind.

I also have modified Apple's Date Book stack to create a version that keeps track of my Lesson Plans. (See Figure 20.) As in the students' notebook, I now can refind the material that I have already covered. I can also compare, year to year, to see if I am progressing through the course at the same pace. Another feature allows me to use HyperCard's Find function to retrieve in an instant notes about some lesson I did last year. I now use this feature instead of the old, paper version that I have used for years. It is better in several ways: First, I can read it (imagine how important this is to me). Second, my computer will now find things for me instead of my having to use the let-my-fingers-do-the-walking approach. Third, it will "grow" to accommodate additional pages year after year, which means all of my lesson plans are now going to be in *one* place.

(a)

(b)

(c)

FIGURE 20. *Lesson Plans stack: (a) six-month calendar card, (b) a weekly card with assignments, and (c) one day of a "zoomed" weekly card.*

I also use HyperCard to create a self-grading test. (See Figure 21.) My students now get immediate feedback on their tests, and I do not even have to grade them myself. I simply record their grades from a printed copy of their test. (Yes, we are working on an "electronic grade" book, into which each student's grade will be entered automatically and his or her overall grade will be recalculated while that student is taking the test. Bob Howard has worked out a way to do this after the students are finished taking their tests, but it still takes about 10 minutes for the computer to recalculate their grades. Hopefully, Bob will get this minor problem solved so that we do not have to wait so long.) I am able to put in sounds to reward the students who get As, and everybody in class instantly knows who got the high grade. I can also have students watch a short animation and ask them questions about it. My students can retake the test to improve their grades. If they click the Retake button, the test automatically erases their previous answers before they

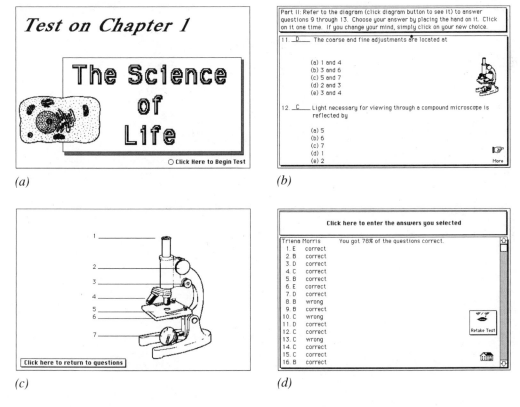

(a)   *(b)*

(c)   *(d)*

FIGURE 21. Test stack: (a) introduction card, (b) notice button for pop-up illustrations, (c) popped-up illustration, and (d) last card with graded results.

begin again. I have found that the students will keep working on the test for the entire class period—trying to get a perfect score. The test has now become a challenge that is fun, in much the same way as all those video games the students enjoy. The text also has become a learning tool because the students keep working to get the right answer.

Another teaching tool is the tutorial-type application that can be created. In chemistry, students can do a prelab-type application to learn about acid–base titrations. (See Figure 22.) In the Titrations stack, the students are again shown a simple animation that explains what a titration is and how to tell when the endpoint of that titration is reached. It gives them the needed background information to do the lab along with the actual procedures. It shows them a data table and how to do various related calculations. And finally, it asks them several questions, which they should be able to answer, and then

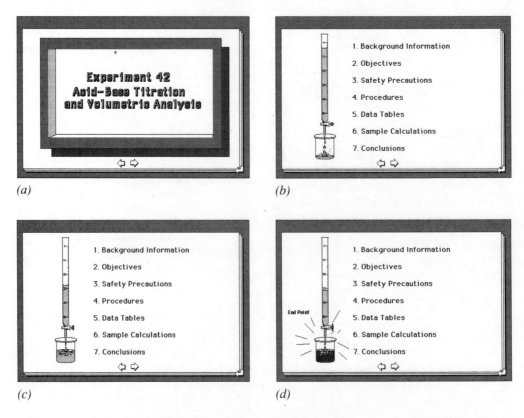

FIGURE 22. Titration stack: (a) introduction card, (b) Card 8 in animation, (c) Card 14 in animation, (d) Card 22 in animation, (e) safety card, (f) procedures card, (g) data card, (h) calculations card, (i) question card, and (j) question card with answer.

Safety Precautions

1. Acids and Bases cause burns; avoid skin contact.
2. When filling the buret with base the funnel may fill up with liquid causing the buret to overflow.
3. Assume that any liquid spilled on the lab table to be either acid or base, and clean up immediately
4. If acid or base is spilled on your skin, flush with water and then inform instructor.
5. WEAR GOGGLES AND APRONS

return to menu

(e)

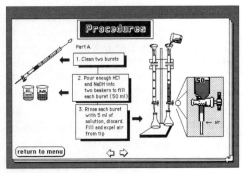

Procedures

Part A.

1. Clean two burets
2. Pour enough HCl and NaOH into two beakers to fill each buret (50 ml)
3. Rinse each buret with 5 ml of solution, discard. Fill and expel air from tip

return to menu

(f)

Data Tables $HCl_{(aq)} + NaOH_{(aq)} \longrightarrow NaCl_{(aq)} + H_2O$

PART A.

PROCEDURES		TRIAL 1		TRIAL 2
1. Final Acid Volume		77	mL	45.6 ml
2. Initial Acid Volume		56	mL	23.2 ml
3. Volume of Acid used	○	21	mL	22.4 ml
4. Final Base Volume			mL	34.7 ml
5. Initial Base Volume			mL	0.0 ml
6. Volume of Base used	○		mL	34.7 ml
7. Molarity of Acid			mol/L	.2 ml
8. Calculate Base Molarity	○		mol/L	0.13 ml

return to menu   clear data table

(g)

Sample Calculations

Item #3: Volume of Acid used

Final Vol. of Acid – Initial Vol. of Acid. = Volume of acid used

Item #6: Volume of Base used

Final Vol. of Base – Initial Vol. of Base = Volume of base used

Item #8: Molarity of Base

Molarity Base × Vol Base = Molarity Acid × Vol Acid
Mb × Vb = Ma × Va

$$Mb = \frac{Ma \times Va}{Vb}$$

return to menu

(h)

Conclusions

1. Describe the apparent relationship between H_3O^+ and OH^- concentrations when an end point is reached in an acid-base titration. (answer)
2. The indicated end-point of an acid-base titration seldom occurs at a pH of 7. What determines the pH of the end point? Explain (answer)
3. The amount of water added to dissolve the solid acid in Part B could have been 35 ml or 45 ml and would have given the same results as with 40 ml. Explain. (answer)
4. The unknown acid in Part B was assumed to be monoprotic. What adjustments would have to be made in your calculations if the acid was known to be diprotic? What would the molecular mass have been (answer)

return to menu

(i)

Conclusions Answers   return

2. The indicated end-point of an acid-base titration seldom occurs at a pH of 7. What determines the pH of the end point? Explain

ANSWER: The actual pH of the end-point in an acid-base titration is determined by the indicator used. For example, the phenolphthalein used in this experiment changes to pink in an excess of the OH ions but this excess does not occur until pH = 8.2. Indicators can be selected for any pH range.

return to menu

(j)

gives them the correct responses. This is not only useful for the teacher while the lab is being discussed, but it is also useful for those students who were absent but need to know about the lab experiment which has been "put away."

In biology, the students can learn about the various parts in both plant and animal cells by using the Cell stack (see Figure 23), designed for drill-and-practice-type work. In this stack, students are asked at the start, "How many organelles do you wish to identify correctly?" This presets a number into the stack script. When this number is reached, the student may quit this activity. The stack randomly picks out organelles for the student to identify by moving the Hand Pointer button to different organelles. Students get two tries at answering correctly before the stack tells them the correct response—thereby teaching the correct identification and the correct spelling of the organelle's name. With slight modification, this stack can then become the actual identification quiz. Students practice using a stack that functions exactly like the quiz that they will take eventually.

I have discussed many ways that we use HyperCard in ACOT. I find it to be an excellent tool for teaching and one that has and will continue to change drastically the ways in which students learn. It can easily be used by the students in a presentation-type manner as well as by the teacher to create learning tools. HyperCard is one of the most universal tools I have for my classroom; however, I did have to spend numerous hours learning how to get HyperCard to work for me.

The operative phrase is "work for me"—because HyperCard has changed the ways I present material to students. It has improved the manner of idea presentation so that my students can better understand and comprehend various concepts. It also has given my students the ability to organize and present ideas in a manner that makes sense to them.

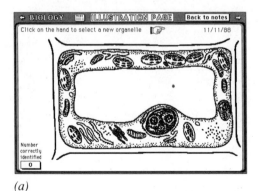
(a)

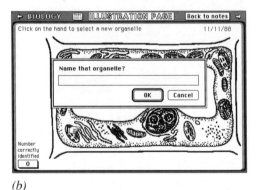
(b)

FIGURE 23. Cell stack: (a) Card 1, view 1, and (b) Card 1, view 4.

And when students actually use an idea or concept in their projects, those ideas and concepts will belong to those students forever.

HyperCard does require a lot of work on the part of its users. Users must learn to think in a logical and sequential manner, often outlining their ideas prior to beginning work. They must learn some of the HyperCard scripting language, and they must learn to solve problems. In science, I can say that they actually use the scientific method to solve these problems. When things don't work as expected and the user must look at the "small" details, HyperCard presents the challenge to do it right. Although HyperTalk is easier to understand than conventional programming languages, it is no less demanding in its logical sequence style.

HyperCard is a tool that empowers the students to find better ways to do various activities. I find that my students have become more organized because of various applications that have been created using a tool that allows them to "do it their way" each and every time. (I, too, have become more organized using HyperCard.) My students are also more eager to "go beyond" the assignment, to investigate further an idea or concept. They are now showing me better ways to do particular assignments, and they are often challenging me to "teach" in a better way. I am now in a classroom that comprises a "community of learners," in which "good enough is no longer good enough." And we have just begun to see the possibilities of what is to come.

HyperCard:
A New Deal
in the Classroom

Robert Campbell and Patricia Hanlon

ROBERT CAMPBELL

Robert Campbell was librarian at Lowell High School, San Francisco. He retired recently after 36 years in California schools, 4 of them as an English teacher, 5 as a writer–researcher of educational proposals, and 27 as a school librarian.

PATRICIA HANLON

Patricia Hanlon is an English teacher at Lowell High School, San Francisco. She has also taught in junior high school. She is a fellow and member of the advisory council of the Bay Area Writing Project.

As a high school teacher, I didn't have to define HyperCard before I could use it.* Some people haven't used it, or haven't used it for anything very interesting, because they haven't been able to define it. (Is it a database? A graphics program with incidental word capabilities? A word processor with bells and whistles?) Before I ever heard of Hyper-Card, I had already identified some items that I needed and wished for in the classroom and that technology might someday provide, so when HyperCard came along and I saw that it fulfilled many of these wishes, that was all the definition I needed.

The school librarian and I had already started a project, first with just stuff we were collecting about John Steinbeck, *The Grapes of Wrath,* and the 1930s. To put it simply, we wanted to store information that we found (including text, graphics, motion, music, sound interviews, and the like), organize and save it, find links between the data and save them, and use it all for teaching. We did not formulate what we wanted very precisely at first—"library in a box" was our code name for it—but the *functionality* we were after included the characteristics of a database, a research instrument, a word processor and editor, a painting program, and an audiovisual appliance. And we wanted these powers for our students as well as for ourselves.

Eventually, we found ourselves using HyperCard with the Macintosh Plus and a video-disc player to build a design example we called Grapevine. Terms like "hypermedia" and "interactive multimedia" came into use, and the struggle to define them began, and continues. For us, by this time, the definitions were superfluous—except that every time we were asked what we were doing, it wasn't possible to answer on the spot by demonstrating Grapevine!

You can avoid some confusion if you do not call a computer or a computer program, like HyperCard, a *tool.* A computer is better compared with a *motor,* which can be used to drive tools or whole workshops. And just as a food processor is not properly a single tool but a set of tools to carry out related tasks (blending, chopping, shredding, grating, and so forth), a word-processing program, driven by a computer, is also a *set* of tools to perform operations. In this sense, HyperCard is also a processor—a set of tools.

What is it that HyperCard processes? Information, of course. And, you might ask, which processes does HyperCard perform on information? Why, it stores, retrieves, organizes, links, finds, displays, arranges, decorates, and formats information. And "information" here means just that, but in any form you can imagine, except possibly intuition: words, numbers, symbols, still and moving pictures, maps and charts, music, sound effects,

---

* Although this essay is coauthored, its point of view (first person singular "I") is that of the teacher (Patricia Hanlon). When "we" is used, it refers to the teacher *and* the librarian (Robert Campbell).

human speech. All this relates very closely to teaching and learning because *processing information* is a large part (but not all) of teaching and learning. If processing information in these limited ways were all there is to teaching, then a computer with HyperCard would be a "teaching machine." Because there is a great deal more to learning than processing information, such as critical thinking, for example, or because a higher level of processing is required, HyperCard with a computer (and with a videodisc player if possible) is simply a very useful kit of tools for one key aspect of teaching and learning.

Now that we have, at last, a definition of HyperCard, let us descend rapidly, as on an express elevator, from these upper floors of abstraction to the bargain basement of public education, the classroom, and see some of the practical applications of this technology that a classroom teacher might make, given the equipment.

The equipment lent to me by Apple Computer beginning with the spring semester of the 1988–89 school year allowed me to begin testing its use for simple class presentations and student browsing. In other respects the classroom is a typical one with no special features. I share it with other teachers. You, too, would need the following equipment:

Apple Macintosh Plus or SE
Hard-disk drive
Pioneer LaserVision Player LD-V4200 with cable to the Macintosh
Monitor with cables to the videodisc player
Speaker with cable for the sound from the Macintosh
Kodak DataShow with cable to the Macintosh (for projecting the computer screen)
Overhead projector
Stand or cart for overhead projector
Screen for the overhead projector
VCR with cables to the monitor
Table or cart for the computer equipment
Cassette tape recorder

I also had access to the following devices in other locations:

Printer
Apple Scanner
MacVision video digitizer
MacRecorder sound digitizer

In addition to the equipment I had Grapevine, our HyperCard program, installed on a hard disk; a large file of digitized Grapevine sounds on hard disk; and our 12-inch videodisc with about 1000 still images and about 10 minutes of motion. The motion segments on the videodisc included some with a sound track.

All of the above made it possible to do "information processing" in a great variety of ways—more ways, in fact, than my students and I attempted in that single semester. I will make some observations on the processes that we were able to practice and mention later those we might go on to in the future.

By using this equipment we had a way to save the results of student research, write comments on the research, write and save class notes, and edit and update these notes. I could print them out and distribute them. I could and did create lessons illustrated or cued with *cards* (screens) in HyperCard, and I often made running class notes on the computer. (Note: A group of cards is called a *stack*.) The semester objectives for the students did not run the gamut of computer-related skills to the more advanced ones, such as painting, scanning, digitizing, or scripting in HyperTalk. We concentrated on the essentials of browsing in Grapevine, using keywords, existing buttons, and the Find command to locate information; looking at its graphics; listening to its interviews and folk songs; dipping into its bibliography and biographical information; investigating the built-in links; and following existing stories and creating new ones. We could do this for small groups or project the computer screen for the whole class. We mainly concentrated on one means—the keyboard—of putting information into the computer and keeping notes. Students also brought in tapes of music they wanted to use and books with images they wanted scanned as well as video tapes they had made with a borrowed camcorder.

If your classroom, like mine, contains even one computer, your students need some basic computer skills if they are to benefit from some hands-on use of it. You might have students who are computer enthusiasts and owners, and you are sure to have some who are not. If you have any students who know the Macintosh or HyperCard, you are fortunate, because you can put such students to work teaching others. I had no students with these skills during the semester I am describing. The two classes with which I used HyperCard and Grapevine were excellent, one a sophomore English honors class and the other a junior class in U.S. history.

Even if you do have more than one computer available (and if you are not teaching a class in computing), you probably do not want to spend any more time than necessary equipping your students with the skills they must have to work with multimedia. Just what are these skills and how can you help students develop them? Because students will usually be working together, not every student will need all the skills of a proficient user. Depending on time, the teacher or a trained student or aide can help, but the more that students are able to do on their own without worrying about the hardware and the technology, the more creative and flexible they will become.

Within the context of your regular classes, you can find several ways of teaching the students some of what they will need to know. Students need to use the keyboard and mouse. They will have to turn the computer on and shut it down properly; handle disks; and open, save, and close files. They can easily learn how to set up and put away the equipment simply by helping the teacher or a trained aide.

If your school has a computer lab, you might be able to take advantage of it to teach an entire class some of the basics of computers. Surprisingly, even today many students are not comfortable with computers; many others have not had personal use of a computer.

I was somewhat surprised to discover that even though fewer students than I had expected have had much hands-on experience with a computer, students take for granted the *idea* of using a computer in class. Some of the students were at first suspicious of the computer in the classroom. They had experienced dull drill-and-practice programs in school before. The few computer enthusiasts tended to be interested in hardware rather than programs. Before long, though, both the enthusiasts and those students who previously had any sort of negative attitude toward computers were eager to use Grapevine. They were able to focus on the substance of what we were doing and to use HyperCard and Grapevine to help them find the information that they needed to better understand the 1930s. They were excited when the computer helped them to make discoveries or to locate materials and connections that they would otherwise have missed or would have spent a long time searching for. Another pleasant surprise for me was that they quickly began to *expect* the computer to accomplish these things.

The One-Computer Classroom

In a classroom with only one computer, the computer will be in constant demand, so you will want to find ways to schedule its constant use. Individual students or students working in groups will want access to it for study and research, for preparing papers or presentations, and for giving presentations. The teacher will use it for preparing and presenting assignments; keeping, showing, and updating class notes; and for making presentations. If the computer is available before or after class, students will sign up to use it whenever they can. You are lucky if your school allows some flexibility in the students' schedules. In the remainder of this chapter I will touch on these topics: the physical setup; using HyperCard; preparing assignments; tips on making stacks and cards; the teacher's presentations; keeping class notes; teaching HyperCard conventions; time management; students' projects and research; and a wish list.

The Physical Setup

Assuming that yours is an ordinary classroom like mine, you will have to give a good deal of attention to such matters as lighting, seating, equipment storage, and the best arrangement of the equipment for various purposes. To use a computer with HyperCard in a classroom requires dealing with several pieces of equipment and the connections between them; if you include multimedia presentations, several more pieces of equipment are needed, and the connections are numerous and (at first) complicated. (Someday soon all this paraphernalia might be neatly, conveniently, and—one hopes—economically packaged. At the moment, none of those adverbs apply.)

Two presumed attributes of an ordinary classroom are that it has electrical outlets and that it can be made relatively dark. Still, it is best to avoid blithe assumptions. You might have to scrounge for extensions to deliver electricity where it is needed or shades to dim unwanted sunlight. You will need a five-switch outlet or a power strip, preferably with a surge protector.

You will want to achieve the same degree of dimness, or sometimes a little less, that you need for comfortable viewing of a television screen. You neither need nor want total darkness, for making a presentation with projectors and/or monitors usually means that these devices assist but do not upstage the star of the show, the presenter. Ideally, the room light is dim enough to allow a clear, colorful image but bright enough to allow the presenter and audience to interact with each other. Students also need enough light to continue taking notes or to write in response to the material.

If you are imagining that you have the equipment I describe, please also imagine that you find a lockable closet in the room or a lockable cabinet, preferably on wheels. Security is one consideration; another is the need to get the gear out of the way on occasion, especially if, as I did, you share a room with other teachers. This usually meant a minimum of two setups and two put-aways every day. With careful planning, practice, and some helpful students regularly assigned, you will do more than cope, you will manage well. (An advance hint of the conclusion: it's worth all the trouble).

Strange as it might at first seem, but for a lot of reasons, I did not set the computer up at the front of the classroom. I set up the equipment in a corner near the back of my room where the TV is kept and where we usually gather to watch video tapes. It is an area already established as being out of the normal traffic pattern, yet students are used to working in groups of various sizes back there.

If you decide to put the computer at the front of the room, realize that it becomes the dramatic center of the class. Individuals and small groups of students will feel self-conscious working on it. You want to give students a chance to explore, to try new ideas, and, especially, to make mistakes. You want to help students quietly while monitoring the class. This is all much easier to accomplish if the students and the equipment are not the center of attention at the front of the room.

You will have cords and cables to contend with. Do not think that warning students not to trip over cables will prevent them from tripping over cables. Instead, put the computer and the equipment away from the established traffic flow. If you can leave your setup semipermanently in place, you can improvise with gaffers' tape and sections of conduit that look like your door threshold (available at an electronics store). The conduit can be walked on and the cables run through it.

For the Macintosh you need a fairly large table or cart. On the table you can place the computer, hard disk, and speaker for the videodisc player. If you have room on this table, also include the videodisc player with the monitor. Because the cables from the Macintosh control these pieces of equipment, they all have to be fairly close to the computer.

The overhead projector with the DataShow or output for the Macintosh screen can be on a separate cart, but again, close enough to the computer to connect the computer by cable to the DataShow.

When the audience is reading from a screen during a presentation, the situation is far different from a single user or small group reading from a screen in a browsing mode. To ensure that everyone in the larger group gets the information from the screen, various students who are sitting closest to the screen can take turns reading aloud. You probably want to encourage the students to sit in different seats each day and to move themselves or their desks as needed. Sometimes the students gather around the computer, some of them sitting on the floor; others move their desks up closer to the computer, depending on how well they can see and whether or not they are taking notes. Before you begin working, be sure all students are in a position to hear and see easily and to become involved.

Unassisted, the built-in speaker of the Mac can be heard by only a very small group. The best supplementary speaker for the computer is the kind that has its own power and volume controls. You will want to adjust the speaker position and set its volume both within the Macintosh's Control Panel and at the speaker itself to balance it with the sound coming out of the video monitor before you begin a presentation.

Does the Macintosh face the class? If it does, the class can see the screen, although most of them will not be able to see it well enough to read from it during a class presentation. It is true that with the screen facing them, the audience will be less distracted by the tangle of cables and cords at the back of the computer. It is also true that with the Macintosh screen facing the class, the teacher can watch the video monitor and see the Macintosh screen easily. However, the critical drawback in this setup is that the teacher's back is to the class.

The best solution for placing equipment seems to be to place the Macintosh sideways on the table. Although the side view is a bit awkward, the teacher can see the students, and talk to them—and she can still see the Macintosh screen and the video monitor at the same time. Try to arrange things so you can move easily to point to each screen, highlighting features you want the audience to notice particularly. Although the mouse on the Macintosh screen can be used for pointing, the cursor is sometimes too small to be seen well by a large audience. The teacher actually pointing to the larger screen is more effective. You can also model how this is conveniently done because you will want students to feel comfortable when pointing to the screens.

An extension cable for the keyboard and the mouse is helpful, because it lets you work up to about 15 feet away from the Macintosh itself and not be tied to any one area of the room. You can give the mouse or the keyboard to a student who can use them to point from her seat, choose from among options on the screen, type in her notes, or provide an answer for the entire class to see.

Putting HyperCard to Work for You

Don't make the mistake of thinking that you will have to become a computer programmer to put HyperCard to use. The choice you have is not between accepting someone else's HyperCard stack as is or becoming a hacker. You can accomplish a great deal without learning any of the HyperTalk scripting language, and you can do wonders with the very simplest scripts. I don't propose to give instructions in these techniques in this article, but here is a list of them—with and without scripting—that I recommend you teach yourself, using the built-in HyperCard Help stacks.

Without scripting:

Make a card.
Make a background.
Make a field and place it on the card or background.
    Choose a style and font for the field.

Type in a field.
Make a button and place it on the card or background.
   Choose a style for a button.
   Use the button to link the card to another card or stack.
Copy or cut and paste cards, buttons, and fields.
Draw on or paste graphics onto a card or background.
(That's all. You use the menu, so it's easier than it sounds.
   You should be able to learn all of the above in one or
   two short sessions.)

With *simple* scripting, write one-line or two-line scripts for cards, locked fields, or buttons that do the following:

Go to another card, with a specified visual effect.
Hide and show fields, pictures, and buttons.
Play sounds.

With slightly more advanced scripts:

Drag objects on the screen to simulate animation.
Play several sounds in sequence.

After you have succeeded with these operations in a short time, don't underestimate your ability to master the wealth of other functions that are available to you with scripting, if you are interested. *If you are not interested,* don't underestimate what you can do with only those skills listed above.

Preparing and Presenting Assignments

A good way to introduce computers and HyperCard is to present your assignments with them. I write up assignments on several cards in HyperCard and print out copies for the students (which I hold on to temporarily). Then I present and explain the assignment in class with the computer. Students begin to understand Macintosh and HyperCard conventions simply by watching me use them and by asking questions. After the lesson, I give the students their printed copies of the assignment for their reference and to reinforce the lesson. Figure 1 shows one screen from a sample assignment.

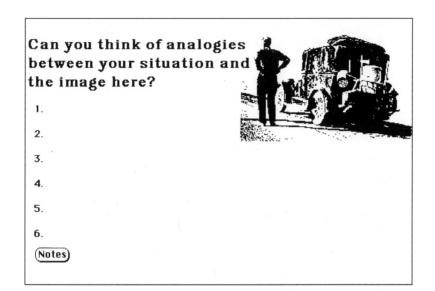

FIGURE 1. Screen from a sample assignment. [Photo: Dorothea Lange, Library of Congress.]

Some Thoughts on Designing Cards and Stacks

Whole books are available on this subject. These ideas and considerations arise from my day-to-day use of HyperCard in the classroom. You will need to prepare one type of presentation for a fairly large group and another type for an individual (or a group of no more than four) doing research or browsing, so I'll take these up separately.

Designing Cards and Stacks for a Large Group

- Cards should have a minimum of text. Think of text for presentation cards as headlines. Use nouns and verbs where possible more than adjectives and adverbs.

- Better legibility is not the only reason to strive for simplicity. A point that is logically developed over several simple cards is easier to grasp and re- member than one squeezed into one intricate card.

- Fonts must be 14 point, at least; usually, larger fonts are preferred.

- Avoid scrolling fields in presentations. (If you must use a scrolling field, then you are obligated to read the text aloud yourself or to have someone close to the screen read it aloud. The best solution usually is to put text on more than one card. No need to be stingy with the number of cards you use.)

- Use a serif font ("HELLO" rather than "HELLO") because the added visual clues help the reader who is not close to the screen.

- Use images or graphics, maps, and charts frequently. If you use them on each card, you will be able to force yourself to develop the habit of not using too much text on a card.

- If a card contains an image, it is usually a good idea to use some text as well, even if the text is just a title. The text helps orient the user, giving the user a context for the images and graphics.

- Some variety in your choice and placement of images adds interest: not always a cartoon; pictures not always in the right half of the card.

- Deliberately vary the amount of text or illustration on each card. This is also a way to control the pace of the presentation.

- Take advantage of HyperCard's ability to drag text and graphics to simulate animation and add interest to the screen. (See Figures 2 and 3.) Your first effect of this kind will seem hard to do, but it gets easier. Here is the script for the button that launches the balloon—a transparent button that covers the balloon at the start.

```
on mouseUp
    choose select tool
    hide menuBar
    set dragSpeed to 75
    drag from 410,215 to 480,341 ——— selects the balloon
    drag from 410,215 to 75,11 ——————— drags the balloon
    show card field "Flying high"
    show card field "Click"
    wait 2 seconds
    doMenu "Select all"
    doMenu "Revert" —————————————————— puts balloon back to starting point
    choose browse tool ——————————————— deselects the screen
    hide card field "Flying high"
    hide card field "Click"
end mouseUp
```

- Use HyperCard's built-in visual effects when you "go" from card to card—dissolve slowly, iris open or close, wipe right, and others.

- Choose a visual effect each time that helps illustrate relationships or themes. For instance, a sequence of cards that begins with "barn door open slowly" might logically end with "barn door close slowly."

FIGURE 2. A card with balloon image, before dragging of balloon.

FIGURE 3. The card from Figure 2, after dragging of balloon.

- To help the audience see a difference between screens, use the "slow" or "very slow" modifiers with visual effects. This helps the audience, especially those at the back of the room, to distinguish more easily between separate screens.

- Use a neutral color between cards when several cards in a sequence are of the same style. Have a card "dissolve slowly to black," for example, before showing the next card—and the break between the cards is more evident.

- If the cards in a sequence are closely related and share a single background, you can put a uniform visual effect in the background script. This way, the cards will be related both in their appearance and in the movement from one card to the next.

- Don't underestimate the utility and power of sound. Multimedia teaches to several senses simultaneously, a major reason for selecting a multimedia presentation. Use sound.

- Sound can be a substitute for text, or you can consider sound as simply a different form of text. Don't overlook the opportunity to augment images and text with sound. The sound can be as simple as a voice reading the main idea of the text or a musical motif that introduces a related idea.

- To conserve memory when you use sound, store the sound stacks on floppy disks and temporarily add these stacks with the sound bites to your hard disk only when you are giving the demonstration that requires them.

- Don't have sound exist in isolation. Your audience becomes accustomed to seeing something on the screen, so when you have sound, be sure to have an appropriate card on the screen, possibly graphics related to the sound, illustrating it or identifying it.

- Use sound as the bridge, a link when you move from one idea to another.

- Use pauses to teach. *Time* is a basic tool in multimedia. Pauses allow the audience to react to the material. This is called *thinking,* and you can encourage it. Pauses help vary the pace of the presentation. When you pause, the audience realizes you expect them to react, so they pay closer attention to see what they might have missed. Of course, as a designer you have to be sure that you have included something for the audience to discover. Otherwise, you are simply wasting their time and, worse even, training them that pauses are not important and can be ignored. Pauses should be as compelling and as carefully crafted for the presentation as are sounds and images.

Designing Cards and Stacks for an Individual or a Small Group

Effective cards and stacks for browsing by a single user or a small group should be designed to be different from those intended for a larger group. In large group presentations, the predominant consideration is the moment, which includes the single card, what the screen looks like, what sound is playing, and what sound and images are coming from the videodisc. In this situation the *presenter* has control over orientation and navigation—where you are and where you are going.

For the individual user or small group (four people or less), more complex points can be made in less space, though clarity and simplicity are still called for. However, because you, the designer, are not directly controlling what the user does, your major concern here is to think more in terms of stacks or paths rather than solely in terms of a single screen. Choosing is essential in interactivity, so you want the user to be able to leave your path at any time. But you want that user to know how to move about and return.

- Give visual clues (sometimes as simple as a title, a label, or an icon) to where the user is and how to get back to the previous cards. Provide a map that shows where all items are in the program. Think about possibly including an index card that lists all the cards in the stack and putting it in the same place in each stack.

- Design the background for groups of cards that are structurally related so that the relationship is also visual: all the cards in the same stack might have the same look to them. You can accomplish this in numerous ways.

- For closely related cards use background fields rather than card fields. Then all text will be placed identically.

- If you don't want all your text in the same place on each card, you can still give your cards a similar look by using the same font in the same style and size on each card.

- Look at each screen separately and ask whether it conveys what you wish it to, whether it says too much or too little, and whether it is interesting and appealing. Now ask whether it connects with what preceded it and what might follow and ask how it contributes to the overall theme of the stack.

- Figure 4 on the following page shows a card at a decision point. Find the places where the user will have a choice. Does the user understand that a choice exists? Does the user know what the choices are?

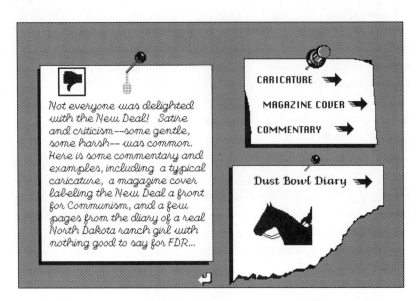

FIGURE 4. A card at a decision point.

- If there are not enough places where choices are offered, add some.

- Analyze the consequences of the possible choices by the user. Are these what you intended? If not, are they acceptable?

- Observe users with your stack. Are they bewildered? Ask for their questions and notes. (You cannot anticipate every possible point of difficulty. Trial runs by users are essential.)

Presenting Lessons with HyperCard

HyperCard is incredibly convenient in the classroom. All the time and energy that you spend on designing and writing up your lessons, if you do it in HyperCard, applies to *presenting* the lesson! You don't have to type your bright idea into your lesson plan at home and then transfer it to the board in the classroom: you simply use the same motor (the computer) that you used to create and save your work to *use* that work with your students.

With HyperCard you can present effective lessons even without multimedia. Create groups of cards (stacks) for the topic you want to develop. You can use these cards to present basic facts or ideas. You can easily add clip art or scanned-in images to illustrate these points. The images can be decorative and appealing, or—more important still—

they can be maps, diagrams, charts, or visual details that help the learner. If a student has created a visual aid for a report—say, a helpful map—it too can be used to enhance your presentation by sharing it with the class. (Should only the teacher get the benefit of students' best work?) Figure 5 shows a lesson screen for a class discussion on the topic of photos; the figure shows two illustrations derived from scanned images obtained from the Farm Security Administration collection at the Library of Congress.

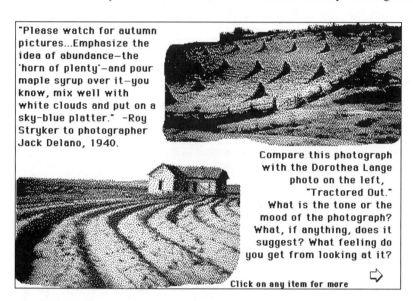

FIGURE 5. A card demonstrating a lesson using photos and a quotation. [Photo, top right: Marion Post Wolcott, Photo Metro, 1986. Photo, bottom left: Dorothea Lange, Oakland Museum, Oakland, California.]

A useful trick when you are presenting a lesson is to put into a card a hidden field that contains questions or ideas for activities that might be relevant to a discussion. It also provides a handy space where the teacher or a student might type notes during the discussion. On each card put a separate hidden field with a button that will display the field at the appropriate moment or hide it at the next click. The entire script for such a button can consist of the following:

```
on mouseUp
    get the visible of field "Notes"
    set the visible of field "Notes" to not it
end mouseUp
```

Figure 6 on the following page shows the lesson card from Figure 1, with a Notes field added.

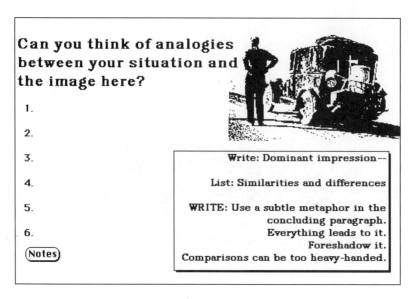

FIGURE 6. *The lesson card from Figure 1, with the Notes field showing.*
[Photo: Dorothea Lange, Library of Congress.]

When you find a topic that students are especially interested in, you can reveal the hidden field and pursue this additional idea. You can add buttons to cards to take you to other cards or stacks that are especially relevant to your topic for the day. Be sure to put in a field that shows the sources of additional information. You might want to use a background button that you name "Source" to establish the idea that students are expected to be interested in the sources of information and to suggest that they, too, should include sources of information in their work. Figure 7 shows a card with a Source button. Figure 8 is the related card, with the Source field containing the source of the text.

During the presentation, stop frequently to ask students to write questions, observations, and points they want to discuss about the information. Pause often to let the students write their questions and work on their notes. This is an important part of interactivity. You are teaching that they will be able to explore their ideas and to find answers to their own questions.

Call on students randomly to read aloud any of the questions they have written out. Ask whether anyone else can answer the question and ask the rest of the group to check their own notes and questions to find related questions. You might also have them work with a partner to discuss one of their questions together and report back to the class.

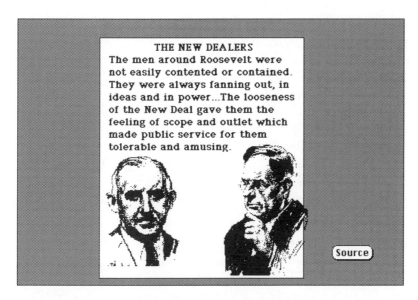

FIGURE 7. A card with a Source button. [Pictured: Raymond Moley and Harold Ickes from Portraits from the New Deal, *National Portrait Gallery, Smithsonian Institution.*]

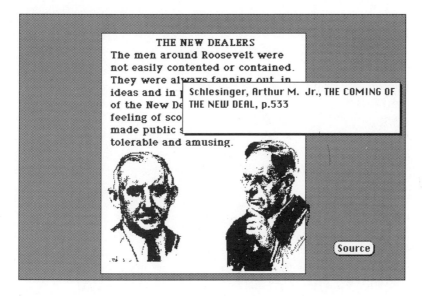

FIGURE 8. The card from Figure 7, with the Source field showing.

You can take advantage of these discussions to teach indirectly the skills for using HyperCard. During a discussion ask students to think of keywords to search on. You can use the Find command to type in a keyword and look for information in the stack. You can also show the class how to go to other stacks to search. Without lecturing or losing the focus on the content of the discussion, you can casually demonstrate various processes as they are needed and informally explain what you are doing and how you are doing it. When a search on a keyword is successful, students will be able to read the entry and perhaps expand the search by suggesting other keywords. You can help students understand how searches like these relate to using the tables of contents and indexes in books and to using the entries in a card catalog. Students soon pick up basic HyperCard conventions in the context of the class work. They are also developing valuable research strategies.

One characteristic of computer programs can sometimes be a disadvantage—but becomes a major strength during a presentation. Unlike workbooks and study guides, computer programs do not reveal their size; the user does not know how much exists beyond the immediate screen. This gives the teacher the advantage of great flexibility in a presentation, because your students do not need to see that you still have 20 cards to review with them or that, because they did so well on the lesson, you don't have to bother with the extra cards you didn't get to. You don't have to say, "We'll finish this tomorrow."

Even though you might not have completed the lesson you had planned, you can bring it to a logical and satisfactory conclusion wherever you happen to be. If a class needs more work on a topic, you have a chance to develop additional materials for review without students feeling that they have fallen short or that you have unfairly added to the lesson. Try doing that with a written study guide! Another benefit is that you can prevent the sometimes embarrassing situation of one class comparing with another how many pages each class finished or which page the class is on. My students, at least, have not yet begun to compare the number of screens of work they have accomplished. Yet going through screens vividly reinforces the idea of moving through content and this process seems reassuring for students.

At the end of a class presentation, collect students' notes. You can use these to assess what students have learned and prepare additions or revisions in the stack for the next lesson. Develop follow-up presentations for later classes, building on the students' questions and comments. You might work with a student in adding her new ideas to the lesson, and perhaps she will even want to present her new work to the class.

Use the notes to suggest to students what other areas they might explore—with your help or on their own. Meet with students in small groups or individually to review areas they're interested in. Students' uncertainties and confusions about a lesson can show up in their notes. You can develop new cards for the next day to expand on a problem area or go back and easily review the cards from the previous lesson. Unlike a chalkboard where work is gone forever, your class notes are dynamic and can keep growing.

The notes can also help you to group students who have similar interests but might not otherwise think of working with each other. Form new groups based on these common interests. Respond to the students' notes and return them with suggestions for further investigation. You do not have to respond in great detail and you do not have to grade them, but you do want to direct students to richer materials and to monitor their progress. The notes are also a fine way of sharing and connecting various sources of information that different members of the class have found.

Time Management

In my one-computer classes, the computer was constantly in use. Computers aside, all my students expect that during class time everyone will be working—either as a class or in groups or individually. Ordinarily, the class convenes as a whole for a few minutes at the beginning and at the end of the period or, on occasion, for a presentation by me, a student, or a group of students. The presence of a computer in the room, then, was not a surprise nor a distraction. It merely meant that when a presentation was given, it was frequently, but not always, done with the aid of the computer and that, during planning time or work time, a person or a group would be at the computer.

Sign-ups to use the computer were essential, of course; they entailed no special management, and they worked smoothly. At the start of each class, we quickly reviewed that day's sign-ups and often adjusted priorities—for example, when someone pleaded a special need. When students feel they have a choice and that they will have their own chance to work on the computer, they usually choose to be generous to one another.

The sophomore English class was, conveniently, the first of the day, so the computer was usually humming long before class started. Other students managed to stay after class or drop by at lunch or other times during the day. Unfortunately, we still never had enough time.

Students' Projects and Research

I can show how HyperCard can work—even in a one-computer classroom—through a few examples from my sophomore English class, as the students discovered the 1930s, *The Grapes of Wrath,* and John Steinbeck.

At the outset I said little about what the content of the unit would be, although they knew we would be reading *The Grapes of Wrath.* I asked the students to look up the basic issues and events of the 1930s in the library and to dredge up from their own minds and the minds of others what knowledge, notions, impressions, and (possibly) memories they could.

A few days later I presented from Grapevine a brief multimedia story called "A Trip to the 1930s." This is an impressionistic overview, which asks: "What were the 1930s *really* like? If you could visit that decade as a time-traveler, what would you make of it?" We hear music of the period ("Puttin' On the Ritz") and get a kaleidoscope of images, on both the computer screen and from the videodisc, ranging from Hoovervilles and people shuffling in breadlines to debutantes and ads for luxury automobiles. We hear eye-witness accounts that contrast memories of poverty and glamor, and we are introduced to some "contact people" (see Figure 9) of the period, including Steinbeck himself.

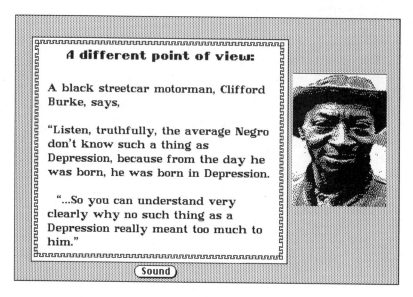

FIGURE 9. A card showing a "contact person" from "A Trip to the 1930s." [Photo: Arthur Rothstein, Library of Congress.]

After a discussion based on their research and the story, I asked the students to find some ideas that seemed worth following up. This generated a list of tentative topics. The next step was for me to list the topics in the computer as the basis for a preliminary search of Grapevine. (We continued informal discussions through all stages of this class activity.)

In class we decided how to phrase topic descriptions as keywords that would zero in on information we sought, through the use of the simple Find command. For example, one selected topic was *family,* which triggered the related words *women* and *depression* and *government programs.*

At this stage I operated the computer; however, I waited to be cued by the students. I went to the Grapevine stack named Expo (for exposition), where (I knew) a wealth of information existed in the form of some 32 cards containing mini-essays on that number of predetermined Grapevine topics. By telling HyperCard to "find *family*" (see Figure 10) and "find *depression*"—after some false leads and occasional irrelevancies—we revealed a hidden field on the same card with its list of "links." These links are references to related information elsewhere in the Grapevine program. One of these links was to the book *Dust Bowl Diary.* (See Figure 11 on the following page.)

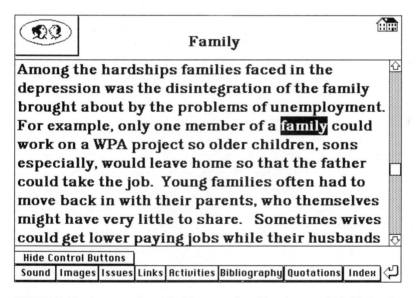

FIGURE 10. A screen from the Expo stack, with a keyword highlighted.

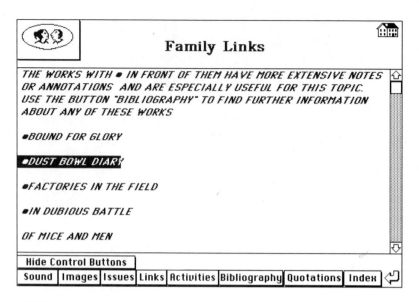

FIGURE 11. *A screen from the Expo stack, showing a linking reference to* Dust Bowl Diary.

We followed up this link by looking at the reference in the Bibliography stack. (See Figure 12.) Here the students discovered that each Bibliography card has a field with one or more topic words and that they could extend the search by using the Find command in this stack, too.

In this way, without having to be adept with HyperCard, they began to learn HyperCard operations, to develop logical search strategies, and to become familiar with the scope, organization, and content of Grapevine. Soon the students made final decisions about what topics to pursue and formed groups. Some students chose to work alone. Now began the sign-ups to use the computer. I was available to help those at the computer whenever I could. As I worked with each group, I trained someone to be able to go to the different stacks in the program.

Now students could attempt searches in the Expo, Bibliography, and Images stacks, as they helped one another. When they had difficulties, they were less often with Hyper-Card conventions than with finding their way around Grapevine. Occasionally, a student or group was lost or confused and had to wait before the teacher could get to them.

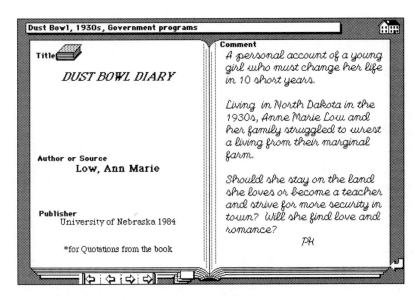

FIGURE 12. A card from the Bibliography stack, showing the entry
for Dust Bowl Diary.

The Images stack is an index to some 900-plus images or sections of motion footage on the videodisc. The digitized picture on each index card is a reminder of what is on the videodisc itself in higher resolution and sometimes in color. These cards, like those in other stacks, carry topic words, so here too students could search for images by topic. Viewing the videodisc image was one kind of productive work; another was using the information on the cards for leads to other images and sources that might be outside Grapevine. Figure 13 on the following page shows a typical card in the Images stack.

Searching in the Sound stack is similar to looking in Images; however, what students usually found was a partial sample pointing to a larger entity. Sound requires so much memory for storage that, evocative and appealing as they can be, the digitized sound clips are no more than brief excerpts from longer interviews or perhaps only a single verse from a folk song. Still, students found it worthwhile to head for the library to do follow-up research and locate the whole interview, speech, or lyric.

Previously, students didn't know what they wanted to look up in the card catalog. Now they know exactly what they are looking for. For example, they knew that they could find "Woody Guthrie" in the card catalog or that they could look under the headings of "music" and "folk songs" to find what they needed for their research on some of the music of the 1930s.

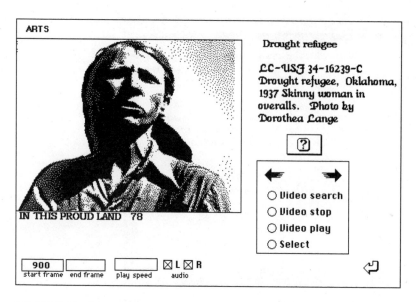

FIGURE 13. A card from the Images stack, showing an entry for
Drought refugee. *[Photo: Dorothea Lange, Library of Congress.]*

Now that students have made choices about what topics to research, and they have
enough facility with HyperCard at least to browse and search, what is the situation like
in the classroom?

While I work with separate groups of students or with individual students, helping them
find materials in Grapevine, other groups or students working individually are doing
their own research, based on what they have already found.

All the students are thinking about how to present their information to the class, using
sound and images to illuminate and illustrate the fruits of their research. They are all
doing a lot of reading. All of them have read *The Grapes of Wrath,* and some of them
have read three or four other books as well. They help one another as they put together
their research—in Grapevine and in the library—with their notes on outside reading.
They ask questions of me and of each other; the answers lead to more questions and further research. Their projects begin to take shape. They remind me of gold prospectors:
each person or group has staked out a small claim on this territory and a lot of energy is
being expended. I observe episodes of suspense, frustration, and sometimes the joy of
discovery as they scramble for paydirt.

One group spends a lot of time with the Steinbeck stack, taking notes and acquiring additional sources of information. The students find references to several important sections

of the book *Steinbeck, A Life in Letters*. The entire group reads parts of this book and discusses it. (This is their own homework assignment, which they decide on and follow through on. This process is a teacher's delight: Students decide what they need to know and what they want to discuss with each other!) One group member buys his own copy of the new book *Working Days,* the journal Steinbeck kept while writing *The Grapes of Wrath*. He wants to be a writer and is interested in Steinbeck's experiences as a writer.

While some students decide to use Grapevine with the videodisc to present their work, others choose to borrow a camcorder to create their own video, showing some of the federal projects of the Depression era in the San Francisco area, including some post office murals and two bridges. Some students do research on the music of the 1930s, which they will present while wearing the appropriate dress of the times. One student uses images from the videodisc to illustrate a poem she has written; she will read the poem to the class while showing them selected images from the videodisc.

As they concentrate on how to present their projects, groups and individuals continue to sign up for computer time. Most of them still need my help to find information and to organize their presentations on the computer. I cannot spend as much time as is needed with each person or group. They somehow manage anyway.

By this time the students have seen that the Stories stack gives them a tool for stringing together a narration or connected exposition with the images and sounds they have discovered. In Stories they need only create a story card and "grab" the cards they want for their presentation in sequence, and then the cards are automatically listed on the right-hand field (with their choice of transition effects on the left). Figure 14 on the following page shows a card from the Stories stack named Depression. The first card to be shown in the narration is named *CCC road sign*, and it is in the Images stack.

At this point the students who plan to make a presentation using the computer want to practice using the mouse and to assemble their presentations with the Stories stack. Some students, like the poet, will use the computer and videodisc player in other ways, some not at all.

When the presentations are finally given, over a period of six or seven days, everyone is more than attentive, and not merely out of politeness. Some projects are very serious in tone, while others contain humor, yet each demonstrates thoughtful research and analysis. The illustrated poem mesmerizes us all. Afterward, students come up to congratulate the poet.

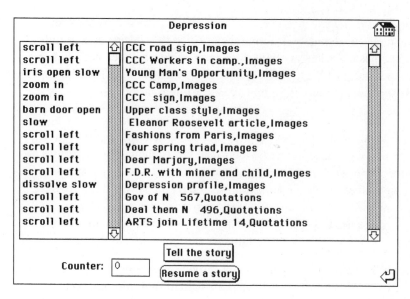

FIGURE 14. *A card from the Stories stack.*

The presentation on the New Deal public works is full of interest because it is about our city—and because it is well researched and designed. The "audience" part of the class is not passive. This group, like all the presenting groups, fields a lot of questions.

One of the groups dealing with music uses an ingenious shortcut: they find a way to synchronize their commentary and images with music that they were not able, yet, to digitize. They simply play it from a cassette. Another group invents an unconventional format to deal with some of the controversial opinions about Steinbeck—a wake, where the "mourners" (!) debate whether or not the novelist was guilty of sentimentality and argue about where he got his knowledge of the Dust Bowl migrants.

All the students are clearly proud of their work. Many tell me that they had fun with the assignment. I believe them because I enjoyed what they did. I know that each future class doing this assignment will do it uniquely, so that my pleasure in them will be repeated, but never exactly duplicated.

A Follow-Up Note

Later in the semester, as we are reading *The Great Gatsby,* the students are angry about the attitudes and the values of the rich and famous as Fitzgerald portrays them. The students, without prodding from me, compare the characters in Fitzgerald's novel with the characters in *The Grapes of Wrath*. The students talk about how the people in Steinbeck's novel are real to them because of the Farm Security Administration photographs on the videodisc and the Woody Guthrie songs. They speculate about how Steinbeck's characters would have felt about the people in the Fitzgerald novel. They relate these two books to the work we have also done with Arthur Miller's play *The Crucible*.

The students talk about how political radicalism grows out of social and economic situations. Suddenly, in early June 1989, the pro-democracy student rebellion in China breaks out. These students in San Francisco are shaken because all year our theme has been "American Dreamers and Doubters." Now, if not before, these students understand that the dreams and doubts we have been discussing in class are universal. Dreams and doubts are as powerful today as they were 50 years ago.

A Wish List

I am glad to have had the opportunity to experiment with HyperCard and some advanced media technology in my classes, and I hope to go on doing so. Still, I have a list of wishes for future classes of this kind. I'm not leaving it simply a private list of what would make me more content as a teacher (though it would); I'm putting it here because it is also a list of things that would make learning in this way even better. I wish that:

- We could have enough time in class for all of the students to have as much time on the computer as they want.
- We could have more workstations in the classroom. How many is enough? What is the optimum number? I'd like a chance to find out. (Right now one computer in a classroom is best for teacher presentations and group presentations. The students who want to write their own stacks simply cannot do it in class. They do not have the skills yet, and they do not have access to the computer to develop their skills.)
- Students could have access to at least one workstation with the program in the library so they could go on their own time and work on their projects or browse through the materials.
- Students could take home a stack to work with or to browse or to add to, much as students now borrow books or video tapes from teachers.
- The time would soon arrive when students will have more advanced computer skills and when they will have greater access to computers.

- Students would be helped to develop—beyond mere "computer literacy" in some general sense—a fundamental competency in using the keyboard and the mouse, in word processing and in *information processing* with programs like HyperCard.

Is It Worth the Trouble?

I have been asked: "If you didn't have the motive of writing about teaching with Hyper-Card in the way you have described, would you still want to take the trouble to teach that way?" My answer is: "Yes, I would, and do." To say that teaching with interactive media helps illustrate and dramatize things is both obvious and an understatement. It seems to inject a sense of immediacy and reality in a subject that is evident in the way students regard what they are studying. Rather than *telling* students that a subject is relevant or significant, we have a way of helping them to discover that for themselves. And in addition to the vividness and impact that learning in this way can have, it is also more effective and precise. Students more quickly grasp the issues and possibilities, and they find information more efficiently. When they find facts or helpful interpretations, or if they gain some insights, they have a powerful way to share them.

With other classes that I had during the same semester, I found it impossible to resist using the computer and HyperCard. When studying units on Native Americans and railroad building in a history class, some students began to bring in important data and graphics. Would it have made sense for me to keep the information to myself or to settle for tacking a few pages of research on the bulletin board? Not when I could shape the information and share some of it through the computer. That sort of activity undeniably does take time and energy—but in this teacher's view, it's no "trouble" at all.

The Use of HyperCard on a University Campus

Jan Biros

JAN BIROS

Jan Biros, who earned an Ed.D. at the State University of New York at Albany, is the manager of special projects in Drexel University's Office of Computing Services. In that capacity she works with faculty developers to distribute and market their software projects. In addition, she coordinates many community-outreach activities with external agencies such as the Philadelphia School District and the Mayor's Commission on Adult Literacy in Philadelphia, which help other educational and nonprofit agencies use the computer, primarily the Macintosh, to better serve their clients and better manage their organizations.

She has helped to initiate and support HyperCard development projects on campus for higher-education courseware applications as well as for adult-literacy and basic-skills applications. She has also helped to organize training sessions and materials in Hyper-Card and advanced scripting; these sessions have been conducted on Drexel's campus and on many other college campuses.

Background

Drexel University is located in Philadelphia, Pennsylvania, and has over 12,000 Apple Macintosh computers on campus. Each incoming student purchases a computer for his or her own use, regardless of major course of study. In addition, over 1000 university-owned Macs exist in public-access areas and administrative offices. Drexel is unique in that it supports a Software Development Group of some 10 full-time programmers and 10 co-op student programmers who develop courseware proposed and designed by faculty members. Over 40 Drexel-developed courseware programs are listed in the Kinko's Academic Courseware Catalogs. Drexel has a strong technical tradition; its largest enrollments are in the colleges of engineering and business administration.

When HyperCard was first announced, everyone thought it was a great idea. It would allow users to perform many interesting, creative tasks—quickly and easily. Users could integrate graphics, sound, and animation and produce wonderful applications, without prior programming experience. HyperCard is a relatively easy product to use if you want to make limited use of its power. However, the average Mac user found it difficult to envision HyperCard's potential. Potential users quickly realized that a fairly advanced skill level is required to produce sophisticated applications with intricate conditional linkages because the user would need to "program" with HyperTalk.

During the first few months of HyperCard use on our campus, the general comment heard from most people was: "Sure it's a great tool, but what can you use it for?" The "purists"—that is, traditional programmers—looked askance at HyperCard because it was not a traditional language or development environment. Because HyperCard has the unique ability to integrate text, graphics, sound, and animation, it requires a set of skills and conceptual frameworks for design that differ from those skills needed for a traditional language environment. To maximize the potential capabilities of HyperCard, the user should possess a well-developed graphic-art and interface/page-design sensibility.

Thus, on Drexel's campus, applications development with HyperCard began outside the traditional development environment, through the efforts of individuals who were experts on using the Macintosh—self-taught "programmers" whose skills had evolved more through experience than through formal instruction and who were experienced in the use of graphics and familiar with design concepts. These individuals developed applications with very specific, practical uses. The applications, which exploited HyperTalk extensively, ran smoothly and were distinguished by their polish and style. They served as terrific examples, demonstrating what could be accomplished with HyperCard. Because of the work performed by our pioneer HyperCard programmers, the University has formalized the support system necessary to introduce more and more users to the power of HyperCard and to stimulate and nurture applications development at all levels of complexity.

Speechware

A faculty member in the neuropsychology department, who works with head-injured patients, theorized the use of the microcomputer as a rehabilitation tool for these individuals, rather than using it in its accepted role as an instructional tool. (See Chute et al., "ProsthesisWare: A New Class of Software Supporting the Activities of Daily Living," in *Neuropsychology* Vol. II pp. 41–57, 1988.) He had a patient, injured in a car accident, who was totally paralyzed except for nominal movement in her thumb. She was unable to communicate. Almost one year later, a medical team was choosing between institutionalizing her or trying to rehabilitate her. Because of her severe handicap, they could not ascertain her level of cognitive ability nor evaluate her chance for improvement. HyperCard was utilized for this patient first as a diagnostic tool and then as a rehabilitative tool. The faculty member worked with one of our developers, who is not a trained programmer, to create a customized tool that allowed this patient to communicate. Because the patient was unable to move the mouse, they provided a microstick. They used HyperCard to create an application that contained common instructions. (For example: I have to go to the bathroom, I need help, and so on.) In addition, they designed a facsimile of the keyboard that appeared on screen. The cursor cycles through the individual letters at a pace determined to be appropriate for her, allowing her to spell words and thereby communicate. The tool—named Speechware (see Figure 1)—allowed the doctors to determine that she was cognitively able and likely to benefit from rehabilitation. The Speechware program dramatically improved the quality of this woman's life. We later discovered that she had wanted desperately to be able to communicate with her three daughters, and Speechware allowed her to do so.

HyperCard's versatility allowed the developer to experiment with various designs to determine the design that most successfully met the patient's needs. Iterations were created easily and quickly. Applications were taken into the hospital, tried out, modified, and then tried again. Only in this manner could such a revolutionary application be developed. Because HyperCard is easily modified, Speechware can also be quickly customized to best meet the needs of other patients, with their individual needs and limitations. Our programmer developed a utility accompanying the Speechware application that teaches the user how to modify the program. Speechware is undoubtedly the first of many HyperCard applications that will be developed for the handicapped and the elderly.

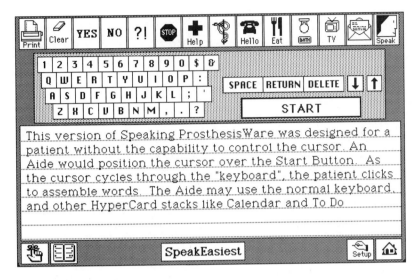

This version of Speaking ProsthesisWare was designed for a
patient without the capability to control the cursor. An
Aide would position the cursor over the Start Button. As
the cursor cycles through the "keyboard", the patient clicks
to assemble words. The Aide may use the normal keyboard,
and other HyperCard stacks like Calendar and To Do

*FIGURE 1. A sample screen from "SpeakEasiest," an iteration of the
original Speechware program.*

Literacy Software

Drexel University, with the support of a state grant, has been involved with the Mayor's
Commission on Adult Literacy in Philadelphia. As part of our role as technical support
center for over 100 agencies attempting to use computers in their literacy instruction, we
are involved with developing literacy instruction programs for adults. Quality software
designed to help adults learn basic math and language-arts skills is a scarce resource. We
decided to see whether we could assist in the development of literacy-program software.
Given very limited resources, both on the part of the literacy agencies we work with and
on our part, we chose to utilize HyperCard. Our literacy computer-support specialist,
a self-taught "programmer" with a strong graphic-arts background, was excited about
what he felt he could create using HyperCard. In about nine months of development, we
created the three programs described below. Because we worked with service providers
who were our content "experts" and consultants, we could quickly implement changes,
additions, and modifications. The inclusion of digitized sound allows the new reader or
nonreader to receive easy-to-follow instructions on how to proceed with the program.
Animation and graphics enable the programs to be interactive and to motivate without
being condescending. The interface in our programs is transparent; the user does not
"see" that the program was developed in HyperCard.

The first program that we completed was an alphabet program. This program helps adults to develop character-recognition and alphabetic-ordering skills. The program also helps adults to become familiar with the position of the characters on the keyboard. Our goals were twofold: to improve reading skills and to learn to use a computer, a keyboard, and a word-processing program, which would provide the adult literacy students with marketable job skills.

Alphabet for Adults is a software tool designed for the most basic adult literacy student. (See Figure 2.) Each letter of the alphabet is presented and named, and then a word beginning with the letter is printed on the screen, spoken, and represented graphically. For each lesson, the student must find, on the keyboard, the letter being learned; after each group of five letters has been presented, the student must put the letters in alphabetic order. The program employs graphics extensively and uses digitized voice to issue directions and to pronounce the letters and words presented to the student. The graphics, visuals, and sound effects are entertaining and motivational, without being patronizing to the student. While the program was intended for adults, it is appropriate for learners of any age.

Vowel Combinations is designed to reinforce vowel combinations for students who are beginning to read at a low level. (See Figure 3.) Seven common long vowel combinations have been selected for this program. The program displays a vowel combination and

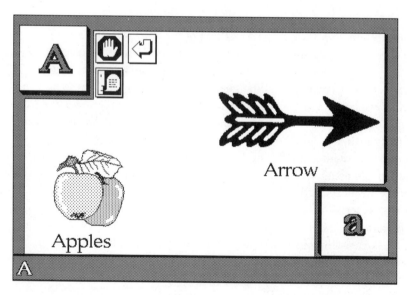

FIGURE 2. A sample screen from Alphabet for Adults.

pronounces it. Next, the program displays a word that uses the vowel combination, which the student can attempt to sound out, and then displays a picture of an object whose name contains the sound. The program provides students with exercises in which they create words by clicking on various consonant and vowel-combination "buttons." A button can be clicked that lists all the words that can be created using the different consonant/vowel combinations. Students can access the list at any point during the lesson, to help them with the exercise. After the student creates a word, the word is checked for accuracy. Correctly built words are pronounced for the student. If a student creates a word that sounds legitimate but is not spelled correctly, the program provides a message briefly explaining what is in error.

Blank-it! is a tool developed for use by literacy tutors and their students. (See Figure 4 on the following page.) It is designed to be used with a language-experience approach to reading and helps automate implementation of the Cloze procedure. The program allows a student or tutor to type an original story or access a previously saved story. (Stories can be saved for reuse.) Font size is easily modified to help visually impaired users. A notebook page on which the tutor can record questions related to the narrative is available for each story. Such questions can be saved for future discussion. After the narrative has been typed in, parts of words and/or whole words can be eliminated for later replacement by the student. Words can be eliminated in a pattern (every other, every third word,

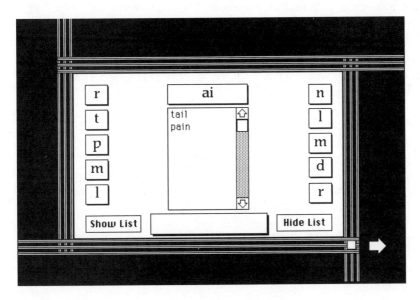

FIGURE 3. A lesson screen from Vowel Combinations.

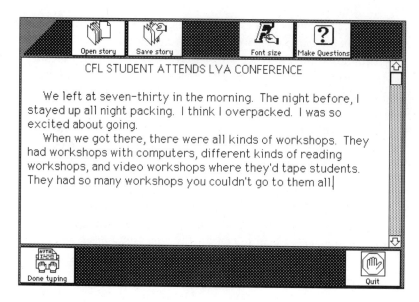

FIGURE 4. The story screen from Blank-it!

and so on); parts of words can be globally eliminated (for example, all *th* or *ie* combinations); or specific letters or combinations can be eliminated individually (*ae* in the fifth word, *th* in the tenth word, and so on). As each letter is eliminated, it is replaced with a dash. The student is then able to go back to the story and fill in the correct words and letters to complete the exercise. As the student tries to fill in the blanks, hints can be accessed by clicking on a button, and a discussion of the process can ensue with the tutor.

ColorCard

ColorCard for HyperCard is a tool developed at Drexel by the creators of Speechware. ColorCard will allow the user to add color to HyperCard stacks on a Macintosh II. (It is not yet ready for distribution but will be shortly.) This package includes a tutorial stack for practice in using color and multi-windowing.

The ColorCard stack permits the user to create a multi-window environment in Hyper-Card. (See Figure 5.) Each window is addressable (in the same manner as buttons, fields, cards, and so on), and each has the capability of displaying any graphic, including full gray scale and 256-color images.

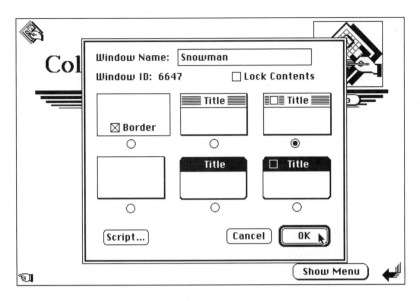

FIGURE 5. The Window Name dialog box from ColorCard.

The ColorCard stack contains tools that permit the user to add windows to cards. Users can choose from six types of windows, including a borderless window. All windows can be resized and moved, and all can contain hidden HyperTalk script. Users can paste any graphic from the Clipboard or Scrapbook into their windows. ColorCard comes with a sample stack, Color Perception. This stack presents some visual color phenomena (such as afterimages, binocular rivalry, color adaptation, and three-dimensional rotation).

As a result of our extensive computer involvement, we at Drexel now believe that the *support* that you provide for users is probably more important than the hardware and software. This is true with HyperCard as well. Users need help in getting started with HyperCard and in advancing their skills as they glimpse the true potential of the program.

We began by offering a one-hour workshop to introduce users to HyperCard. (We also offer one-hour workshops for other software products that we support.) However, we soon discovered that this was simply not enough time, even for the sophisticated Mac users we had on campus. We then developed a full day of training, which assumed no knowledge of HyperCard and which took users up to basic scripting. The entire day was hands-on. By the end of the workshop, participants had created two stacks of their own and had extensively enhanced an existing stack by creating many dynamic links. A variety of types of fields, buttons, graphics, and visual effects were taught. (One of the stacks created for our training session is a presentation stack on desktop publishing; this stack acts as a template in which the user can enter any text and/or graphics and thus have a presentation tool available.)

We created documentation that replicates the instruction so that the user can leave the training and repeat what was done in class. The documentation comes with four disks prepared with sample stacks and stacks used in instruction. The training has been very well received. However, users soon wanted to learn advanced scripting techniques, so we are now developing an addition to our initial training sessions that will concentrate on advanced scripting and advanced development techniques.

We will also begin monthly HyperLunches for those interested in learning more about using HyperCard. The luncheon meetings will be predominantly for faculty members and will have a "show-and-tell" sharing session in which faculty can demonstrate stacks that they have created and discuss how they are using them. The session will include a technical instructional component in which participants will learn new HyperCard skills or shortcuts from those who are at a more advanced level. We will also designate one professional staff person within the Office of Computing Services to be our HyperCard specialist; the specialist will be available to answer more complex questions, help faculty with more significant development projects, and plan and conduct training sessions and workshops for HyperCard.

Currently, the most common use on our campus for HyperCard, beyond the scope of the applications described above, is for organizing and presenting notes and course material in classroom presentations. However, once faculty members begin to work with HyperCard more extensively, a greater variety of applications will be created.* Continuing support will be necessary to help faculty and students use this valuable tool to further enhance their teaching and learning experiences. Users at all levels of expertise must have accessible advice, instruction, and general support to enable them to explore the potential of HyperCard.

---

*Since the completion of this article in early 1989, many more individuals are using HyperCard on campus, and we have several attractive and sophisticated HyperCard courseware products in the offing.

HyperCard, Technology, and Education

Peter Olivieri

PETER OLIVIERI

Peter Olivieri is a faculty member in the computer sciences department at Boston College. He is now serving as the first director of the University's newly constructed Instructional Research and Development Laboratory. The goal of this laboratory is to provide faculty with the resources necessary to introduce technology into the classroom. In addition to his activities as a teacher and at the lab, he directs the Sports Video Production Unit, which is utilizing state-of-the-art computer and video technology for application to athletic events at the college. He also is the editor of Wheels for the Mind, *an Apple Computer quarterly publication (prepared at Boston College) that details the use of the Macintosh computer in the educational environment.*

The Hype over HyperCard

When the Apple Macintosh computer was introduced, many people agreed that it really was "the machine for the rest of us." Finally, a computer had been designed with the user in mind. It was a relatively easy machine to use. Its operation was almost intuitive, and it required no previous exposure to the use of computers. This was particularly true in the educational community where many members of the community, especially faculty, were quite reluctant to venture into the world of computing. The Macintosh computer has ended that reluctance. It has become one of the most widely used computers within higher education.

In the early days, those who had been exposed to computing for some time envisioned yet another breakthrough. Certainly, it was nice to have a machine that now was both accepted and used by members of the academic community. However, there was yet another hurdle to cross. While the Macintosh was easy to use, developing applications programs for it was unusually difficult. The dream, then, was for an applications-development environment that was as easy to use as the Macintosh itself. Realizing this dream was a necessary precondition if there was to be any hope of moving the user community beyond word processing.

Enter HyperCard. When Bill Atkinson first released HyperCard, a feeling of cautious optimism surfaced within the educational community. Was this dream of an easy-to-use development system for the Macintosh not merely a fantasy? In retrospect, a good deal of skepticism existed during those early days. Yet, slowly the fantasy turned into reality as people discovered all that they could do with HyperCard. Faculty members who had used their computers only to type memos and papers were now using them to prepare class presentations, keep student records, develop personal and professional databases, and have some fun besides.

There is no question that HyperCard was, in its own way, truly a revolution. It awakened an enthusiasm in many previously unenthusiastic people. It began to empower people to accomplish tasks that they had thought impossible, at least for them. Oddly enough, HyperCard was particularly appropriate for the educational community, for it was as much about teaching as teaching itself. The important point here is not about the particular product—because products will grow, diminish, disappear, and return. Rather, the important point concerns what the product does. In this instance, it fosters sharing. By providing a vehicle with which users can navigate, in the way that they choose, through information, HyperCard really opened up a new world to both the people who wanted to share their experience and those who wanted to learn from others. In a funny kind of way, it has helped make everyone a teacher (and, indeed, there is a teacher in all of us).

The First Shall Be Last and the Last Shall Be First

Predictably, some difficulties appear no matter how much we would like the fantasy to be perfect. While there were, and perhaps are, some limitations with the product, these changed, and change, over time. New wish lists, new revisions, and new technologies all push a product to be better. In truth, the user community is rarely satisfied. There is always another feature that would make a product "just perfect." With HyperCard, however, most of the difficulties appeared precisely because it was such an easy development environment.

The first wave of HyperCard stacks included many projects that were poorly done. They violated many of the principles of good Apple Macintosh computer design as well as some of the tenets of good teaching. This is not unusual and is to be expected when a tool, previously used by few, finds its way into the hands of many. What is necessary, then, is to learn from this observation and to teach users the appropriate ways in which to share their talents. Instruction should be given on such topics as "Adhering to the Apple Macintosh Computer User Interface," "Principles of Stack Design," "Teaching with HyperCard," and so forth.

That first tidal wave of stackware has now receded somewhat and the more recent stacks evidence a greater concern for the principles of good design. In fact, it seems now that "classes of stackware" have emerged that perhaps reflect the user community itself.

Who Are the Players?

If HyperCard is one of the stars in the production, then who are the players? The players can best be identified by looking at the types of stacks that are available. While the following list is not exhaustive, it does represent some useful categories for discussion.

- Public-domain stacks—These stacks are available either for free or as shareware. Some are great. Some are terrible. Anyone can contribute to this category and can use others' stacks. Adherence to design principles is less rigid in this environment. The players here are "everyone."
- Commercially available stacks—By and large, these stacks provide either actual applications (record keeping, zip-code index, courses) or additional stackware development tools (printing information, merging stacks, adding sound, and so on). Usually, these stacks are developed by people experienced in the "ways of the computer."

- Faculty-developed stacks—These stacks are often for the faculty member's personal use, either at the office or in class. Their depth and design varies considerably. Most often, these are developed by individuals with great disciplinary expertise but little applications-development experience. The exceptional stacks almost always have both a teacher and a technician associated with their design.

If the stacks in each of these categories were closely scrutinized, it is likely that we would discover that the very best stacks are developed through a combination of talents that include teaching experience, subject experience, computer experience, and applications-development experience. Of course, there are many fine HyperCard applications that do not involve teaching (record keeping and telephone lists, for example), but we will focus here on instruction.

Making the Scene: Delivering on the Promise

If HyperCard (or any applications-development system—now or in the future) is to have an impact, it must be capable of "understanding" the environment within which it must live. HyperCard does provide the tools necessary for users to develop their own materials. However, the tools alone are not enough. Why? Let's focus on the educational community and look at its constituents.

Generally, the educational community consists of four groups: teachers, students, staff, and administrators. Although this model does closely resemble that of a school, the same classifications can apply to training programs in industry, in government, or wherever teaching takes place. Of these four groups, the temples of knowledge (certainly in a disciplinary sense) would be the teachers. These are the people who should be in the best position to share their knowledge by helping others to navigate their way through the teacher's wealth of experience. Please note that the word "teacher" certainly includes a host of people not necessarily in the teaching profession and not necessarily formally educated. It is this group that we would most like to empower with technology in ways that would facilitate the delivery of the knowledge that they have accumulated.

Unfortunately, it is precisely this group that is least able to allocate the time necessary to grapple with the nitty-gritty of applications development. There are a wide variety of reasons for this that include spending time on the teaching itself, doing research in one's subject area, performing tasks more directly associated with one's promotion, and lacking time to experience the rigors of tapping (and learning) the features of HyperCard or of the computer. This last reason is an especially important one. For any serious applications development, it is very, very useful to have some computer-programming experience. It is not the structure or syntax of the particular language that is important. Rather, it is the logic and experience gained in problem solving with a computer that is most valuable. The best HyperCard stacks often use aspects of HyperTalk (a script-writing language) that most teachers would not typically have thought to use or been exposed to. That is not to suggest that an advanced degree in computer science is necessary. However, some experience certainly is. Whatever the reasons, suffice it to say that many teachers will rarely have the time to develop applications other than slide shows, brief demonstrations, and personal databases.

This reality would not be so terrible were it not for the fact that it is an obstacle to exploiting the great contributions that teachers can and are willing to make. Not to worry! There merely needs to be some attention focused on creative ways to merge the power and potential of HyperCard with the power and potential of the teacher. There are five ingredients that would help to bring this about:

1. A technology lab for teachers
2. SWAT teams
3. Experimental learning labs
4. Vendor commitment to developing tools
5. People networks

Technology Lab for Teachers

First, it would be nice to have a physical place that teachers could visit to get exposed to and to experiment with new technology—both hardware and software. One of the biggest problems that needs to be addressed is that of educating teachers. Many of them are simply not aware of what can be done. It is important to provide excellent materials that demonstrate the potential for using simulation, knowledge navigation, self-learning, interactive videodiscs, and multimedia in the classroom.

When the Apple Macintosh computer was first introduced, we decided to open a Faculty Microcomputer Resource Center. It was a modest facility containing about 10 Macintosh computers, laser-printing resources, and a lot of sample software. The facility, for faculty only, is accessible 24 hours a day, 7 days a week, by utilizing a card-key system. Since its opening, the number of card-key holders has grown to over 400 faculty members. The facility itself has been an enormous success and has been one of the major factors in the introduction of computing to the faculty. Literally dozens of other colleges and universities (and at least one high school) have introduced similar facilities.

Because much of the work that went on in this facility was related to word processing, it was felt that something else was needed in order to move faculty to the next level of computing—that of utilizing the technology within the classroom environment. Thus, we are in the process of putting together an Instructional Research and Development Laboratory that will provide faculty with the resources—both technological and human—that will be of assistance in introducing multimedia technology into the classroom. This facility will provide access to a wide variety of video and audio equipment as well as to computer hardware and authoring software. The "research" component will focus on evaluating whether or not different strategies actually have an effect on learning.

SWAT Teams

Second, teams need to be put together that combine the resources of available time, computer expertise, disciplinary expertise, and teaching expertise. A team might simply be a small group, consisting of a faculty member and a programmer, working together on a particular project. A team might also be an organized SWAT team (Sharing With Applied Technology). The SWAT team might be an institutional group of up to four people. It should be headed by a faculty member and include, as appropriate, a curriculum-design person, a technical person, and a "delivery" person (someone schooled in the art of showmanship). SWAT teams may, of course, vary in their composition. The job of the SWAT team is to be a proactive force in the development of applications in the educational environment. Instead of sitting back and waiting for the application idea to wander by, the team would go out and visit the teachers, departments, and so forth, and live for a while in their environment. After an appropriate exposure to what is taking place (in a course, in some research, in a department, whatever), the team could join with a particular teacher and develop—under the teacher's guidance—an application that would facilitate the sharing of knowledge.

This "cooperative approach" to development is by no means a new one. Stanford University, Dartmouth University, Drexell University, and a host of other institutions have well-organized programs in this regard. It is mentioned here for two reasons. First, it is important to emphasize that the development of educational applications is a joint venture that will require a wide variety of expertise—expertise that may change over time as new technologies emerge. Second, these teams must be "proactive" in their approach—that is, they need to visit the various academic departments, sit in on their department meetings, and learn what their technology needs are. They then need to invite the departments to their facility (the technology lab mentioned above) and demonstrate the technologies and tools that are currently available. A wide variety of creative ideas and projects will likely emerge if this proactive approach is used.

Experimental Learning Labs

Third, experimental learning labs are needed. Some might consider these to be "computer classrooms." Rather, the intent is to move well beyond the traditional use of the computer in the classroom. These labs would be places were a variety of technologies could be tested and then tried out in actual classroom situations. Such facilities would expose students to many HyperCard courseware experiences and to an extraordinary array of delivery technologies. Envision a lab that, at different times during the month, might have a Macintosh computer on every student's desk, or a large-screen, computer-based presentation technology, or a network of CD-ROMs, or a lab of interactive videodiscs. Only the best applications and technology would gravitate to the classrooms at large.

We are currently building an experimental learning lab (intentionally not called a computer classroom). Our intent is to develop a facility that is modular in design. On one day, it might be a lecture hall with a computer up front along with a large-screen projector and an intelligent podium; on another day it might have a personal computer at every desk; on yet another day the desks might be arranged in "language lab" style for individual instruction. The Board of Trustees might meet there and use the polling units at each desk to vote on various proposals presented. Individual and group audio and visual resources will be built into the room. We want to be able to try out a wide variety of ways in which technology might aid in both teaching and learning.

Vendor Commitment to Developing Tools

Fourth, there needs to be a continual commitment on the part of the computer vendors and commercial developers to provide tools that can facilitate the development process. As we move into a multimedia learning environment, these tools will become even more critical. Such tools might include HyperCard version 11.5, audio interactive systems, student laptop computers, networked videodiscs, new telecommunications tools, and the like. The current Macintosh computer–user interface has been fantastic. Yet, in comparison with the way we, as human machines, operate, it is quite crude. It is still not easy to use technology. It is still not easy to acquire knowledge, to learn.

People Networks

Finally, there needs to be a formal network of people working in these areas. The potential exists for much wasted duplication of effort. There is the possibility of a lost opportunity to expose a group of students to a set of concepts simply because one did not know that something was available. Envision, if you will, a dial-in network where you could interactively search across the country for a teacher (developer, technician) who had developed "Applications of Technology in the Arts" or a "Biology Simulation of the

Growth Process" or for someone who has experience with "Using HyperCard with a Videodisc" or who was interested in working with another teacher to turn a not-yet-fully-formulated idea into practice.

What Is in Act II?

It is an exciting time for teachers and for learners. Consider for a moment what technologies you were using in 1970. What was your teaching (learning) like before the Apple Macintosh computer? For most of us, there has been a dramatic change. Well, it will only get better. Perhaps some of the following are on the horizon.

Classrooms

The traditional classroom environment will likely change. While there will always be "classes" and "lectures," other forms of "delivering the product" will emerge. With the introduction of audio and video capability into the classroom, classes will become centers where students are challenged, involved, and, yes, in some ways entertained (in the positive sense of the word). One can envision facilities where a computer, hidden within the tabletop, gives the student the capability of retrieving any portion of the "textbook" material related to a course; a polling keypad at each seat allows the instructor to query the entire class and get a feel for their understanding of a particular topic; an instructor station can react to audio input; interactive classroom simulations allow the students to control an experiment, live and in color, on a 12-foot-by-12-foot screen. A switch at each station allows a student to obtain printed (or disk) copies of the instructor's lecture, their peers' comments, any graphics displayed, or a videotape copy (or, soon, a videodisc or CD-ROM copy) of the entire proceedings of the class. During the class, students can, from their seats, call up the library and retrieve some information relevant to a point that they want to make in the class. In fact, that point can be made by having a student direct a video clip—retrieved at that very moment from the library—to the large screen up front for all to see. Stranger yet is the fact that most of the technology that has been described above currently exists.

Libraries

Libraries are moving rapidly toward becoming technological providers of information. A decade ago, very few libraries would have considered any need for input from computer scientists, systems analysts, information systems specialists, or people involved with technology. Now, however, the arena is quite different. At our campus library, for example, the traditional card catalog is no longer used. Access to the collection is completely on-line. That is, library users enter the information they are looking for into a computer terminal, and the computer aids them in their search. In addition, there are CD-ROM clusters, multimedia facilities, extensive computerized databases, remote access to these facilities via a computer on your desktop, and so on. These are all working now. Plans are underway for developing expert systems to aid users in their library research, videodisc-based kiosks to guide users to the library services, and extensive authoring (by library staff) of materials to aid the teacher, the student, and the researcher.

In the future, we will likely see the library as a central resource of much of our information needs. From our desktop—at home, in the office, in the dormitory—we will be able to view films, to obtain copies of articles, and to create lectures "live" that contain text–graphics–video–audio components. We will be able to send a customized list of our needs to an "intelligent agent" in the library's computer that will work on our behalf and alert us (electronically) when something arrives in which we might be interested.

Technology

Technology is more difficult to speculate about because it changes so fast. Perhaps the only sure thing is that technology will become easier to use. It is likely that it will be as easy to create materials that combine text, video, and audio as it is to do word processing today. We will be able to record and retrieve events from wherever we are: in the library, in the classroom, in the office, or at home. An audio interface with the computer will be commonplace, and software advances should be able to provide us with our own personalized intelligent agent who maintains our "electronic household" for us. Video via telephone will be commonplace. Television sets will be thin, wall size, of extremely high definition, and will contain a built-in computer and a CD-ROM–like reader and recorder. In fact, we are now on the threshold of most of these technologies. We will let you speculate on technologies that will provide more direct links between mind and computer, robots that increasingly act like ourselves, computers that organize and discover, books that are read in seconds, and learning experiences that, literally, place you in the center of the action.

Lifelong Learning

What will remain the same is that we will never stop learning. What will be different is that it will be easier to learn more. Most of us have wished that we could explore other areas of interest—in science, in sociology, in education, in the arts. There never seems to be enough time, enough energy, and perhaps not enough perseverance to pursue such explorations. One can envision the day when you can explore—via interactive video— any area of your choice. More importantly, you can be guided through that exploration by those who have been acknowledged to be excellent teachers, researchers, and theoreticians. How exciting it will be to visit (or call) your local library and borrow a "disc" that contains an "experience" brought to you by an expert in that field—not simply a lecture but a dialog with the in-class teacher, active participation in simulations and experiments, answers to your questions, and recommendations for additional paths you might be interested in following (that you might never have thought of).

Learning experiences will be very different. They will be customized. They will be interactive. They will be easy to access and use. They will be multimedia. They will be entertaining.

It is unfortunate that for many of us, "learning" enters a somewhat reduced mode after high school, college, or graduate school. That leaves a lot of years when there could have been new explorations, new discoveries, new creations, and even new knowledge. Technology might provide some of the means to truly contribute to lifelong learning—to bring out the teacher and learner in the rest of us.

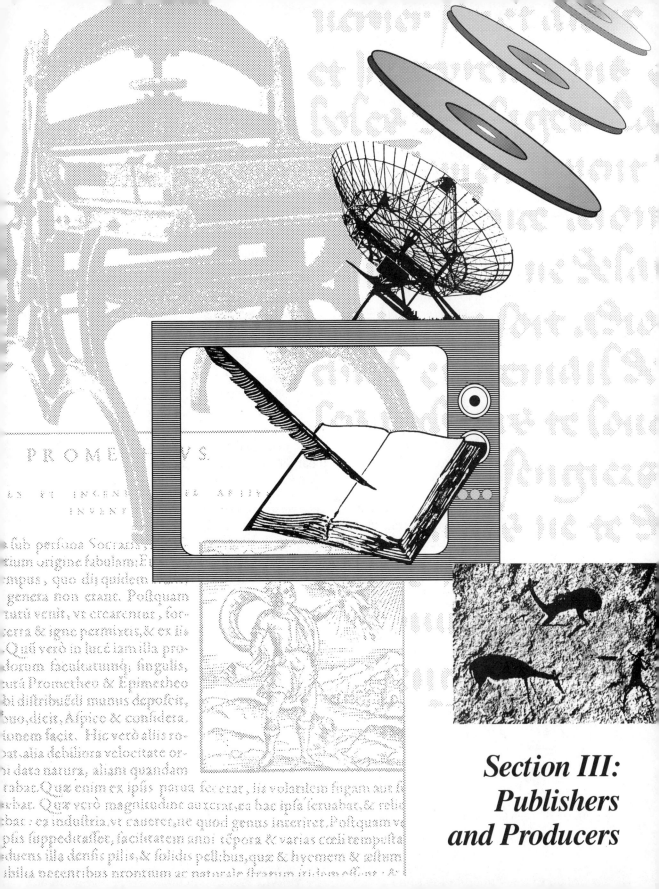

Section III:
Publishers
and Producers

Without additional multimedia publishers and producers, we will not see a sufficient number of multimedia applications available for teachers and students. In this section, publishers and producers look at HyperCard and other multimedia tools. The articles include first-hand experiences of using multimedia and also broad views of what requirements must be met to place multimedia in the mainstream of education.

Monica Bradsher, an editor at National Geographic Society, bravely demonstrates the results of a naive user's first entry into HyperCard. She also describes several multimedia projects at National Geographic Society. She believes the impact of hypermedia on education will depend on ease of use and on meeting the needs of teachers.

Tim Walker describes a case study of a multimedia producer, Optical Data Corporation, using HyperCard for the first time. He is vice president for product development at Optical Data Corp. Reading his chapter is like reading notes in a designer's log book of what worked and what did not work. In his conclusion he emphasizes the importance of the user as the designer when HyperCard is used.

Walter Koetke is director of research for Scholastic Inc. In his article he describes a demonstration of a classroom multimedia station based on the United States Constitution. He also describes the HyperCard multimedia interface as the fourth plateau in computer-based educational technology. The first three plateaus were mainframes, minicomputers, and microcomputers. When used as an interface to multimedia containing moving images, he believes HyperCard will be a critical part of a powerful tool for teaching and learning.

Hugh Osborn takes the broad view and examines where the evolution in multimedia will take us. He comes to the task from the point of view of a television producer. He talks about media, computers, motivation, and informal education. If developed with care, he believes that multimedia can foster learning.

The Teacher as Navigator

Monica Bradsher

MONICA BRADSHER

Monica Bradsher is managing editor for software in the Educational Media Division of the National Geographic Society (NGS), where she has played a leading role in developing computer courseware and the National Geographic Kids Network®. Monica is a graduate of Swarthmore College and holds an M.Ed. from the Graduate School of Education at Harvard University. She was a classroom teacher for 10 years—in Massachusetts, Hong Kong, Virginia, and Washington, D.C.—before joining the Society staff in 1980 as a filmstrip editor.

She shares a lively interest in foreign affairs with her husband and two grown sons. When the boys were young, the family lived in Moscow and in Hong Kong, each for five years. She returned to the Soviet Union in 1988 for a five-week stint as an educational-software specialist in Tashkent with the United States Information Agency's cultural-exchange exhibit, "Information USA." That trip led to two trips in 1989. Three Moscow schools now participate in the NGS Kids Network as part of a collaboration with the Academy of Sciences of the U.S.S.R. The NGS Kids Network is expanding rapidly and now includes schools in many nations.

One question raised in this conference has been why it is that we remember some things and not other things, why some lessons do stick and others don't. A lot of the answer seems to lie in what's sometimes called the "teachable moment," and such moments often occur outside of school. Before addressing my main theme, I'd like to share with you one of the teachable moments in my life.

About 15 years ago, my family and I attended the funeral of one of my in-laws. In the South, funerals continue to be a major social event. After a few hours of meeting visitors in the mortuary, my kids were going crazy with boredom and the effort of being appropriately solemn. So I took them down a hall and found a canteen. (It seemed so incongruous to find a Coke machine in a mortuary!) While I was persuading the machine to give us a drink, part of my mind kept returning to the kinds of questions that funerals invariably raise: If I were to die tomorrow, is this the way I should have spent my life? In other words, I was experiencing a teachable moment. I was ready to consider deep philosophical issues that normally don't command much of my attention.

Just then, a man spoke up. He'd been sitting there watching me keep peace between my sons. "Y'all a teacher?" he asked. I said yes, surprised he could guess so readily. "Bet you're an English teacher," he drawled. Reluctantly, I admitted to that, too, expecting to be quizzed on some fine point of grammar. "I had an English teacher in tenth grade," he explained, "who made me sit in the front row right under her nose.... And whenever she talked to us, she spit."

It isn't often, fortunately, that someone teaches you quite so clearly just how you appear to the world. I want to share that story with you because I still consider myself a teacher, even though I've been with National Geographic for eight years, and because I haven't forgotten that teachers struggle against tremendous odds to gain the respect and status they deserve.

I'm also afraid that this speech might turn out to be another teachable moment for me! I probably know less about HyperCard than anyone here. I came mainly because I wanted to hear what the rest of you have to say. We're doing some interesting things with computers at National Geographic, including an interactive videodisc product, but so far all our efforts have focused on the Apple II computer line, not on the Apple Macintosh.

Just as in my teaching days, Sunday evening was the only time I had free to prepare this presentation. It was too late to make overhead transparencies. I have slides about our other projects—National Geographic Kids Network®, the Geography Education Program, Computer Courseware Kits, our new Weather Machine® telecommunications service—but nothing about hypermedia.

I could hardly represent National Geographic without images of some sort. The only solution seemed to be to make my own images on my Macintosh. Such a sense of desperation is highly motivating—another teachable moment. The time had come to teach myself to create a HyperCard stack. At 4:00 a.m I was still at it. What you will see is a naive user's first entry into HyperCard.

Planning in a New Way

One good thing I discovered was that I could plan my presentation in a new way. Usually, I start by jotting down ideas and organizing them into an outline—a logical, linear progression. That's such hard work, forcing thought into an artificial structure, but it has always seemed to be a necessary step in explaining things to others through any traditional medium, whether lecture, print, or audiovisual. Feeling lazy, I decided to start with the fun part, drawing pictures. I actually began with an elephant, but (as you'll see) the elephant is somewhere in the middle of this stack. I added cards in different directions.

I mention this because I think that HyperCard might still be underrated as a tool for thinking. For certain learning styles, it might prove critical to have under one's control the possibility of starting in the middle, building a web of relationships, and exploring that web to discover structure. Not all children learn in a logical progression. Many are more like magpies, picking up some brightly shining isolated fact to add to an unrelated collection of knowledge. Only later do they begin to see relationships among those facts. Without help at the right—teachable—moments, some children will never make certain crucial connections in their thinking.

Another thing I discovered about HyperCard was that moving beyond making simple stacks to creating scripts for complex programs is a giant step. I'm not sure how long I will need to take that step, but I am sure that one of the first things I'm going to do when I get home is to start teaching myself to mock up program designs. I'm not a programmer. Years ago, I learned just enough BASIC to teach a little introductory course on computers for sixth-graders. That was before the first Apple computer. And I haven't made much progress since then because a discouraging gap always existed between what I could create myself and the kind of programs I wanted children to have. Letting others do the programming seemed the only choice. HyperCard might change that for me and for many teachers.

In a recent issue of *Apple Viewpoints,* Alan Kay presents a timeline of major breakthroughs in computer history. In his formulation, HyperCard ranks as an "icebreaker."

An earlier icebreaker, MacPaint, opened the way for software tools that have launched the revolution in desktop publishing. Exactly what software will follow in the wake of HyperCard is still unclear and is the subject of much speculation. I'd like to address instead the question of what impact Hypermedia might have on education.

I hope I'm not the only one here who is old enough to have a sense of déjà vu when confronted with projections of a computer revolution—or any kind of revolution—in schools. The revolution that was supposed to occur when schools began to use computers might be happening, but it's moving in maddeningly slow motion. The real question about hypermedia is, "Now that we have a chance to do it over again, how should we do it differently?"

Education and Inventions

Because schools seem to change so slowly, I think it's helpful to take a longer view of the effects of inventions on education. Certainly, we shouldn't confine ourselves to the history of computers or even the history of television and other electronic media. The shape that schooling takes reflects to some extent a society's definition of good education, of what an educated person should be like as well as what he or she should know. Inventions have always had an impact on that definition, but not without a lot of controversy, not without serious opposition.

Consider the effect of the invention of written language. Preliterate societies still exist in the world today. In some Islamic countries, for example, you can find villages in which no one knows how to read or write. But they do have little schools where teaching is going on, where children are learning to recite the Holy Koran. Knowing the entire Koran by heart is considered the highest attainment, the mark of a truly educated person. That's a feat few of us could achieve, to know by heart a book as long as the Old Testament. We don't develop our memories to that degree because we have other uses for our time.

Introducing instruction in reading and writing in a preliterate society often provokes opposition. If people can look up any verse, they won't feel the need to learn to recite verses by heart. And if they don't memorize verses, perhaps they will reject our values and no longer be morally upright members of the community! Similar objections have been made to nearly every innovation in education, that the new will harm the social fabric, that the invention will somehow hurt our children.

All of us here are innovators to some degree, so we tend to reject this sort of opposition. But the guardians of tradition are not entirely wrong. Nearly every innovation has had a cost as well as a benefit. In the case of written language, the cost was a decrease in our facility for memorizing, a loss greatly outweighed by the advantages of enlarging our collective memory through written records. Much the same can be said of the more recent inventions shown in Figure 1.

The value of movable type and of printed books in extending learning to large numbers of people is unquestioned. But the mass-produced books lacked some of the beauty of illuminated manuscripts. No doubt many of Gutenberg's contemporaries warned that a printed Bible would command less respect and so undermine morality.

The camera expanded our ways of knowing the world. In the hundred years of the National Geographic Society, photographic illustrations have put great beauty into the hands of the masses and expanded the horizons of ordinary people. Most art teachers, however, will tell you that the impact of photography has not been all good. Knowing how to execute accurate renderings is no longer part of the definition of an educated person. A "D" in an English class might get you into trouble at home, but who cares how well you did in an art class?

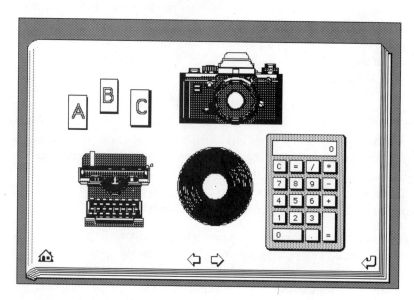

FIGURE 1. Education has gained—and lost—something from each of these inventions: movable type, the camera, the typewriter, the phonograph, and the calculator.

The phonograph and its successors give music classes a library of performances to study, but learning to play an instrument is no longer a social necessity. I can play the stereo— so I don't need to learn to play the piano to entertain my guests.

As for the typewriter, ask any curmudgeon about the current state of penmanship in this country. And if you want to see a real donnybrook, mention the word "calculator" at a school-district curriculum meeting: "Sure, it's important to develop problem-solving skills. But if you let those calculators into classrooms, the kids will lose their incentive to learn the multiplication tables!"

Computers, like these earlier inventions, are beginning to have an effect on society's definition of good education—and computers have been targets of similar opposition. But the effects of inventions are never as deep or as sudden in education as either the opponents or the innovators predict. We do still have piano lessons, and we do still learn cursive writing. It's doubtful that calculators will eclipse drills in multiplication or that spelling checkers will eliminate spelling tests. Bruce MacDonald, one of the teachers who pilot-tested National Geographic Kids Network software, describes a certain kind of parent as a "spelling Nazi." Anyone who has ever taught knows exactly what he means. Spelling Nazis are merely one of many forces that slow changes in curriculum and teaching methods.

Surveys show that large numbers of teachers have yet to touch a computer. The revolution has fallen short of expectations. Will hypermedia have any better luck?

The nineteenth-century model of schooling persists despite growing evidence that a factorylike education does not address the needs of today. (See Figure 2 on the following page.) In most places, we still have a kind of assembly line, grades K–12, that's supposed to turn out a finished product, a citizen who has a certain body of knowledge. We still divide kids into convenient "packages" containing 30 students and spend a vast amount of time lecturing to them, regardless of individual learning styles and needs.

But there's less and less agreement on what body of knowledge should be learned, and there's a growing consensus that schools should prepare the young for lifelong learning. The combination of stiff, foreign economic competition and the changing demographics of our country has convinced many people that we must find new and better ways to prepare students, especially girls and minority students, for scientific or technical careers.

With so much pressure for change, it's tempting to think that the factory model of schooling has outgrown its usefulness and will soon be replaced. On the other hand, many have a vested interest in maintaining the present reality—teachers' unions, politicians, publishers, spelling Nazis. Taxpayers' investment in existing school buildings and

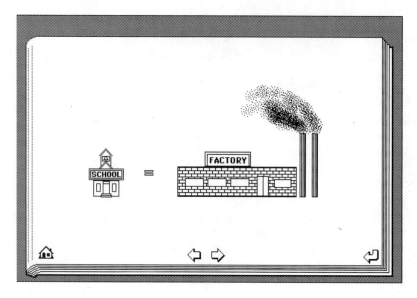

FIGURE 2. To a large degree, our schools still reflect the attitudes prevalent during the Industrial Revolution.

popular nostalgia for the good-old school days add to the inertia. The result is that, for all the multiplying problems, schools change slowly if at all. The more they change, the more they stay the same.

The Perpetual Pendulum

So many controversies about education hinge on whether the top priority is to ensure the production of a certain kind of citizen or to help each student realize her or his full potential as an individual contributing uniquely to society—hence the continuing tension between rote learning and critical thinking, between calculating correct answers and hypothesizing about real problems, between covering the syllabus and investigating a few topics in depth. (See Figure 3.) The pendulum has swung back and forth between content mastery and process skills, between "the Basics" and "Relevance."

If you have any doubt that a power struggle is going on, consider the conflict between proliferating state mandates and the new trend toward school-based management or between proponents of standardized tests with accountability and champions of subjective evaluation with greater autonomy for teachers.

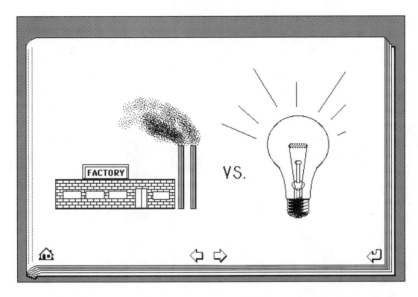

FIGURE 3. Current debates about computers tend to polarize around two persistent philosophies of education: a factory orientation and a more humanistic outlook.

Strangely enough, advocates of each of these opposing views of education see the computer as the answer to many problems. (See Figure 4 on the following page.) That people so opposed in philosophy agree on anything should make us suspicious—particularly when the effect of all that advocacy of computers has had so modest an impact! Are they talking about the same machine?

I'm sure you recall the old fable of India about the blind men who reported their impressions of an elephant. (See Figure 5 on the following page and Figure 6 on page 321.) One, who had felt the breeze from the animal's flapping ears, said that an elephant resembles a fan. The man who grabbed the tail said that an elephant is a kind of rope. The one who held a leg said that elephants are as strong as tree trunks and must support the weight of the world. The blind men seemed to describe several different creatures, but they had encountered the same animal.

Similarly, when educators talk about computers, it's sometimes hard to believe they have considered the full virtuosity of the machine. A computer is not a one-trick pony—like a phonograph that can play back only recorded sounds—yet some teachers still view the computer primarily as a super calculator, of little interest to those who have no pressing need to crunch numbers.

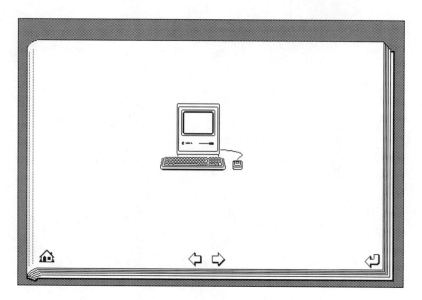

FIGURE 4. An unlikely savior for each side in the philosophy-of-education debate: the microcomputer.

FIGURE 5. Here's my original elephant. This is not a political statement. Nor am I implying that microcomputers are white elephants!

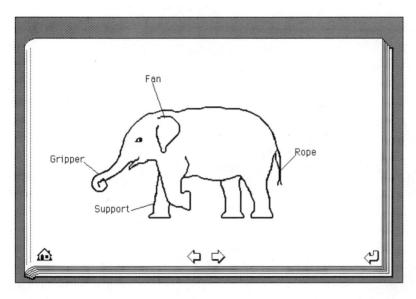

FIGURE 6. The personal computer resembles an elephant in that it can be viewed differently by different people.

Perhaps unconsciously, advocates of computer-assisted instruction (CAI) uphold the tradition of the school-as-factory model. (See Figure 7 on the following page.) For them, the computer offers a low-cost alternative to the fallible teacher. Good tutorials protect children against the variability of teachers. Some children need sustained repetition—drills—to master essential facts. The computer can be relied upon to be a consistent, patient drillmaster. Its calculating power can provide instant feedback, showing whether the child has found the right answer. And its large memory capacity can store—in organized, accessible fashion—all the factual content that ought to be covered. People in this camp want to reform education from the top down. They seek quantitative proof that children learn more material faster from computers than from other media.

Equally vociferous, computer fans in the humanist–progressive tradition will tell you that the only proper use of a school computer is as a tool that empowers the learner by allowing her or him to communicate through writing or music or graphic arts or to explore the world through simulation or surrogate travel. (See Figure 8 on the following page.) Some people further narrow the acceptable field of computer use to Logo or some other programming language that gives the learner complete control over the machine.

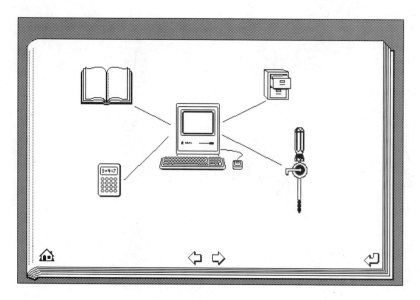

FIGURE 7. Policymakers in the school-as-factory camp tend to evaluate school computers in terms of productivity. They want to know whether computers can produce employable citizens faster and at less cost.

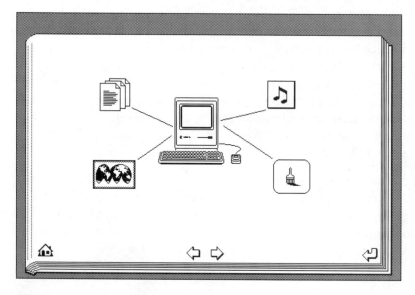

FIGURE 8. Humanistic advocates of computers tend to define them as tools for self-expression and discovery.

Proponents of this point of view tend to want to rescue learning from the deadening influence of authority figures in the form of teachers and administrators or embodied in CAI programs. If only we can put this marvelous tool into the hands of children while they are still young, the thinking goes, we can preserve their innate curiosity and imagination from the crushing influence of formal schooling. This is the philosophy of re-forming education from the bottom up, going directly to the children.

Both camps make a couple of mistakes, it seems to me. One, already touched on, is de-fining too narrowly what a computer can or should do in schools. Surely, a place exists both for good tutorials and for good paint programs. A more serious mistake is the ten-dency to view the computer as a way of circumventing teachers.

Teachers and Technology

Whether the reform is to be from the top down or from the bottom up, the teacher seems to be assigned to an uninspiring role. In the factory model of state mandates and CAI, the teacher is expected to stand back and let somebody else decide what's to be taught, what's to be tested, and how.

Or, on the other hand, the teacher is supposed to stand back and allow the kids to explore on their own with a computer. Some very good teachers stand back and let learning hap-pen. That's my style, too. However, that kind of inquiry-based learning doesn't happen automatically. You have to do a lot of planning and subtle structuring to create the atmosphere in which it works.

Most teachers don't stand back obediently. After they close that classroom door, they teach in their own way. The top-down people look at the product: If the graduates aren't quite what the plan called for, it must be because the teachers didn't follow directions. The bottom-up folks create a wonderful program for the kids, but somehow the teachers manage to mess it up by not presenting it the way the creators envisioned it.

This pattern of trying to circumvent teachers and then blaming them for the way things come out is not confined to the area of computers and software. The solution is always the same: teacher training.

I think teachers have reason to be skeptical about the benefits of technology. A trip to the Soviet Union this spring gave me new understanding of that skepticism. Talking to teachers there about computers was like going back 10 years in our country. Soviet teachers wanted to know if computers were physically harmful. They said that Japanese computers had been shipped to them without software, and the teachers were given no training. The computers bore no obvious relationship to the established curriculum. Teachers complained that central authorities made decisions that only teachers, who really knew the children, should make.

In the Soviet Union, resistance to computers is not confined to teachers; it's expressed by all those who fear the changes Gorbachev is introducing. Here's a whole society that has had a system much like tenure. They've had no incentive to take risks, few opportunities for individual advancement, low pay, and lots of bureaucratic hassles. Now they're being asked to show initiative and to use technology—and they're terrified. They're thinking: "If you just lie low long enough, the authorities will change their minds again, and all this will go away." Sound familiar?

Many teachers are still engaged in passive resistance toward computers, but over the years different groups of teachers have been won over to using them. (See Figure 9.) The first were those who just loved the machines for the sheer wonder and novelty of what computers can do. Then some teachers began to see computers as an avenue for career advancement, often as a way to get out of teaching! The number of computer-using teachers grew larger when it became clear that drill-and-practice software freed them from showing flashcards.

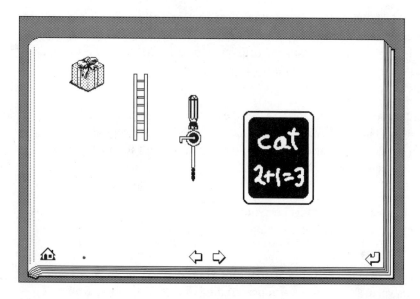

FIGURE 9. Successive changes in teachers' perceptions of personal computers: as a novelty, as a way up the career ladder, as a babysitter (drill and practice), and as a magic slate (word processing).

Word processing probably has been responsible for the largest number of conversions. Not only does word processing help teachers write reports to parents and supervisors, it also helps them with one of their hardest tasks—teaching writing. Word processing has some of the advantages of a magic slate—and more. A word-processing program permits easy revision, compactly stores written work, and enables even young children to produce "writing" that looks neat and is inviting to the reader.

Software designers, whether they are working within the CAI mold or are producing a nonlinear hypermedia product, can easily fall into the trap of thinking themselves better teachers than the ones in the classrooms. Certainly, we all do a fine job of teaching our own children, and we teach each other every day. Such informal teaching is satisfying and effective in its place, but it's not quite the same as what teachers are expected to do hour after hour and day after day.

Teacher-proof materials are doomed to languish unused in school media centers. The advantages that designers and publishers have over teachers are the luxuries of time and proximity to such resources as pictures and good reference libraries. The teacher, on the other hand, has the advantage of being there, knowing the kids, and managing the atmosphere for learning. The teacher is an indispensable part of education in all kinds of schools and in various societies. But just what should the teacher's role be? That has varied.

I've noticed that several speakers complained that there's no chalkboard here. Do you wonder why we feel that need so acutely? Think again about that primitive school in a preliterate society. Often you'll see a teacher squatting down with a small circle of pupils. They take turns drawing pictures in the sand. The act of pointing seems to be an important part of teaching and learning. Perhaps that is one reason the Macintosh interface is so powerful—pointing with the mouse seems natural. I think we feel a need for a chalkboard because drawing and pointing are essential methods of teaching.

Somehow over the centuries, we put the sand for drawing up on the wall in the form of a chalkboard behind the teacher's desk where the children can't get at it easily. In most classrooms, it's still a special treat to be allowed to draw on the board with the teacher's chalk. Having a large class of 30 or so students makes it difficult to let everyone have a chance at this important sketching-and-pointing activity. In the factorylike school, the teacher has been expected to be the authority, the foreman, the fount of all knowledge, the keeper of all right answers. So only the teacher could do the pointing.

Considering the explosion of knowledge and the accessibility of information, how can anyone hope to know it all? Yet many teachers still have difficulty admitting that they don't know all the answers. Having the answers is the most obvious distinction between teachers and students. It tends to legitimize the teacher's authority in a society where age alone no longer guarantees respect.

Interactive multimedia products have the potential to help teachers conduct a class. When Peter Jennings used a HyperCard reference stack during coverage of a political campaign, we saw a new role definition that teachers might go for: anchor person. Teachers could be the ones who have information resources at their fingertips, not necessarily in their heads, the ones who can cut to an entertaining snippet of motion video, the ones to model investigative learning by querying the database or interviewing guests. But the students, like reporters, have a role in the show. Using a computer and videodisc player, they can prepare and deliver parts of the lesson in the form of presentations that will hold the attention of the rest of the group.

As a presentation device, the computer-plus-videodisc-player gives the teacher a chance at last to compete with television without sacrificing curriculum or classroom control. Many teachers are willing to give up the burden of being captain in favor of the role of navigator. As navigator, the teacher guides the class in deciding which pictures to view, what factual knowledge to consider. A good navigator can change course settings to take advantage of favorable winds. If a teachable moment comes along that is somewhat off the subject of the day, a rich multimedia product should allow the teacher to guide students to the resources they need to satisfy their intellectual curiosity.

GTV—An Interactive Multimedia Project

National Geographic's first computer-driven videodisc project, called GTV™ (geography television), is a collaboration with Lucasfilm, Ltd. The project has been supported in part by a grant from the state of California. GTV is designed to allow teachers and students to initiate many new connections between bits of information, between photographs and text, between geography and history.

Viewed without computer mediation—Level One—the two double-sided videodiscs in this product take viewers on a journey through time for a look at American history from a geographic perspective. Relationships between certain landscapes and events are fairly explicit in the videodisc narration. Adding the computer's power—Level Three—allows the teacher to explore more landscapes, more events, and more relationships than could be addressed in any traditional presentation of comparable length.

A Macintosh version of the GTV software will be available. Working with HyperCard would make the developers' tasks easier. We all look forward to a time when many K–12 schools will have Macintosh computers with hard-disk drives and with CD-ROM drives. Nevertheless, it is possible right now for teachers with an Apple IIGS to begin to explore the power of interactive videodiscs. This new medium is especially helpful in teaching geography, a discipline whose essence is in finding relationships between location or place and just about anything else—landforms, flora, fauna, climate, culture, economic activity, political struggles, military conflict, and so on.

In pilot testing, teachers have responded most enthusiastically to such options as building presentations of their own or having students use GTV in small groups to prepare reports for the rest of the class. As longtime masters of the filmstrip medium, our staff passed on to teachers one of our simplest and most valuable tools—the light table. We always spread our slides, or transparencies, on a light table as an aid in arranging pictures, figuring out the order of presentation. Using the GTV software, teachers see a "light table" on the computer screen. They can manipulate icons representing images or segments of the videodisc programs. They can tell the computer how long to let each image remain on the screen and whether to include any music or narration with it. And they can run their "slide show" to preview the presentation they've prepared.

At the National Geographic Society, we're guided by certain goals set by our president and chairman, Gilbert M. Grosvenor. Four years ago, when he launched our campaign to improve geography education, he made clear that reaching teachers was essential. Teachers' responses to the annual Summer Geography Institute at our headquarters have been touching. They frequently express surprise and gratitude that someone is paying attention to regular classroom teachers. We also involve teachers as consultants and pilot testers at each stage of development of our new products.

Mr. Grosvenor charged us with changing the perception of geography as a course in merely memorizing place names and locations. Our goal is to spread recognition of the capacity of geographic study to cross disciplinary boundaries and find more complete explanations of how the world around us really works. The new electronic media offer an unprecedented opportunity to restore geography to its rightful place as an exciting, integrative way of organizing knowledge.

GTV adheres to the criteria listed in Figure 10 on the following page. It is based on the California Framework for History and Geography. It allows classes to rearrange pictures and information to discover new connections in ways that other media can't match. It is highly interactive—whether it's being used by a teacher with an entire class, by an individual preparing a presentation, or by a small group exploring together.

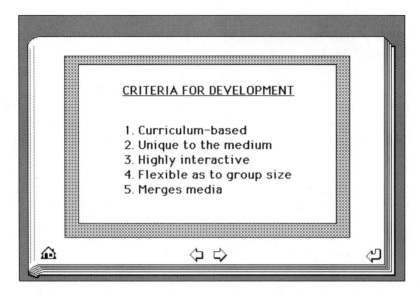

*FIGURE 10. National Geographic's computer-related products have
in common certain criteria that will be important to the success of
interactive multimedia in general.*

The interrelation of computer software and videodisc is more powerful than use of those media separately would be. There is no point in buying expensive equipment and materials unless these new tools perform in ways that more traditional media cannot. It isn't enough that a computer might do something a little faster than a more traditional method could.

In addition to GTV, some of our other new products have the same ingredients—a combination of media and meeting teachers' needs, although no videodisc is included. The Weather Machine, a software tool for studying the atmosphere, has been a success at our pilot test sites because it allows teachers and students to create accurate, colorful weather-map displays for presentation to the class. Through telecommunications, classes can receive today's weather data today—and in a form they can manipulate and study. The teacher becomes the data navigator, helping students discover relationships between variables and see patterns that are clues to forecasting.

In collaboration with Technical Education Research Centers (TERC), in Cambridge, Massachusetts, we're developing the National Geographic Kids Network, a new curriculum in science and geography for grades 4–6. Kids and teachers in this network collect data, share it with schools nationwide through telecommunications, and look for patterns in the combined results (displayed as maps and as graphs on their computer screens). For example, the first curriculum unit that we developed centered on the issue of acid rain. The teacher must be navigator, not captain, in this curriculum because the experiments investigate real issues for which the answers are not yet known.

The enthusiastic response of teachers to The Weather Machine and to the National Geographic Kids Network makes me optimistic about the future of computers in schools. In spite of the challenges inherent in telecommunicating through antiquated school telephone systems, teachers persist. Many of them have previously seen no need to use computers, but the humanizing aspect of the network—sharing data and letters with other teachers and kids—seems to provide the incentive to spend the extra time required to become familiar with a computer and with software. Similarly, the incentive of being able to tailor beautifully illustrated presentations to the needs of a class—or to the teachable moment of an individual student—seems to be overcoming teachers' reluctance to tackle learning about videodiscs.

How should we do it differently this time around? Treat teachers as navigators. Respect their need for materials that don't require hours to learn or to use. Give them the resources to lead students on journeys of inquiry. And let's be sure the role is indeed that of navigator. No teacher wants to be merely the deckhand who cleans up—after the kids, with their computers, have had all the fun on their own!

HyperCard and Videodisc: A Case Study in Design

Timothy Walker

TIMOTHY WALKER

Timothy Walker was trained as a social psychologist at Harvard University, where he specialized in linguistic anthropology and mass communications. He spent a number of years as a secondary-school teacher and media-production specialist, and has designed courses in anthropology, media studies, radio and television production, and photography. He subsequently completed a master's program in inter-active telecommunications at New York University, where he focused on computer-assisted, videodisc-based learning environments. As a doctoral candidate at the Massa-chusetts Institute of Technology's Media Laboratory, he studied with Seymour Papert's learning and epistemology group before joining Optical Data Corporation as vice president of advanced software development. His research interests center on the topic of media literacy.

Introduction

What follows is a brief case study of one HyperCard product—a reflection on design, redesign, and the perennial tension between vision and reality. To begin with, Hyper-Card is a design medium that embodies its own designer's vision. In creating his "software erector set," Bill Atkinson was philosophically in tune with hypertext pioneers such as Vannevar Bush and Doug Englebart, sharing their dream of empowering human thought, creativity, and exchange. HyperCard is most remarkable because it is a product that contains within itself the tools of its own production. These tools allow users to customize a HyperCard stack and to superimpose their own "data strata" on top of one information base. In theory, at least, authorship and readership can mesh seamlessly.

This does not mean that Atkinson's vision will be successfully embodied in every Hyper-Card stack on the market. The fact is that many more people will be simply users of stackware than will have the time, ability, or inclination to bend HyperCard's raw power to their own ends. HyperCard thus poses a supreme challenge to any designer who shares the "hypertext philosophy," which is, in essence, that users should become designers. Advancing this vision of Hypermedia clearly depends on "good design"—in this case, on successful solutions to the dilemma of how to design stacks that are both robust and malleable. For the past two years, this has been a central concern in the process of shaping VideoCards™, a HyperCard-based "front end" for Optical Data Corporation's science databases.

Optical Data Corporation—the country's leading producer–publisher of optical video-discs—pioneered the archival videodisc for education in the 1980s with a series of basic science collections. Videodisc players use laser technology (similar to that of an audio compact-disc player) to display video images, either as still frames or in motion. Perfect still frames and virtually instant access to any image are the technology's key advantages over videotape. One archival videodisc can store an hour of motion video—over 100,000 individual frames. Optical Data's discs typically provide several thousand still frames, with the remainder of each side used for motion clips.

For years, Optical Data had published separate, print-based image directories that cataloged the contents of each educational science disc. Teachers using these materials accessed individual frames and movies by looking up frame numbers in the print directory and then pushing buttons on a hand-held, remote-control unit to call up the visuals. The discs had instant appeal as multimedia resources, but the sheer size of the resource was often overwhelming. The true promise of videodiscs lay in computer-based management of the image archive; however, no affordable system yet existed for classroom use. An Apple II could do little more than "push the buttons" for the teacher. Then, along came WildCard.

In early 1987, Apple Computer's Mike Liebhold demonstrated how he'd used WildCard (later renamed HyperCard) to develop graphic "tours" for Optical Data's Earth Science videodisc. (See Figure 1.) Clicking on "buttons" scattered across an Apple Macintosh computer-based map of the United States, he instantly called up a series of Landsat satellite images on the TV monitor. Clicking on a "lightning bolt" icon, he triggered a flash and a peal of thunder. Here, it seemed, was an ideal "front end" for archival videodiscs! The simple, concrete metaphor of a stack of file cards mapped perfectly onto the way consecutive single frames were laid out on a videodisc. The built-in tools (and the videodisc drivers that enabled WildCard to control a disc player) provided a whole new range of interactive design options. By June 1987, development of a prototype, commercial front end (for the same Earth Science disc) was under way at Optical Data.

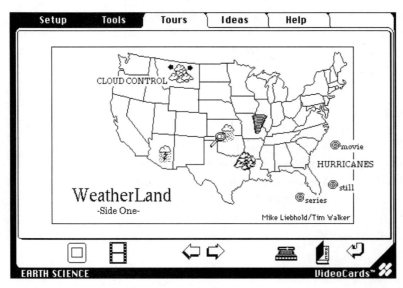

FIGURE 1. Mike Liebhold's "WeatherLand," an example of a graphic "tour" designed by using HyperCard.

Designing a Front End

Our earliest design decisions were not really decisions, but rather assumptions derived from the architecture—the "data structure," if you will—of the videodisc archive itself and from the parallels between "cards" and "frames." At Optical Data we had developed a standard organizational format for our visual databases, using title frames to denote clearly defined topic–subtopic relationships among groups of images. The front end we were building for Earth Science would resemble an "electronic card catalog": a massive stack with some 7000 cards, one for each still frame (or cluster of frames) and one for each of the several dozen short movies on the disc. The data on each card would be imported from the text files we'd compiled for the print-based directory. Button links would enable users to navigate from one topic to another, following an index structure tied to the title frames on the disc itself. These were givens.

Beyond the form of the card catalog itself lurked tougher design choices. What would teachers (and students) want to do with all this data? What tools and features would they expect (or tolerate) in a "hypermedia" environment—something few had even heard of? How much could we assume they would know about basic HyperTalk commands, let alone about Bill Atkinson's vision? In the months prior to HyperCard's official release, these and other basic questions were difficult to answer—and, given the attendant secrecy, virtually impossible to field-test!

Hence, the answers, as often as not, had to stem from intuition. One early, irrevocable choice was to opt for a set of separate stacks, functionally distinct from the main Data stack. The notion of these ancillary stacks as "containers" for specialized functions suggested the visual metaphor of tab folders, located at the bottom of the screen, which replaced HyperCard's menu bar along the top of the screen. (See Figure 2 on following page.) It was a utilitarian device, to be sure, but one which both reinforced the grouping of special functions and complemented the basic card metaphor.

To ensure the consistency of the VideoCards interface, every card—throughout all the stacks—shared a visually identical background. By clicking the "tabs," users could access the following ancillary stacks:

- The Setup stack, which guided the user through the initialization sequence.
- The Tools stack, which included an animated control panel for the videodisc, a text-search utility, a card-marking/presentation tool, and a list of HyperTalk videodisc commands.
- The Tours stack, containing (initially) Mike Liebhold's simple graphic browsers.

- The Ideas stack, conceived as a sort of on-line, updatable user newsletter.
- The Help stack, with a stack map and explanatory cards for each major feature.
- The Open stack (accessible via the *blank* tab), which users were encouraged to adapt to suit their own needs.

A number of design decisions made at this early juncture were rooted in a supremely idealistic view of HyperCard's acceptance and currency among a true "community" of users. We envisioned a distributed network of HyperCard-literate educators, eager to have their students confront the intellectual challenge of constructing new elements for the database. For example, in addition to the descriptive elements on each data card, we provided two unlocked, empty text fields so that users could enter new information of their own. The Ideas stack initially contained a single essay on the "philosophy" of hypermedia—an exhortation to users to provide feedback and (more concretely) examples of the Tours and data enhancements they'd come up with. Future versions of the database, we declared, would benefit from the contributions of this active user network. The Open stack offered "room to grow"—for those users who wished to add custom features. The information provided on videodisc scripting presumed an audience of HyperCard do-it-yourselfers.

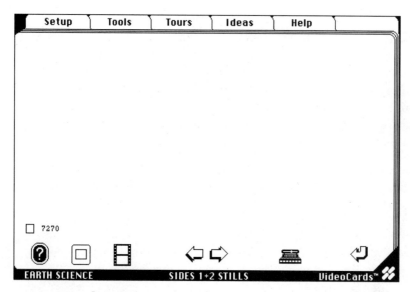

FIGURE 2. The VideoCards background, showing "tabs" that appear on all cards.

This is not to imply that the idealism behind this original design ultimately impeded the product in any way; to the contrary, here was a rare instance of a commercial software product developed in vitro, shaped in disproportionate measure by the optimism surrounding HyperCard itself in its prerelease phase. The very pace of progress (with a debut product literally the outcome of a one-person, three-month development effort) seemed to support our underlying assumption that users would quickly attain HyperCard proficiency.

When the VideoCards front end was unveiled alongside HyperCard at the 1987 MacWorld Expo, it attracted its share of attention—and has been attracting attention ever since. HyperCard-videodisc applications have proven to be surefire "demo winners" across the board. For a number of months, basking in the success of VideoCards' initial reception, we focused on replicating the Earth Science model for each of Optical Data's other science archives: life science, physical science, astronomy. The replication involved 22,000 still frames and 7 hours of full-motion video, indexed in 12 megabytes of stackware (over 20,000 cards in all).

VideoCards version 1 was a fully functional information-management tool, supporting presentation, browsing, and directed research. For presentations, the Apple Macintosh computer functioned as a desktop audiovisual controller and a set of electronic "cue cards" rolled into one. Users could browse in a number of ways: for example, by exploring the sample Tours or by using the animated Control Panel to skim through videodisc images and then pull up data cards for specific visuals. Various tools supported basic research functions. The Search & Show feature quickly compiled a list of every instance of a specified term in the database. The Mark & Edit feature allowed users to build their own lists of pertinent images while browsing, simply by clicking a box on each data card. In each case, the resulting lists enabled rapid image retrieval. Simply clicking the appropriate line within a list called up the videodisc frame or data card or both.

For all its features, version 1 was as remarkable for what it promised as for what it delivered. That is to say, much of its strength lay in pointing the way to novel classroom applications. As a product inspired by Atkinson's vision, it offered teachers and students not so much a vast archive of unassailable data as a template—a shell within which the act of extending and enriching the basic data set could become an educationally rewarding activity. We hoped teachers would encourage their students to personalize the data cards by typing their own descriptions and annotations into the open text fields provided. Student reports prepared as text files and appended to the VideoCards database could become part of an expanding classroom resource. We anticipated a flurry of activity as users constructed their own Tour cards: exploded diagrams, time lines, map browsers, and the like, using buttons to access videodisc images.

A Critical Reassessment

It was not until the spring of 1988, when work on the companion front-end stacks had culminated in the release of VideoCards databases for each of ODC's archival discs, that we found ourselves with some breathing space, and we began to reexamine our earlier expectations. Had things panned out as planned? Certainly, the product continued to "show" well and was attracting considerable attention to Optical Data's videodisc offerings. On the other hand, despite brisk sales activity, follow-up calls turned up only a handful of teachers actually using VideoCards in the classroom. The typical early adopter, it seemed, was an ed-tech specialist or district computer coordinator who was getting great demo mileage out of the product but who had little to say about how "average users"—teachers and students—might be faring.

Despite this lack of clear feedback, it was also becoming clear that the average user was having considerably more difficulty mastering HyperCard than most early developers had anticipated. Although hordes of hackers had crammed electronic bulletin boards from coast to coast with examples of rudimentary stack design, high-quality stacks were rare. For computer neophytes or nonprogrammers, HyperTalk was proving a rather high hurdle. One conclusion emerged from all this: we could make absolutely no assumptions about the prior experience of our "typical" user. Some educators using VideoCards had never touched an Apple Macintosh computer before; others were accomplished Hyper-Talk scripters. Yet the product's real promise depended on the user's ability to enhance it and modify it, using HyperCard tools. How could we ensure that VideoCards would not daunt the neophyte, while conveying the exciting possibilities to more advanced users? Certainly, good print documentation could go far to address these needs—and we had prepared none for VideoCards version 1!

If documentation was clearly a crying need, we had begun to suspect that the software itself might already need revision. While our early start with HyperCard had enabled Optical Data to be "first out of the chute" with VideoCards, the lack of field testing during this formative phase was beginning to show. Many of our original assumptions about users' familiarity with HyperCard, or their shared grasp of Atkinson's philosophical premise, proved to be incorrect. For the first time since the generation of the basic model the summer before, questions of design were coming to the fore. Clearly, it was time to reinvent the product—if only to promote its basic goals more effectively.

Reactive Changes

An informal field-test arrangement with a local high school proved a milestone in the overhaul of version 1. We looked on, recording speak-aloud protocols, as a series of teachers and students attempted to cope with VideoCards: hard-disk installation, software initialization, overview and help screens, tool cards, data cards, navigation iconography, and the like. These sessions—the first serious testing the product had undergone—were invaluable, and led to a series of what might be called reactive changes in the VideoCards software. Over the next several months, the Setup stack and its initialization procedure were completely revamped; the Control Panel interface was reworked; other tool cards were redesigned for greater consistency; and on-screen messages were reworded for greater clarity.

The redesigned Setup Stack still did double duty, providing a one-time software initialization sequence and a subsequent entry point for all users. Now, however, the two functions were neatly partitioned. Opened for the first time, the stack prompted the user through a series of four steps, such as clicking a button to install a Home Card button, choosing a player, and so on. If the user quit before completing all four steps, then the software was "smart" enough to resume the sequence the next time the stack was opened. After completion, however, the initialization prompts were hidden from view. From that point on, users entering the database were presented with only two choices: to consult an on-line VideoCards overview or to proceed directly to the Control Panel.

As work began on comprehensive print documentation, the role of on-line documentation and help came under scrutiny. We revamped the Essential Info section—the series of a dozen overview cards in the Setup stack—on the assumption that first-time VideoCards users would have had no prior experience with HyperCard. The first things introduced were Command-Spacebar—used to reveal HyperCard's menu bar—and the convention of clicking right and left arrows to step forward and back between cards. A HyperCard QuickRef card then listed 14 basic keyboard commands and encouraged users to try them out. As a backup measure, we decided to print out the Essential Info section as part of a VideoCards QuickRef card, to be included with the documentation.

Another approach was to make tools and buttons literally "self-explanatory." For example, our field tests had revealed that novice users had difficulty understanding how to use the Control Panel (see Figure 3 on following page) to manipulate video images. For some people, videodisc concepts like "step forward," "search frame," or "display on" were brand-new. For others, the tricky part was using the mouse to move the animated "slider." Because the Control Panel was effectively the center of VideoCards activity, and was the first screen many users were likely to view, helping users to master this feature was essential. Our solution was to rescript the Control Panel buttons (see Figure 4), so that holding the shift key down while clicking a button displayed a brief message

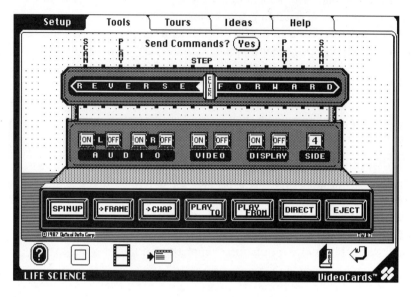

FIGURE 3. "Old" control panel: VideoCards version 1.

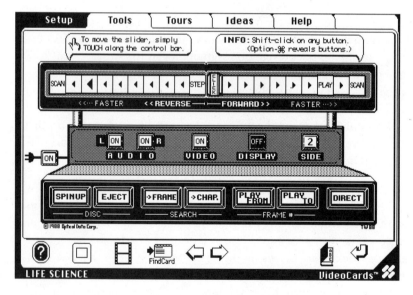

FIGURE 4. "New" control panel: VideoCards version 2.

explaining that button's function. Two conspicuous "dialog balloons" provided hints on how to manipulate the slider, how to reveal buttons, and how to see button explanations. Then we crossed our fingers, hoping users would notice the balloon messages!

In version 1, the VideoCards Help Stack had provided the only published instructions on such tools as Search & Show and Mark & Edit, using multiple cards to explain each feature. The main problem, of course, was that in order to learn anything, a user had to leave the tool cards behind to go to the Help cards! Printed instructions would alleviate this problem, for users could try out the tools as they read the documentation. So rather than duplicate on-line what print could more usefully convey, we decided that version 2's Help stack should provide more of a schematic overview of the software, with a single card for each key feature or tool, as shown in Figure 5.

We also devised a way of incorporating guided tours into the Help stack, so that certain Help cards could actually demonstrate the features they described. A user could click a Show Me! button, then sit back and go on a "talking tour" of a particular feature, such as Mark & Edit. Each tour visited a series of actual VideoCards screens, with an oversized hand "pointing" and "clicking buttons" and a Macintalk voice explaining each action. Despite the crude synthetic speech (using digitized speech would have consumed too much disk space), the technique approximated a look over the shoulder of an experienced user—something no documentation could provide.

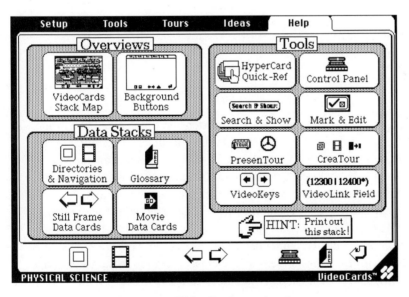

FIGURE 5. The Help menu in VideoCards version 2.

"Proactive" Changes

As we revised the VideoCards software in response to field testing and more accurate user profiles, we also upgraded it by incorporating a wish list of features that would extend the usefulness of each multimedia database and the range of activities each could support. The principal changes affected three VideoCards stacks: the main Data stack, the Tools stack, and the Ideas stack.

Each Data stack, as has been noted, served as the electronic card catalog for a particular videodisc archive. The data on each card had been derived from earlier print-based directories—which invariably provided little more than caption-length information for each image. One of the most obvious challenges, then, was to find ways of building up the data component by enhancing the descriptions. In a way, taking on this task ourselves was a departure from one of VideoCards' initial purposes, that of providing a framework for user enhancements. We reasoned that users could always add their own information; they'd simply be starting with a richer data set. Furthermore, we had evolved an approach that we hoped would compound VideoCards' utility as a browsing environment.

The approach was a set of guidelines combined with a simple format through which our content consultants, working in a standard word-processing environment, could contribute new text to each database, using five standard categories:

- Description
- Things to Notice
- Question and Answer
- Keywords
- See Also

The Description component was, of course, a simple extension of the original caption. Notice lines, on the other hand, were worded so as to draw a student's attention to specific elements of a visual, such as an important aspect of an organism's anatomy or a key detail of a mechanical apparatus. Questions and Answers were one-line teasers, again relating to specific visuals, while See Also links specified related images or motion clips on the disc. Keywords supplemented the actual descriptive text with other pertinent terms—providing "landing pads" for text searches using HyperCard's Find command. Together, the elements were intended to reward visual database browsing by stimulating students' curiosity, inviting them to pay closer attention to the visuals, and prompting them to think more deeply about what they were seeing.

As our consultants shipped back their text files, the new information (arranged by frame number and category) was ported into the Data stacks—but not into the same old Data stacks! (See Figure 6, below, and Figure 7, on following page, for a comparison of the old and new data cards.) While Description and Notice lines could reside comfortably in the main data field on each card, each of the other elements called for its own special field. For example, we invented a simple two-line Q/A field, with a question shown on the top line and the second line empty. Clicking on a question popped the answer into the second line; moving the mouse pointer out of the field hid the answer again. Another invention, the See Also fields, displayed lists of one or more associated frames or movies. To traverse a link, the user simply clicked on the desired item; each field's script contained its own list of destination card ID numbers. Any See Also field could easily support additional links, either from a consultant's text files or by using a manual link-making process.

Perhaps the most exciting new scripting went into several additional tools designed to enhance the user's ability to build personal information structures. One of these building blocks, the VideoLink field, enabled frame numbers entered into ordinary text passages to function like buttons, which, when clicked, cued up individual video frames or even played motion segments. New frame-number links could be entered automatically by clicking with the Option key held down. Simple cursor movements alternately locked

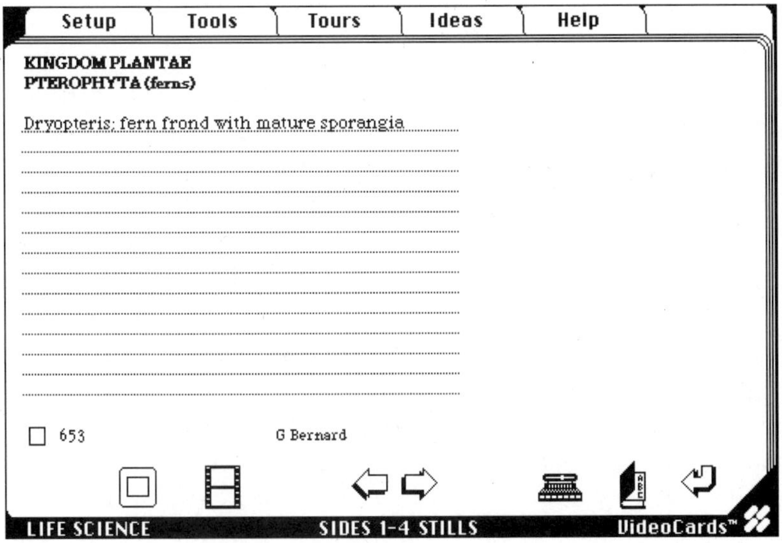

FIGURE 6. "Old" data card: VideoCards version 1.

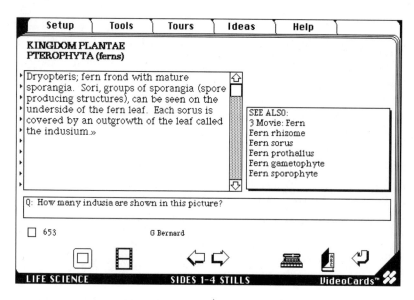

FIGURE 7. "New" data card: VideoCards version 2.

and unlocked the field, toggling it from a read/write mode to a read-only mode. While requiring virtually no HyperCard fluency, VideoLink fields served equally well for logging or annotating video material, inserting video figures into a text report, or authoring lesson sequences.

Another set of tools, dubbed CreaTour, was intended for users with advanced HyperCard abilities who wanted to create their own stacks, incorporating video-display capabilities. VideoCards' existing Mark & Edit feature already allowed users to gather specific still frames and movies into lists and to rearrange the visuals simply by cutting and pasting lines within or between lists. CreaTour now enabled users to create "video buttons" (see Figure 8) from these list sequences—buttons which could be pasted into separate stacks for stand-alone applications.

The key to stand-alone capabilities was having the user begin by generating a stack using CreaTour's Spinoff card, which invisibly exported a number of essential handlers as it created the new stack. The spun-off stack sprang into existence with a single card, featuring a VideoLink field as well as buttons for navigating back to the host stack's CreaTour cards. The stack's author could customize it in any number of ways, always able to draw upon the multimedia database. The stack itself could function independently of VideoCards—could, for example, deliver a self-contained floppy-disk–based lesson.

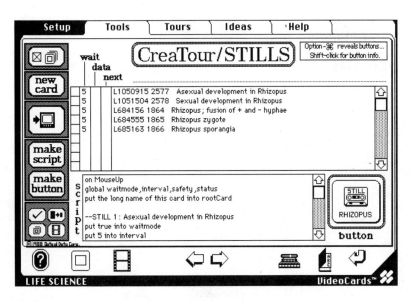

FIGURE 8. The Creatour/stills card, which allows users to create "video buttons."

At a June 1988 workshop in Upland, California, a number of VideoCards version 1 users brought their Apple Macintosh computers to a sneak preview of the new CreaTour tools and traded thoughts on classroom applications. At the outset, each participant received a floppy disk with a simple stack: a set of a dozen or so cards, each with a topic heading and a blank text field. As discussion proceeded, participants typed their comments into the appropriate topic field. At day's end, floppy disks were collected, and the entire set of comments was pooled into a master stack. Over the next several months, this IdeaBase stack—and the underlying concept of collective contributions—evolved into the official VideoCards version 2 Ideas stack.

The current IdeaBase shares the simple design of its Upland ancestor and invites all VideoCards users to participate in a straightforward exchange process. (See Figure 9 on the following page.) The user enters personal comments, questions, or tips onto the appropriate topic card and then mails a floppy-disk copy of the stack back to Optical Data. There, the new material is filtered into an actively maintained master compilation stack, and an updated copy of the compilation is returned to the user. As a model of information exchange, the IdeaBase holds out great promise.

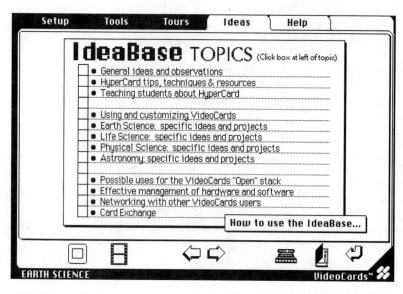

FIGURE 9. The IdeaBase menu, which invites the user to participate in an exchange process.

Conclusion

At this writing, in early 1989, VideoCards version 2 has just been released, and its designers (now redesigners) have earned another breathing space. This time, we're not looking over our shoulders at a trail of first-generation flaws, but looking forward—to the fulfillment of second-generation promises. There is now every expectation that VideoCards' users will finally include average teachers and students, rather than only technology coordinators. A product that might have languished as a demonstration piece has been refined into a state-of-the-art tool, with enough documented features to keep its users productive for many school years.

Was the initial release of the software premature? Probably so, by conventional software standards. VideoCards version 1 was a remarkable product—but it had never been field-tested and had no documentation to speak of. It was in many respects still in an experimental stage. Yet, we've had no complaints from the early adoptors on our decision to release version 1. Most were already using Optical Data's videodiscs, and VideoCards converted these visual databases to multimedia databases. A year of field experience has engendered more powerful, better-designed, and better-documented software, just as the broad cross-section of educators is gearing up for classroom multimedia adoptions.

Seen in perspective, the development cycle sketched here included most of the phases that comprise conventional software development. But HyperCard, as the development medium of choice, imposed a distinctive stamp on the process—from the relatively small effort needed to embody unique functions in our initial prototype, to our ability to rework the product from the ground up. The first year of HyperCard's release was an experimental one for every developer. We've all learned a great deal about how average teachers and students will approach HyperCard; the revamped VideoCards 2 reflects much of this new knowledge.

Earlier, we framed a key challenge for stack designers: to create stacks for average users that incorporate the vision of the user as designer. VideoCards 2 rises to this challenge by providing a range of tools that will enable many users—not just HyperCard experts— to enjoy the rewards of manipulating information and building their own multimedia stacks. We can expect that, over time, users will grow with HyperCard as we ourselves have grown with it. They will come to appreciate its central philosophy—the vision of continually and collaboratively improving on a basic design. For it was HyperCard as a design medium that made us certain we had to redesign our product. How could we settle for less than the best, when the tools were right in our hands?

HyperCard:
A Multimedia Interface

Walter J. Koetke

WALTER J. KOETKE

Walter J. Koetke helped introduce computers into United States public-school classrooms with a pioneering effort in the 1960s in the Lexington, Massachusetts, school system. He joined Scholastic Inc. in 1983, where he is currently director of research and development. He is a frequent speaker at national conventions and has written computer-curriculum material, two textbooks, as well as many articles and columns. He is a graduate of the Massachusetts Institute of Technology and earned a master's degree from Harvard University.

Any discussion of HyperCard in K–12 education should include at least a glimpse of reality. And the reality of public education in the United States right now is frightening. Let's look at just a few facts.

A 1988 survey published by the National Geographic Society evaluated the basic geographic knowledge of 18- to 24-year-olds from 8 nations. The United States ranked eighth. Some of their findings for our young adults included: two of three could not locate Vietnam on a map; one of four could not locate Russia; and one of seven could not locate the United States. Our level of literacy is even worse. Approximately 29 million people in the United States are functionally illiterate, meaning that they cannot read on a fifth-grade level. They cannot read a newspaper, address an envelope, complete a job application, find a number in the telephone book, order from a menu, or read a note from their child's teacher. Our national high-school dropout rate is now almost 30 percent— over 50 percent in most major cities. And according to a 1988 study, 20 percent of 18-year-olds who did graduate could not read their high-school diploma.

A 1986 study of 21- to 25-year-old college graduates conducted by the Educational Testing Service revealed that 40 percent of the graduates could not calculate the change they should receive when paying a restaurant check, and 60 percent could not calculate a 10-percent tip.

Perhaps we've been emphasizing other things in our nation's classrooms. After all, many educators will tell you that problem solving is more important than an ability to calculate. But a 1986 study of 17-year-olds showed no gain in problem-solving skills since 17-year-olds were last tested in 1978. The same study showed a significant increase since 1982 in the percentage of girls who agree with the statement, "Math is more appropriate for boys than for girls." If these issues are really our priorities, we're not doing very well with them either.

Similar statistics exist for any subject area you choose. The point is clear: Public education in the United States is not doing the job that needs to be done. Public education is failing at a time when its success is more important than ever if the United States is to remain competitive in a global economy. It's failing us at a time when flexible individual skills are vital for those who must find their way through a rapidly changing job market. Please note that I do not intend to blame teachers for the shortcomings of public education. They are certainly one part of the problem—but only one of a great many parts. If we hope to fix those shortcomings, then teachers must become a major part of the solution. Any technology that we hope to use to improve learning must be adopted and used by classroom teachers. If they don't accept it, it really doesn't have a chance.

Perhaps that's enough of reality. Is HyperCard going to solve the problems of K–12 American education? Of course not! The problems are very complex and the solutions are neither simple nor well defined. Is HyperCard going to solve even one of the major problems? I doubt it. So why has HyperCard captured the imagination of so many educators? Are they eternally optimistic, desperately grasping at straws, or falling for media hype? Or does HyperCard really represent a powerful tool for educators?

I believe that HyperCard is an important key to effective use of multimedia in the classroom and that appropriate use of multimedia can be an important factor in improving the effectiveness of learning for many children. Certainly it is merely one of the pieces needed to solve a complex problem, but it can help—and it can do so right away. Some of my reasons for this belief follow, but before you read on, take a moment to complete a very brief assignment. Write a two- or three-sentence description of a memorable event in your life that happened before you were in junior high school. That's all. Just write two or three sentences, then read on.

During the 1986–87 school year, Apple Computer, Inc., Scholastic Inc., and Optical Data Corp. collaborated to produce a demonstration of a classroom multimedia station based on the United States Constitution. The result of this collaboration was a demo that is even more effective than anticipated. The demo uses a HyperCard-based interface for the Macintosh and a Pioneer laser videodisc player. So do many others. The demo uses a relatively wordless interface based on a museum metaphor—a rather self-explanatory, easy-to-use interface with many positive features. But the interface wasn't the key to the demo's educational effectiveness. A good interface should be very easy to use and quickly become transparent to the learner. If these characteristics aren't present, then the interface becomes a negative factor in the educational effectiveness of the package.

The key to the demo's effectiveness is the extensive use of moving images and sound. The videodisc included moving images such as news clips of James Meredith entering the University of Mississippi, related speeches of President John F. Kennedy and Governor Ross Barnett, re-creations of some of the conditions of slavery, and authentic music from an early period in American history. Fabrice Florin of Apple's Multimedia Lab was responsible for the superb video editing on this demo—the importance of which on multimedia development projects cannot be overemphasized. Poor video editing will almost certainly override all other aspects of a multimedia project, no matter how well they are done.

The effectiveness of this demo was apparent in the eyes of many of the students and teachers who used it. Those eyes often included a few tears. Users were clearly moved by the material presented. Why? They've used the Macintosh, HyperCard, and even multimedia before. What's so special about this particular application? The key seems to be the moving images and sound.

Perhaps the importance of moving images and sound should have been anticipated. After all, we've learned more about the brain in the last 10 years than in all the years of previous research. Current research indicates that emotion is not only involved in memory but is also the basis on which our memory is organized. If we can affect a learner's emotions, then we will certainly have a significant impact on learning. Image recall is our most reliable and generally accessible memory, and moving images and sound are a particularly effective way to elicit emotion—and that's exactly what good multimedia should provide.

Did you do your assignment? Did you write two or three sentences to describe a significant event that happened prior to junior high school? Think for a moment about what you did. What process did you use to write your sentences? Most of you recalled an image, then wrote two or three sentences that described that image. Even though you were asked to write sentences, you recalled an image of a situation and only afterwards used language. And nearly everyone recalled an image of an emotional event. Moving images and sound are powerful tools for learning!

When you consider multimedia projects and products, remember that moving images and sound together are the key to emotional impact. Sound alone can have a major impact, but motion video or still images alone cannot. Sound alone is probably just as effective as sound with still images. This is an important distinction, as several early and currently available multimedia products combine sound with still images. While these products might have several legitimate educational applications, they do not represent the type of multimedia product being discussed here as they are not likely to impact the emotions of the user.

Many techniques of accelerated learning key on image and sound. If you're not familiar with the common sense, the nonsense, and the important new ideas of accelerated learning, the book *Accelerated Learning* by Colin Rose (Dell Publishing, 1985) is highly recommended. HyperCard-based multimedia provides an ideal opportunity to implement some of these ideas so they might reach an increased number of learners. I believe that properly produced multimedia has an excellent chance of significantly improving learning for many children in most classrooms.

A word about other motion video and sound already available seems appropriate. After all, 16-millimeter films and television are readily available to many teachers, yet neither has had a significant impact on learning. Perhaps the use of motion video and sound are not enough. I believe that well-made films and well-executed television can have a significant impact, but HyperCard-based multimedia includes a critically important additional component—*interactivity*. Interactivity means teacher and/or learner control. A classroom teacher is not likely to use a 20-minute film or videotape if he or she really only wants the class to see three 45-second clips. Finding the three clips and showing them takes too much time and effort. However, if those clips can be accessed with one or two "clicks," their likelihood of use in the classroom is very high. And students can review those clips on their own time to whatever extent they choose—a luxury rarely possible with film or television.

This demo project was also particularly effective as a presentation tool. Multimedia presentation tools for teachers have an excellent chance of succeeding, whereas one computer in the classroom does not. There are several reasons for this. First, the basic mode of teaching in grades 7–12 continues to be lecture. If one wants this mode to change, then one must meet teachers where they are and help them change at a reasonable pace. Providing an effective tool that truly helps them accomplish those tasks with which they are already familiar is an excellent start. Second, interactive multimedia happens to be a very effective presentation tool—in nearly all subject areas. In addition, when interactive multimedia is used as a presentation tool in front of the classroom, the entire class is benefitting from the expense for the hardware rather than just one or two students who are using a more typical classroom computer.

The same demo also modeled two other applications that showed considerable promise for enhancing education. Users are able to use the HyperCard multimedia demo in a browsing mode—a mode that lets you wander and explore, much as you might do in a museum or library. Users are also able to use the demo as an audio-visual production tool. They can select motion video, stills, and sounds that they want to use in their own presentation, arrange them in whatever order they deem appropriate, and then create a tour of those items or record those items on video tape for separate presentations.

HyperCard-based, interactive multimedia systems that make appropriate use of motion and sound have enormous potential for improving learning—or so it seems. However, despite a great deal of enthusiasm on the part of those who have used such a system, no research-supported evidence exists to show that this is an excellent or even a good way to learn. In most cases, users to date have been reviewing material that they already know rather than learning it for the first time. I have no doubt whatsoever that multimedia systems are an extraordinarily effective way to review material—but are they an effective way to learn something new? We don't really know yet. The demo already discussed includes a single screen with a profile of Martin Luther King Jr. and a menu of his most famous speeches. When adults who are browsing see that profile, they almost always stop and select one of the speeches. Those adults recognize King's profile. That's a noteworthy tribute to both the power of imagery and the impact of King—most adults recognize him from only his profile. And they have at least heard of the power of his speeches. However, what about the learner who has never heard of King and who certainly wouldn't recognize his profile? Would that learner stop and listen to one of his speeches? Probably not. Not unless that learner was also being guided by an effective teacher.

In fact, researchers can correctly point out that we don't even know for sure whether exposure to external images is the most effective way to create internal images. Sound silly? It isn't really. Think of the image that you recalled earlier in order to write the two- or three-sentence description. Were you part of the image? For many of you, the answer is "yes." Where did your image come from? You thought you were recalling an image from the past—but you were part of the image. Unless you had an out-of-body experience, that well-remembered image was not something you actually saw. Our internal images really aren't always created solely by external images.

I anticipate that the use of HyperCard as a multimedia interface will carry computer-based educational technology to its fourth plateau. The first three major categories of computer-based educational technology were: mainframes and large time-sharing systems; minicomputers from Hewlett-Packard Co. and Digital Equipment Corp.; and microcomputers such as the Apple II series, the IBM PC, and the Commodore 64. In each case, the educational applications and the number of users of each type of hardware reached a plateau until the next category was available. The application of HyperCard as a multimedia interface is sufficiently powerful and different to become the fourth step in this evolution.

Knowing about the three previous plateaus should be helpful. Each category of hardware produced very similar results within the educational community. The results included: a promise that far exceeded the reality; an initial emphasis on computer literacy and programming; later emphasis on curriculum support; an increased number of users; more effective, easier-to-use applications; a need for new research as existing research no longer applied; and a complete replacement of the previous category's software.

Let's not repeat all of our mistakes. As we begin to develop and use HyperCard-based multimedia products, let's not promise more than we can deliver. Wouldn't it be nice to promise even less and then let users be surprised! And let's not attempt to teach everyone how to program using HyperTalk. HyperTalk is a wonderful language that appeals to many people; so is French. More people communicate using French than there are Macintosh computers communicating using HyperTalk, but we don't often hear serious suggestions of requiring that everyone learn French.

Is HyperCard going to be important in K–12 education? Indeed it is. When used as an interface to multimedia containing moving images and sound, it will be a critical part of a powerful tool for teaching and learning. And as the driving force within this new application of computer-based technology to education, it will help expand the number of educational users of computing facilities in general. These are two rather significant steps forward.

Media Computers, Motivation, and Informal Education: Gutenberg 2000?

Hugh Osborn

HUGH OSBORN

Hugh Osborn is an independent multimedia designer and producer based in New York City. He designed the landmark "Diagnostic Challenges" patient-encounter simulator for Smith, Kline & French Laboratories in 1980, while working for WICAT Systems of Orem, Utah.

He was a Fellow (1985–87) in the Learning Lab at WNET, New York's Public Broadcasting System (PBS) station, where he investigated multimedia versions of PBS series.

He was a research associate (1987–88) at Teachers College, Columbia University. Most recently, he has designed and produced "Stamps: Windows on the World" and codesigned "Berlitz CDI Spanish," which are Compact Disc Interactive titles published by American Interactive Media, a Polygram Records subsidiary in Los Angeles.

He earned a B.A. in philosophy, with a minor in systems engineering, from Swarthmore College in Pennsylvania.

For the last quarter century, the world of multimedia has been little known. It has been the province of specialists, whose work was obscure and poorly understood. Now, however, the popularity of HyperCard has brought this subterranean stream to the surface. Teachers, students, business professionals, and others all over the world are creating stacks that contain buttons, links, indices, and related exotic creatures.

Where will the evolution of multimedia take us? In this paper, I present one view of the continuing development of multimedia[1] and its impact on how individuals learn and how we evolve as a society. I argue that the multimedia programming available in the next few years could fill a desperate need in the United States—the need to reengage our citizens in the world of ideas. If we can advance the state of the art in multimedia to this next stage, we will have an important tool in the effort to reverse the strategically disastrous decline in American education.

I will examine what I consider to be key pressure points in bringing about the next stage in the evolution of multimedia:

- *Media computers*. First, a foray into hardware and software. We will look at an extraordinary technological convergence and an example of the kind of programming that it will make possible.

- *Motivation*. Next, an examination of the catalytic aspect of multimedia and where it might enter our lives.

- *Informal education*. Finally, a look at how multimedia might affect some of the social dynamics that are eroding America's tradition of learning.

My conclusion is that multimedia, if carefully developed as a publishing medium, could play a transformative role in our society over the next few decades—as we progress as a society toward "Gutenberg 2000."[2]

---

[1] A note about terminology: As is often the case in new fields, no consensus exists in the multimedia field about what various terms mean or what to call certain items that clearly need names. "Multimedia," "hypermedia," and "intermedia" are often used interchangeably to describe the same thing. In this article, I use the term "multimedia" to describe any software using the four essential communications media—text, audio, images, and logic—whether on a media computer or an analog video–computer hybrid. I use the term "hypermedia" to describe a subset of multimedia that has "hyper" characteristics: various modules linked in a nonhierarchical, nonlinear structure. I stress hypermedia products throughout the article, although many of my points are true for nonhyper multimedia products (such as games with no sizeable knowledgebase).

[2] Some of the ideas in this article were developed in conjunction with Professor Robert McClintock and Christopher Pino at Teachers College, Columbia University.

Media Computers

If multimedia programming is to have a significant impact on communications—if a large-scale publishing industry is to be developed—appropriate hardware must be available to play it on. The issue of a platform points to the essential nature of multimedia: synergy. Multimedia combines the four primary communications media: text, audio, images (still and moving), and computer logic. To reach the potential of multimedia, these component media have to be mixed—the way that the primary hues on an artist's palette are mixed to create an infinite variety of color. This implies that the media have the same base, that the artist is not mixing watercolors and oil paints.

Existing hardware systems that play all four media tend to use two bases: a digital computer to supply text, logic control, and some graphics; and an analog video device to present audio and full-color images. Generally, these systems are too complex and expensive to be widely accepted; they require dual viewing screens or costly video overlay devices. They do not meld the media but rather graft video to the computer. Although appropriate for many kinds of educational and commercial applications, these hybrids are not likely to become a popular consumer platform for multimedia.

A nonhybrid, single-base platform is not far off. Two trends in technology are leading us to this promised land. The first is that digital microchip technology has been creeping up on media capabilities. The audio and graphic output of the Apple IIGS is an excellent example of the kind of multicolored realistic pictures and high-quality sound of which computers are becoming capable. These capabilities are approaching those of television: full-color pictures and motion with audio.

These interactive media are hungry, especially video and audio—a 20-megabyte (MB) hard disk can hold only 30 minutes of low-quality digital sound. To the rescue comes the second technical advance—the optical digital disc, an immense storage bin for digital data. The most ubiquitous version, the compact disc, can store 18 hours of speech-quality sound, 7000 pictures, enough text to fill 600 books, or, with special decoding chips, 90 minutes of full-screen motion with audio.

A Focal Point: The Networked Media Computer

Media microchips and optical digital storage are the advances needed to create an all-digital, single-box, multimedia publishing platform. I call this platform the networked media computer (NMC) and consider it to be the next important step in the evolution of multimedia. This all-digital multimedia platform will have several advantages over the hybrid systems of today. It will be faster, cheaper, smaller, simpler to operate, and capable of riding the ever-advancing tidal wave of digital technology.

In order to provide a highly flexible palette for software creators, media computers must have, at a minimum, the following characteristics:

- *Compressed audio.* A basic demarcation between computer software and television programming is audio. Intelligent use of audio can completely alter the way a viewer perceives a program: The time sense can be controlled by the program instead of by the user. Yet large amounts of audio are required for sound to be more than a parlor trick, thus requiring compression of the data to at least 10 kilobytes (KB) per second for speech quality.

- *Mass storage.* The requirement for audio leads to a need for optical storage approaching a billion characters. The most likely candidate for this is, of course, the compact disc, which stores 650 MB.

- *Natural color graphics.* Although some superb programs have been done on monochrome systems, especially on the Macintosh, an important line is crossed when all pictures can be represented.

- *Motion.* Many things can be communicated only by motion of 15 frames per second or more and with audio. Motion capability also allows access to the huge stores of existing video footage.

- *Large amounts of RAM (random-access memory).* To handle the kinds of techniques that are required for user-friendly programming and other informational approaches, a reasonably large working memory is needed. Consumer products can have as little as 1 MB of memory, but other systems will generally have at least 4 MB of memory.

- *Communications.* Networking users is an important part of the multimedia programming described later in this article. Communications, even if only at the modem level, are therefore a requirement.

- *Hyperauthoring.* To produce programming inexpensively, hyperauthoring systems like HyperCard must be available. Also, end-user authoring, a driving force in the success of HyperCard, is a requirement.

The development of "media computers" with these characteristics is occurring on two fronts: the computer industry (led by Apple, IBM, Intel, Microsoft, and NeXT) and the consumer electronics industry (primarily Philips with their Compact Disc Interactive, or CD-I, home media computer). Special attention should be paid to Apple and Philips because of their high-level corporate commitments to and large investments in media computing.

The broad interest in media computers on the part of hardware companies will, within two years, lead to several different kinds of products appropriate to a variety of environments. By 1992, the consumer electronics industry will provide low-end hardware for the home costing less than $1000, and computer manufacturers will create mid-range systems costing from $2000 to $5000 and high-end, powerful systems in the $3500 to $10,000 range. (The computer manufacturers may also enter the home market for multimedia, although rumors to this effect have not been confirmed as of this writing.)

The Omnibus Medium

What kind of software can be played on a media computer? Anything. Because media computers can display text, audio, motion, and still pictures and because they can use computer logic to tie these media together, their software can use virtually all the techniques of any known information or media discipline: database, Hollywood feature films, CAD (computer-aided design), slide shows, artificial intelligence, Public Broadcasting System documentaries, real-time computer animation, cartography, any form of print, audio recording, sound synthesis, and so on. Media computing software—true multimedia—will be an omnibus medium: the medium that encompasses all others.

This is an astonishing point, a milestone in the history of communications. We can barely begin to imagine the chimera and completely new creatures that will grow from the extraordinary cross-pollination of information disciplines that will occur in media computers. Experience with the Apple Macintosh computer has shown the kinds of software creations possible when one versatile platform is used in a variety of disciplines: database packages that support graphics and sound, CAD three-dimensional graphics programs that become desktop-publishing tools, music games that are also synthesizers and musical theory tutors, and many others.

Multimedia software is certain to evolve in creative directions when true media computers become available; however, determining the exact route of this evolution is difficult. All new media are originally used to mimic the old until geniuses come along who can see what the medium can really do. Who can predict what new forms of communication will be created?

Hypermedia

The strand of multimedia I will focus on for the remainder of this article is called "hypermedia."[3] In narrowing my focus, I do not mean to imply that other forms of multimedia will not have an impact; however, my instinct is that the forms that will be

---

[3] Many readers are familiar with the concepts behind hypermedia. I include this overview for those who are not.

as important as hypermedia have not yet been invented. Thus I will concentrate on one of the few glimpses of the future we do have.

As a concept, hypermedia is nearly 40 years old. It was first described by Vannevar Bush in his famous article "As We May Think"[4] and developed and demonstrated in the 1960s and 1970s by Doug Englebart and Ted Nelson. But only now, with software advances like HyperCard on powerful and inexpensive computers, can we start to implement hypermedia. And the hypermedia systems being developed now are only shadows of what true media computers will allow us to do.

The core concept of hypermedia is interconnectedness, an idea that reflects the way humans think. Our minds do not seem to work in a linear fashion—they jump from idea to idea—yet most of our media are linearly organized. There is a good reason for the linear organization of ideas expressed in books, films, and television programming. These media are linear in format and are essentially patterned on speech—a linear enterprise. The one exception to this linearity is the reference book, a random-access medium. In fact, the general metaphor used to explain hypermedia (or hypertext, its all-text form) is an encyclopedia. The body of any entry in an encyclopedia can contain a reference to any other entry, and a nonlinear skipping among entries to follow whatever train of thought occurs to the reader is encouraged by the encyclopedia's basic form.

Jumping around among entries in a set of 20 or more books can be unwieldy, but computer-controlled jumping within indexed text data is a much simpler exercise. Hypermedia extends this ability to programs comprised of all forms of media. The jumps are called *links,* and they are automatically executed by the computerized substrate of the program. Hypermedia programs often have no linear path or organization (except an alphabetical organization), so the organizing principle of the session is created by the reader or viewer.

There have been several interesting demonstrations of hypermedia. All good HyperCard stacks include implementations of hypermedia concepts, usually in the form of hypertext—hypermedia without full-color images or significant audio. Among the experimental systems with some form of true, single-screen hypermedia, the MIT Media Lab programs stand out as the best examples. Some commercial computer–videodisc programming has interesting hyper-ish structures, but most follow more traditional hierarchical instructional systems design (ISD) approaches: menu-based formats following programmed instruction principles.

---

[4] Bush, Vannevar. "As We May Think." *Atlantic Monthly* 176, 1 (July 1945); 101–108.

Here I will focus on a kind of hypermedia that could have tremendous impact on the multimedia market. There is no easy term to describe it; perhaps the closest I can come is "structured hypermedia knowledgebase," a cumbersome phrase to be sure. However, it is a kind of hypermedia that is becoming more defined by work at the Apple Multimedia Lab and elsewhere, and it is a form of communication that might hold a key to the future of learning. It is best illustrated by an example.

"Beyond Einstein"—A Structured Hypermedia Knowledgebase

"Beyond Einstein" was created in 1986 in WNET's Learning Laboratory in New York. WNET is a flagship Public Broadcasting System (PBS) station, creating some 40 percent of PBS's domestically produced material. The station set up the lab to explore the conversion of its extraordinary video assets into multimedia formats. Tom Anderson, the lab's director, and I created "Einstein," a short demonstration program, to show what a future PBS-quality home/school hypermedia program might look like.[5] The subject was quantum physics, a topic selected for several reasons:

- One of our theses was that hypermedia could bring complicated subjects within the grasp of laypeople, so we selected a subject with some intellectual depth. Quantum physics certainly fit the bill.

- The quantum universe is a fascinating place—if one has the tools to start to peek into it. It is a world where ghost matter is "allowed" to exist until it is caught by the Uncertainty Principle, where scientists probe infinitesimal, nonmechanistic entities with the most gigantic and expensive mechanisms ever made. Yet few people know much about this world. The increasingly technical and arcane nature of physics prevents most non-scientists from being able to understand the physical world around them. We thought this "science gap" could be bridged.

- A consequence of the science gap is the decay in the feeder system for higher science education in America. Currently, there are about 35 percent fewer American physics doctoral candidates in the U.S. than there were 20 years ago. (The shortfall is covered by foreign students.) In large part, this is because of the way science is taught in this country: Often, science seems uninviting to younger students. Highly motivating programs at the

---

[5] Full credits include: Tom Anderson of Commonwealth Strategies (Boston) as project director (and also, reluctantly, "on-screen talent" for the videotape); I was the assistant project director; Gary Zamchick was the art director; and Christopher Pino was the programmer. The main source material was from "The Creation of the Universe," a PBS special written and narrated by Tim Ferris and produced and directed by Geoff Haines-Stiles. (See: Anderson, Thomas, "Beyond Einstein." *Interactive Multimedia*. Redmond, WA: Microsoft Press, 1988.)

grass-roots level—high school, early college—might help cause an increase in the percentage of American physics doctoral candidates.

Because of its many interlinking historical, practical, philosophical, and scientific facets, quantum physics is a good subject for a hyperlinked program. By the time we worked out a structure that met our various needs, we had designed what I am calling a structured hypermedia knowledgebase. This was expressed in the following ways.

1. Hypermedia

The design of "Beyond Einstein" comprises from 150 to 200 multimedia modules (although only a few of these were produced for the demo). They typically consisted of:

- A few minutes of video or audio with synched stills for a total of several hours on the disc of audio/visual presentation.
- Several minutes of audio bites for introductions or to support text, graphics, simulations, and so forth.
- From 10 to 20 pages of text with graphics. The text explanations were multistaged: Up to three levels of technical expertise were provided, including mathematical treatments at the deepest level.
- Simulations and other interactive sequences.

These modules also had a "hyper" structure: They could contain links to parts of other modules. A glossary could be summoned by pointing to any term; it, in turn, was linked to all other uses of that term in the program.

2. Structures

Unlike an encyclopedia or some of the free-form approaches to hypermedia, "Beyond Einstein" had a structure—or rather several of them. To create an overall organization, we split the subject matter into a two-dimensional matrix of four periods along the x axis and four themes along the y axis. (See Figure 1 on the following page. The diagrams shown in this essay are, unfortunately, line re-creations of beautiful, shaded graphics in the original program.) The themes were:

- The physics itself
- The people involved in the quantum revolution, the places they worked, and the tools they used
- The grand ideas and issues of quantum physics
- The applications of quantum physics

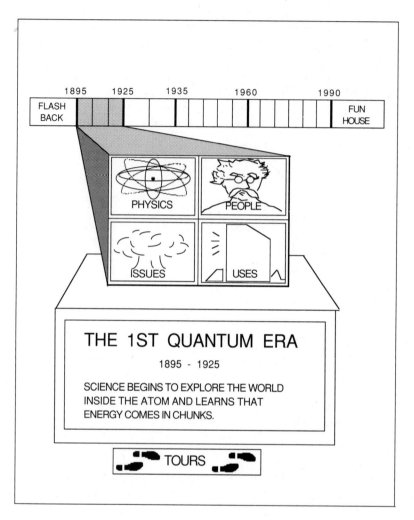

*FIGURE 1. Overall organization of the "Beyond Einstein"
demonstration program.*

The *x* axis represented the twentieth century, divided into four eras because each era contains roughly an equal density of quantum physical achievements and discoveries. Each of the 16 era–theme combinations that resulted from this structure contained from 5 to 20 modules on subjects relevant to that time period and subject. Examples are shown in the Menu in Figure 2.

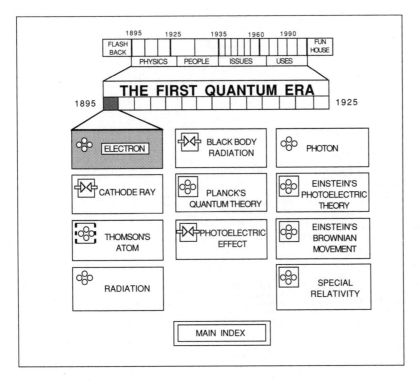

FIGURE 2. The index screen for the first quantum era.

There were also three other overall structures:

- A semantic net at the end of each of the main content modules. This provided a glimpse of the relationship of that subject to others in the program and could link the user to other modules. (See Figure 3 on the following page.)

- Tours that tied together modules into a relatively coherent linear narrative structure.

- The glossary mentioned above.

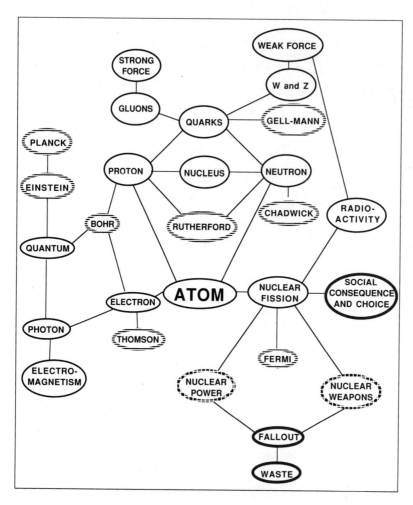

FIGURE 3. The semantic net for the Atom subject module.

3. A knowledgebase

We designed "Beyond Einstein" to encapsulate knowledge in a way that parallels a data-base structure. An employee database contains "raw" information about employees—name, address, salary, and so on—for each employee. This information is represented in one form internally and in another on different reports or screen queries. Thus, the inter-nal representation allows great flexibility in external presentation.

The same is true in a knowledgebase. The 200 modules and their parts are like the records and fields in the database. (This is database talk; each employee is a *record* in the database, each piece of information about the employee is a *field*.) The Tours, semantic nets, and other accesses of the media modules all presented the same content (the modules) in different lights and in different formats. In a sense, the viewer could "triangulate" the content by accessing it different ways.

Databases can be quite extensive—and so can knowledgebases. "Beyond Einstein" could easily have been part of a multidisc knowledgebase with thousands of modules covering all of science. As it was, the program we specified could be used for dozens of hours without exhausting it.

A verbal description of "Beyond Einstein" cannot impart a sense of the experience of interacting with it (or even of watching a tape of this interaction). Because we were able to use footage from "The Creation of the Universe," a superb PBS documentary, many of the motion sequences had top-quality visuals, editing, and audio (with music by Brian Eno). Many of these borrowed sequences were $4000-per-second computer animation, including a 2-minute zoom into the atom complete with glowing electron shells, multicolored quarks, and shimmering gluon nets. The graphics we created were full color, shaded, and often animated, adding to the visual richness of the program.

The reaction to "Beyond Einstein" has been extremely enthusiastic.[6] Many viewers claimed that viewing the program had affected their ideas about knowledge and learning. We often heard comments like, "If I had only been able to learn like this in college." Generally, viewers thought that the methods used in "Beyond Einstein" would be a fantastic way to learn.

Several recurring themes ran through viewers' responses. First and foremost, viewers of the tape wanted to get their hands on the real interactive program and start *exploring*. Second, structured hypermedia was generally perceived as a truly new and different way to communicate; it was not seen as enhanced linear video or computer programming. Third, many viewers felt that the medium seemed to provide a more rounded learning experience than other media (often this response included classroom learning). People used terms like "complete learning environment" in describing the experience.

---

[6] It would be irresponsible to present these reactions as having been scientifically measured. Viewers watched a demonstration tape rather than interacting with a final product; no statistical instrument was used to gauge reactions; and my report of viewer reactions is suspect in its objectivity. Nonetheless, I do not think I greatly overstate general viewer responses to "Beyond Einstein."

Motivation

The most enthusiastic comments about "Einstein" were about the *form* of the program, not the execution. In other words, what people really responded to is probably endemic to hypermedia. It is difficult to confirm this, having had extensive experience with only one program, but these responses are consistent with reactions to other projects, especially Apple's Multimedia Lab's HyperCard-videodisc programs.

This leads to an obvious question: What excites people about the experience of hypermedia programs such as "Beyond Einstein"? There are probably many factors. However, seven characteristics seem to me to be paramount. These are:

1. *Visual representations of knowledge.* In traditional educational publishing, text is the primary communications medium, with illustrations, diagrams, and pictures used as amplifiers (often as an afterthought). Given the extraordinary visual-processing ability of the human brain, this seems misguided (though understandable, given the technology of printing). In hypermedia, the emphasis changes: Visual representations become a primary function, complementing both text and audio narrative.

2. *A broad base of accessible knowledge.* Hypermedia can provide a huge store of information. Up to 20 hours of audio or 8,000 images or 250,000 pages of text can be stored on a compact disc, so programs can be created that have epic scope. "Beyond Einstein" and other discs on the subjects of classical mechanics, astrophysics, and relativity could cover the scope of modern and classical physics. Versions of existing multi-disc CD players could be used to increase the breadth and/or depth of the knowledgebase by an order of magnitude.

   The real significance of this feature is that hypermedia programs can deliver extraordinary depth of experience without the user running out of material after a few hours of involvement. It is not unusual to have a book or documentary on a subject excite you, only to be unable to find other materials of similar quality to follow up on the interest. Hypermedia knowledgebases can be huge, with the attendant promise that any insights exist in a wide-open landscape, not a small cul-de-sac.

3. *Indices.* Two- and three-dimensional metaphorical graphics can be created that act as indices to other media sections in a program, even to other indices. Thus, a history program could lay out a multiscreen timeline that represents all the essential events within the period the program covers.

Each event representation or icon could act as a link to additional media about that event. "Beyond Einstein" used timeline indices with audio captions (activated by resting the cursor on a button) that previewed topics and noted relationships between them. Viewers could profitably spend time on the index screen itself, before activating the buttons and entering the modules.

Well-designed indices make explicit the organizing principles of the knowledgebase. They allow viewers to internalize a structure or build a mental model because they can directly interact with a graphic representation of the principle. In this sense, indices are powerful mnemonic devices that can be used to present multiple perspectives to the user.

4. *Exploration.* The reigning metaphor in hypermedia access is "navigation." As implied by this metaphor, users are explorers, following their curiosity wherever it may take them. If motivation flags, guides or tours are available to suggest paths that might be of interest and, in some cases, to introduce a narrative structure. The significance of navigation is that viewers become willing learners, rather than students to be instructed by the program. The difference in the motivation of viewers—and thus their retention—is immense.

5. *An editorial style that emphasizes insight, discovery, conceptual knowledge, and relationships.* In creating "Beyond Einstein," we purposely avoided the sort of dry, academic style that stymies so many budding physicists. We found that the best approach was one borrowed from good educational television programming. The best of these programs draw the viewer in by carefully couching materials in terms of insights and relationships—a perfect approach for structured hypermedia.

A prime example of this is "The Ascent of Man," the phenomenally popular Jacob Bronowski extended film essay on Western culture and thought. Bronowski used interesting camera work, striking locations, and carefully designed sets to engage the viewer in a process of discovery through a network of ideas and insights. He was successful in keeping millions of viewers on the edges of their seats, despite the fact that the subject matter was not exactly traditional prime-time material. In hypermedia, the structure of an "Ascent" might be different—the network of insights could be made graphically explicit and explored in different ways under user control—but the filmic techniques would translate well.

6. *Simulations.* In addition to navigational interactions, viewers can play with simulations, toolboxes, games, and other activities. One example in "Beyond Einstein" was a simulation of an early Niels Bohr model of the atom. The viewer could set up and watch a quantum leap and observe the color of the resulting photon (light particle). In simulations, the viewer can observe and directly tinker with relationships. Playing these "what if" games is one of the most effective forms of learning and can strongly reinforce the material presented in the knowledgebase.

7. *Communications, networks, groups.* Although not demonstrated in "Beyond Einstein," networks will be an important part of future hypermedia experiences. Being part of a group of kindred souls is a vital part of any extended journey. Extensions of the electronic bulletin boards that exist today, future networks will provide expert feedback, group simulations, and forums for discussion. Clearly, no technology can listen and respond like a human, and learning will always involve the need for human communications, with both peers and experts. Networks can be devised by hypermedia designers to fill this need, especially as two-way video and simultaneous voice/data communications services become more widespread.

Because of these characteristics (and perhaps others I can't discern), hypermedia seems a very natural way to learn. Young children have a primordial drive to play and learn, but often the traditional instructional methods they encounter in schools suppress this drive. Traditional learning is *work* for many people, and the media by which they learn do not seem to tap into the same motivational vein that successful early learning does. Hypermedia can create an explorable playground out of conceptual subjects, resulting in programs that are, in a sense, engaging educational toys for the intellect, whereas much of traditional education is the equivalent of flash cards.

Hypermedia knowledgebases must be experienced to be understood—and claims about their resonating with essential human cognition cannot be verified in the near future. However, if my assertion that hypermedia is inherently motivating is correct, it has some important implications. These will become clear as we look at how hypermedia programs might enter our lives.

Whither Hypermedia?

How might hypermedia programs like "Beyond Einstein" enter the mainstream of American media? Clearly, the content of the hypermedia programs mentioned above overlap with the school curriculum. Educational institutions will, I predict, continue their evolutionary adoption of technology, including many forms of multimedia. However, several factors will inhibit the rapid adoption of hypermedia in schools.

- *Interaction time.* True hypermedia exploration requires hours of interaction time, far more than can be supported by even the most computerized school system today. The average access time for schools that have computers is about 12 minutes per day.

- *Conservative tendencies of publishers and schools.* Given the large scope and editorial nature of hypermedia, it is likely that production of educational programs would fall to the large educational publishers, an industry that is not especially innovative. The editorial content of most national textbook series is subject to political influences in certain large states, primarily those in Texas and California. This process does not usually result in the adoption of radically different educational approaches.

- *Educational philosophy.* The current mood in education is away from the Dewey-inspired, "softer" approach to education and toward a "back to the basics" tightening of standards. (For example, national examinations are being seriously discussed.) Good hypermedia is not as clearly goal-oriented as is, for example, programmed instruction. Hypermedia might not satisfy tight, traditional means–ends equations for cost justification.

If hypermedia programs were created by educational publishers in the context of the current national mood, there seems to me to be little chance that the fragile "joy of learning" could be retained. This is not a blanket indictment of the educational publishing industry, but simply a realistic assessment of the requirements of developing a new medium within the current dynamics of the production and distribution of educational materials in public schools.

Colleges and universities have more leeway to experiment. In fact, much of the most innovative work in hypermedia production has taken place at universities such as MIT, Stanford, and Brown. However, the university publishing market is small and is characterized by a large number of competing texts in any field. Yet, colleges and universities will be important early markets for the more general hypermedia products designed for use in survey courses.

The most appropriate and important initial market for structured hypermedia is in the home. If, indeed, hypermedia programming can be as motivational as our experience with "Beyond Einstein" indicates, then it should be capable of sparking a publishing industry consisting of several definable markets.

- *Middle-class parents concerned about their children's education.* The malaise of the nation's schools has not been lost on parents, many of whom are terrified by the prospect of sending their children to substandard schools. But these parents have no tools with which to work after their children outgrow Fisher-Price toys.

  The most important characteristics of this group are: (1) no lack of concern for their children's well-being but a lack of time to devote to intensive educational parenting, (2) a desire to have the time they do spend with their children be enriching "quality time," (3) a concern about the effect of television on their children, and (4) relatively ample funds.

  Programming for this group should encourage hypermedia navigation as a substitute for television watching, and it should contain family activities and encourage outside activities (hobbies, museum attendance, field trips, and so forth). This programming must, above all, be *fun,* otherwise it will create family discord rather than harmony. No child wants to find homework under the Christmas tree.

  A real possibility is that new versions of "enhancement programs" will grow up to boost public-school education by taking children in after school. This could happen at several levels, from parents babysitting for local children to extensions of Scholastic Aptitude Testing tutoring companies. These groups would be freer to use hypermedia programming, given that they would have less evaluative pressure.

- *Children selecting programs for themselves.* The programs mentioned above assume parental screening and purchasing of hypermedia products. If the programming is enticing enough, children might select the program as a result of what they have heard by word of mouth. This is the coveted "Nintendo effect," and the programs that will inspire it are more likely to be lower-cost multimedia games rather than conceptual hypermedia. However, this distinction will probably erode as new forms of hypermedia are invented.

- *Adults purchasing for themselves.* This is the "PBS plus" market: the "learning junkies" who view Public Broadcasting System programming plus others who are like-minded but do not watch much television. This group, which overlaps with the first group mentioned, is a primary market for hypermedia. It includes precocious eight-year-olds and adults of all ages. The largest subgroup consists of college-educated adults who have an ongoing interest in the world, but at least two other major subgroups exist: blue-collar workers and seniors.

In a recent discussion at Teachers College at Columbia University, Bill Moyers told of a group of plumbers at a factory who were flipping through television channels at lunch. They happened to stop on one of Moyers's programs in which a discussion of philosophical ideas was underway. They watched the whole program, astonished that, as they put it, "a whole world of ideas existed" that they had never heard about. They have been avidly watching his programs and reading up on "ideas" ever since. They wrote to him: "We are plumbers during the day, but at lunch and in the evenings, we are Philosophers At Large." It is not clear how large this group of casualties of the educational system is, or how to market to them, but my guess is that they are a large market.

Seniors are another huge and growing population group with a set of needs that exactly matches the characteristics of hypermedia. Having retired from the world of work, they have the time, and often the money, to explore all the corners of the world they never had a moment to investigate while they were raising families and working.

Informal Education

If good hypermedia (and, certainly, other forms of multimedia) can spark a deep motivation to learn, and if this is successfully exploited by a thriving consumer publishing industry, what wider significance might this have? I contend that the issue of motivation in learning is central to a number of social ills in the U.S. today. Given this, the wide dissemination of effective hypermedia programs could have a transformative effect on our culture. (Here I practice sociology without a license.)

Our educational system has nearly broken down. This fact has been documented in a myriad of government and foundation studies and is reflected in statistics quoted regularly in our popular press. (A recent article in *Time* magazine reports that 37 percent of our 18-year-olds are illiterate or high school dropouts or both.) This affects our society by wasting the potential of our individual citizens, by eroding our economic base at a time when education is a strategic commodity, and by undermining the foundations of a Jeffersonian democracy, which posits an educated, informed citizenry. Exploring some of the causes of this breakdown will illuminate how hypermedia could play an important role in reversing the "rising tide of mediocrity" bemoaned in "A Nation at Risk," the famous 1983 condemnation of American education issued by the U.S. Department of Education.

I want to address three interrelated factors by no means meant to be comprehensive: quality of teaching, informal education, and television. Then I will suggest ways in which multimedia programming, hypermedia in particular, can help alleviate these problems.

Problem 1: Teaching Quality and Low Student Motivation

An obvious factor in the degradation of educational quality in the U.S. is a decline in quality of teachers. College-educated women who, in years past, would gravitate to teaching because they had few alternative careers can now become brain surgeons or investment bankers. Teaching has not kept up with other professions in terms of salary and has little (although growing) status. Many contemporary teachers have undergraduate degrees in education instead of a substantive "content" field such as mathematics, history, or literature. Given that teachers who are able to excite students in an area are usually those who have a deep knowledge of and love for that subject, the lack of commitment to excellence in an area of study on the part of contemporary teachers is worrisome.

Problem 2: Breakdown in America's Informal Educational Network

The decline of informal education is as important as the degradation of teaching quality in formal education in America. Information picked up from parents, friends, relatives, town elders, preachers, community leaders, and others reinforces the knowledge imparted by teachers. More importantly, hearing information from these sources reinforces the *value* of knowledge gained in schools, by showing that discussions about the world are not limited to textbooks and classrooms.

However, American families are under far more stress than ever before. Leisure time has been reduced by 37 percent in the last 20 years, and more and more families consist of single-parent or dual-working-parent households. Thus, parents have much less time to dedicate to the raising of a family. Mom, who used to be an informal teacher, is now a wage earner. Grandparents, who lived next door in bygone years, now live in another state.

Similarly, churches, which used to provide a sense of community and enlightened religious training, are losing sway with many American families. The decline is steepest in the old-line Protestant churches, the teachings of which are in line with traditional Western humanistic values and which tended, therefore, to reinforce the educational experience. (Their decline is mirrored by the ascent of evangelical strains, which are expert at packaging and marketing religion on television but which greatly restrict the domain of intellectual investigation—take, for example, the growth of "creation science.") Because religious education is virtually taboo in public schools, many students get no exposure either formally or informally to this important component of culture.

Peers can also be an excellent source of knowledge, but only if one's peers are interested in learning and discussing. A declining educational level can thus set up a vicious circle: As interest in learning declines, so does the system of reinforcements a peer group can provide. This further weakens the motivation to learn.

Problem 3: Television

The growth of popularity of television coincides closely with the degradation of our public schools. This cannot be a coincidence. Although still controversial, the truth of the hypothesis that television has negatively affected the quality of education seems, to many people, undeniable.

One major problem with television is the sheer quantity of time it expropriates. This displaces learning activities. Children (and adults) watching television do not play games, do not read, and rarely think. Many of the traditional activities of childhood have been replaced by hours a day of "vegging out" in front of the television. This problem is exacerbated by "latchkeyism," parents who don't mind having their children watch television because it keeps them inside the house and out of trouble when the parents can't be home.

A more serious problem with commercial television is that it beams into American living rooms an artificial culture invented by marketers intent not on creating worthwhile artistic experiences but on manipulating viewers' buying patterns. Television is such a huge portion of the average person's conscious experience that the popular television culture resulting from this dynamic has virtually become American culture. The reins of icon- and value-generation have gone from village elders, artists, philosophers, and others grounded in Western culture to Madison Avenue statisticians and copywriters.[7]

---

[7] Neil Postman's book *Amusing Ourselves to Death* (Penguin Group, New York, 1985) provides a good dissection of television culture and how it can blanch the substance from public discourse. Postman claims that Revolutionary America was the most literate "country" and era in history, that our roots and government derive from a population that devoured books and political discourse. This contradicts the notion that the educated, literate portion of the populace has always been minuscule, that things are no worse now than they have ever been.

In the culture viewed on commercial television, what has happened to learned people, to inquisitive people, to knowledge? They have been deemed not a popular image, or at least not an entertaining one. Thus, many children grow up without seeing reflective, knowledgeable people depicted on television. Given that characters on television show no interest in history, science, literature, or geography, why should we expect our children to care about these subjects?

A final problem with television is that it reduces attention spans and increases the expected level of sensorial stimulation. As marketers learn how to keep us glued to the tube, we increasingly expect messages to be delivered in short, glitzy packets: 23-minute sitcoms broken up by flashy 15- and 30-second commercials, intense 3-minute MTV rock 'n' roll experiences, 150-second reports on the 80,000 people who died in Armenia, and political discourse reduced to sound bites and punchy messages. Even "Sesame Street" is widely criticized for setting up a three-year-old's expectations that the world comes in 5- to 60-second packets and that each packet will be different from the previous. Reading and other sustained, quiet activities like doing homework suffer as a result of these expectations of rapid pace and media glitz.

So why should we expect children to learn, given that:

- Mom and Dad do not have the time to be supportive of educational activities and are often not even home.
- Learning about the world is not "cool" in the culture depicted on television.

- Schools are not very interesting and teachers not very inspiring.
- Television is more fun than homework and certainly less work.

It seems unrealistic to hope that, with no new factors in the educational equation, we will return to a simpler, more disciplined society in which parents spend more time with children, people read more and watch television less, and learning is valued and sought after by children and adults alike. There is not likely to be a spontaneous increase in personal striving to traverse the hard road to knowledge. The distractions are too many and the support network too thin. However, if we can make the road to knowledge easier, if we can make traveling that road enjoyable, then solutions for many of the problems outlined above start to take form. There is reason to believe that hypermedia *can* make that road easier to travel, that the highly motivational character of good hypermedia programming will be a key factor in fixing the breakdown of education in America.

How might this be? In several ways:

1. Fight the addiction to "high-bandwidth" media
One way to combat addiction to high-glitz, small-packet television is to fight fire with fire. Hypermedia programming can include full-screen television, video effects, and dazzling techniques to capture the interest of the viewer. But more importantly, active participation in programming and exploration of knowledge can be substituted for passive viewing. After a sustainable interest in a subject has been kindled, the internal motivation of the learner to follow up, combined with bibliographies and activities suggested in hypermedia products, will help engage the learner in "low-bandwidth" media—such as books, museums, hobbies, and friends.

2. Provide an array of flexible educational alternatives
Hypermedia learning environments can be centerpieces in a spectrum of educational approaches that complement formal education. These include:

■ *Informal learning at home.* Consumers can explore any subject that interests them, as described above. This is true for adults, children, and families. Given how powerful a hypermedia environment can be, having this alternative channel to knowledge could dissociate learning from schooling in the minds of children (especially teenagers), making it socially acceptable.

■ *Interest groups.* Networking, especially upcoming voice/data and video links, will encourage groups of learners to discuss the subjects they have in common. Experts can join the network, answering questions and providing updates for a fee, greatly enhancing the value of the network.

■ *"Booster" or "latchkey" schools.* Hypermedia (and multimedia in general) could play a big role in private institutions created to "turbo boost" public education on afternoons and weekends and during the summer. These entities, enlightened cousins of S.A.T training schools, may well spring up as a response to voucher programs being discussed widely in the U.S.

■ *Accredited home courses.* Hypermedia learning environments are perfect for home courses accredited by remote institutions. Learners could tie in to established educational centers, perhaps visiting them for orientation and discussion. This approach is especially useful for out-of-the-way locations.

3. Capture and disseminate breadth, depth, and quality

Hypermedia programming can capture presentations by the best teachers, thinkers, scholars, and mentors of our time. When a superb hypermedia program is created about an essential subject, it can become an international treasure, something that thousands or even millions of people can spend time learning from and then use as a resource for the rest of their lives. Such programs can serve the function that an inspiring teacher or a classic book serves in exciting a person about an area of study. Indeed, teachers, especially those who are not yet confident in their subject matter, could use such programs to spark student interest.

4. Energize informal education

If hypermedia programs can make learning more fun and knowledge more accessible, then they may reverse the slide in informal education in America. This could have several components:

- The development of interest groups could lead to peer subcultures that engage in networked hypermedia activities such as historical simulations, mathematical games, discussion groups centered on hypermedia products, and group experiments. This could result in a heightened sense of learning opportunities at all stages of life, making the perceived "entry fee" to the world of knowledge much lower.

- Hypermedia and multimedia products can help parents work with children productively and encourage families to learn together. Products that allow parents to participate in their children's learning experiences without an extraordinary investment of time will fill a crying need and find a willing market. Games in which family members take different roles are one way of accomplishing this; "parents-only" sections of programs that suggest activities and ways of working with children are another. Multimedia products will also be created that help parents manage a multi- and hypermedia curriculum for their children.

- Hypermedia products can also reinforce cultural and community activities that do exist. Programs can suggest activities that involve museums, libraries, hobby shops, night schools, concerts, and other available local resources. These institutions can be active participants, working with publishers to carve a role out for themselves in programming concerned with their area of expertise.

- Most importantly, hypermedia knowledgebases and other multimedia products can raise the level of public consciousness of ideas. Exploring the world of thought could become a widespread hobby, or at least an accepted pastime. If this form of learning weans large numbers of people from television, especially latchkey children, the nature of informal education and the public image of all education could be changed significantly. This would be hypermedia's greatest contribution to lifting the educational malaise in the U.S. today.

Gutenberg 2000?

At the center of this glowing scenario is motivation. If hypermedia is as naturally motivating as early experiments suggest, it could spark a revolution. The key to Gutenberg 1450 was the accurate replication and dissemination of information. As we approach the year 2000, we are awash in information yet unable to learn effectively. As a nation, we are thirsting for a thirst for knowledge. If we can develop a thirst for knowledge, we will thrive as a nation and as individuals. Thus, the key to Gutenberg 2000 is the motivation to learn. If developed with care, the technologies and methodologies I have discussed in this article can help create this motivation and foster learning in our homes and schools, in our children and in ourselves.

Closing Comments

This last section is entitled "Closing Comments" rather than "Summary" because the ideas presented in the book are too diverse to summarize in a few pages. Instead, we collected comments from various authors on three ideas that appeared in several articles.

1. *If multimedia is to reach its incredible potential, hardware and software for end users must be made easy to use.* Today, multimedia is a collection of hardware and software that gives exciting results for those who have the time and the inclination to tinker. Today's users must endure the trials of linking separate hardware with special cables and of using software that is not easy to master. However, even in this early stage of development, the results are better than anything seen before. Multimedia capabilities are now in the hands of many end users who are genuinely excited about the results—and that fact is truly significant.

2. *Learning with interactive multimedia gives us additional options on how to learn the material we choose.* We can select a linear path through the material, or we jump from one idea to another. In addition to the teacher, the main tool for learning throughout the ages has been the textbook. We who are literate have been conditioned to learn from it. With the capabilities of interactive multimedia, teachers and their students will no longer be tied primarily to learning through textbooks. Thus, multimedia blurs the distinction between learner and teacher because we all become fellow travelers through the information we choose. Each of us can be a learner one moment, browsing a multimedia database, and a teacher the next moment, adding new material and drawing inferences about the ideas in the database and then sharing our insights with others. Imagine a learning environment that is "patient," individualized, easy to use, entertaining, challenging, and multimedia in nature. That is where we are headed.

3. *Simply because we have the technology to create powerful interactive multimedia does not mean that we will make it happen.* It will take talented and creative individuals in many fields to produce the hardware, software, and distribution mechanism so that all of us can enjoy quick access to multimedia information and tools to explore and present ideas to others.

Interactive multimedia is teaching: sharing insights on how the world goes together, browsing and collecting information, making connections, and sharing thoughts with others. Multimedia will change the way we think and learn, and we can see it coming.

The challenge is exciting. We should welcome it!

The manuscript for this book was prepared and submitted to Microsoft Press in electronic form. Text files were processed and formatted using Microsoft Word.

Cover design by Greg Hickman
Principal typography by Lisa Iversen

Text composition by Microsoft Press in Times Roman with display in Times Roman Bold, using the Magna composition system and the Linotronic 300 laser imagesetter.

OTHER TITLES FROM MICROSOFT PRESS

CD ROM 2: Optical Publishing
Edited by Suzanne Ropiequet, with John Einberger and Bill Zoellick

"Recommended reading for any information professional."   Online

The second volume in the CD-ROM series focuses on optical publishing with CD-ROM. Topics include licensing and copyrighting; organizing and indexing data; collecting and preparing text, images, and sound; and designing software and integrating systems. Case studies track the evolution of two products from ideas to commercially available CD-ROM publications. A glossary and resource section provide additional information.
368 pages, softcover 7⅜ x 9¼ $22.95   Order Code CD2OP

MICROSOFT® CD-ROM YEARBOOK 1989–1990
Microsoft Press
Foreword by Bill Gates

The MICROSOFT CD-ROM YEARBOOK is a dynamic source of structured information and perspectives on this industry. You can use the book as a reference for current facts, figures, and dates, or you can dip into it for fascinating articles, reviews, and analyses of the entire industry and its products. This 1989-1990 edition features a look at the CD-ROM industry past and present, as well as a tour of who's doing what in CD-ROM, including publishers, libraries, the news media, the medical and legal professions, the home-entertainment industry, and corporations. You'll find the directory of CD-ROM titles, companies, and conferences invaluable—over 250 pages. MICROSOFT CD-ROM YEARBOOK—timely information on the people, products, and issues of the optical-publishing industry.
960 pages, softcover 8½ x 11 $79.95   Order Code CDYE

COMPUTER LIB/DREAM MACHINES
Ted Nelson

"An exuberant, multifont compendium of computing proverbs, anecdotes, jokes, predictions, and politics. Still as fresh and relevant as it was a dozen years ago. COMPUTER LIB is a browser's gold mine."   PC World

This is a time whose book has come. First published in 1974, COMPUTER LIB/DREAM MACHINES became the first cult book of the computer generation. Embraced by hackers and quoted by the press, it inspired thousands in the computer industry. Written at the dawn of the computer revolution, COMPUTER LIB predicted the major issues of today—design of easy-to-use computer systems, image synthesis, artificial intelligence, computer-assisted instruction, and hypertext, Nelson's vision of a nonsequential way to store data. Now republished by Microsoft Press with new commentaries, insights, and reconsiderations, COMPUTER LIB/DREAM MACHINES brings this wildly Utopian introduction to computers to a new generation.
336 pages, softcover   9¼ x 9¾ $18.95   Order Code COLIDR
A Tempus Book

PROGRAMMERS AT WORK
Interviews with 19 Programmers Who Shaped the Computer Industry
Susan Lammers

"PROGRAMMERS AT WORK...does for the budding software writers what the Paris Review interviews did for would-be fiction writers. It provides comfort, inspiration and a sense of community with those who have already succeeded in the field...It is not to be missed."   The New York Times

PROGRAMMERS AT WORK is a collection of captivating interviews that probe the minds of nineteen of today's most notable programmers. The interviews highlight the forces, the events, and the personality traits that influenced today's software movers and shakers. How do these programmers approach program design? Is programming a talent or a learned skill? An art or a science? And how do these programmers envision the future of computing? Although each interview reveals an individual success story, the collection, taken as a whole, provides a colorful portrait of the microcomputer industry. Included are interviews with Andy Hertzfeld (Macintosh Operating System), John Warnock (PostScript), C. Wayne Ratliff (dBASE), Jonathan Sachs (Lotus 1-2-3), and Bill Gates (BASIC). A lively appendix provides some actual code and worksheets from these software wizards.
400 pages, softcover   7⅜ x 9¼ $9.95   Order Code PRWOTE
A Tempus Book

Microsoft Press® books are available wherever fine books are sold, or credit card orders can be placed by calling 1-800-MSPRESS.